ROUTLEDGE LIBRARY EDITIONS: CHINESE LITERATURE AND ARTS

Volume 19

PROSCRIBED CHINESE WRITING

PROSCRIBED CHINESE WRITING

ROBERT TUNG

LONDON AND NEW YORK

First published in 1976 by Curzon Press Ltd

This edition first published in 2022
by Routledge
4 Park Square, Milton Park, Abingdon, Oxon OX14 4RN

and by Routledge
605 Third Avenue, New York, NY 10017

Routledge is an imprint of the Taylor & Francis Group, an informa business

© 1976 Robert Tung

All rights reserved. No part of this book may be reprinted or reproduced or utilised in any form or by any electronic, mechanical, or other means, now known or hereafter invented, including photocopying and recording, or in any information storage or retrieval system, without permission in writing from the publishers.

Trademark notice: Product or corporate names may be trademarks or registered trademarks, and are used only for identification and explanation without intent to infringe.

British Library Cataloguing in Publication Data
A catalogue record for this book is available from the British Library

ISBN: 978-0-367-11183-0 (Set)
ISBN: 978-0-367-77167-6 (Volume 19) (hbk)
ISBN: 978-0-367-77169-0 (Volume 19) (pbk)
ISBN: 978-1-003-17009-9 (Volume 19) (ebk)

DOI: 10.4324/9781003170099

Publisher's Note
The publisher has gone to great lengths to ensure the quality of this reprint but points out that some imperfections in the original copies may be apparent.

Disclaimer
The publisher has made every effort to trace copyright holders and would welcome correspondence from those they have been unable to trace.

SCANDINAVIAN INSTITUTE OF　　　　　　　NO 21
ASIAN STUDIES MONOGRAPH SERIES

Proscribed Chinese Writing

Robert Tung

Second revised edition

Curzon Press

This book is published with the help of
a grant from the University of Copenhagen.

Scandinavian Institute of Asian Studies
Kejsergade 2, DK—1155 Copenhagen K,
Denmark.

First published 1976
Second revised edition 1978

Curzon Press Ltd : London and Malmö

© 1976 Robert Tung

ISBN 0 7007 0090 0
ISSN 0069 1712

Printed by Craftsman Press Ltd., Bangkok

TABLE OF CONTENTS

FOREWORD VII

INTRODUCTION IX

APPENDIX XIX

CONVERSION TABLE FROM PIN–YIN TO WADE–GILES
TRANSCRIPTION SYSTEM XXXXIX

NOTES TO PROSCRIBED CHINESE WRITING

Wong Shih-Wei, *Wild Lilies* 1

Ting Ling, *Thoughts on March 8 Day* 11

Ai Ching, *Understand and Respect Writers* 17

Hsiao Chun, *Sketches of Chirping Cicadas* 21

Hsiao Chun, *On Love and Tolerance among comrades* 24

Hsia Yen, *From Choosing Theatrical Programmes* 29

Meng Chao, *Secret of the Palace of White Ants* 32

Meng Chao, *Chang Hsien-chung Kills or Kills Not?* 35

Chin Mu, *Chrysanthemum and Goldfish* 38

Chin Mu, *To Imitate Steps at Han Tan* 43

Chin Mu, *The Complication of River Branches* 46

Chin Mu, *Poisons and Medicines* 50

Wu Han, *Humans and Ghosts* 54

Wu Han, *Hai Jui Scolds the Emperor* 58

Teng To, *Stories about Bragging* 63

Teng To, *Show Concern for All Things* 66

Liao Mo-Sha, *Report What Comes Handy* 69

Chang Pai, *Manner of Contention* 93

PREFACE TO THE SECOND EDITION

In preparing this second edition for the press, opportunity has been taken to correct a few misprints which have occurred in some of the transliterations given under the heading of *Notes to Proscribed Chinese Writing*.

The page numbers of these *Notes* correspond with the page numbers of the Chinese texts so as to afford a convenient means of cross-reference; they are not the folio numbers for the respective pages.

ROBERT TUNG
1977

FOREWORD

Apart from the inherent interest of the texts themselves, PROSCRIBED CHINESE WRITING is designed as a textbook for students who have studied the Chinese language for one or two years and who are now ready to read the literature. It is a collection of essays written over the last 30 years by Chinese scholars, all of whom have been criticised by the Chinese Communist Party or by the Government. The work of these authors constitutes an important part of Chinese literature which the world must not continue to ignore. Several Western scholars claim that Chinese literature has been strangled by the repressive actions taken by the Communist authorities. I trust this book will prove the existence of literature as a dynamic force still alive in China today.

The glossary at the back of the book defines words strictly within the context of the appropriate story, thus saving students the trouble of choosing the correct definition from many possible meanings offered by a dictionary. For example, the expression " 用心 " in Teng To's article *Stories about Bragging* is defined as "intention", without listing other possible meanings, such as "diligent", "attentively", or "(to study) hard". Similarly the character " 講 " is translated as "to be interested in" and "to be particular about" instead of "to talk". Again, in Wu Han's article *Humans and Ghosts,* the phrase " 對不起 " is translated "to do injustice to", "to be unfair to" or "to mistreat", rather than "sorry" or "to be unable to face a person owing to some fault".

I have adopted the Peking-sponsored pin-yin system for transliteration, with the exception of relatively well-known names and place-names. I have included, however, a conversion table for those more familiar with the Wade-Giles system.

The articles, placed in context by short explanatory introductions, are arranged according to their dates of publication. Then an appendix explains why the authors won official Chinese disapproval.

The publication of this book would not have been possible without the help and encouragement of Søren Egerod, professor of East Asian languages, University of Copenhagen and head of the Scandinavian Institute of Asian Studies. I am also grateful to Dr. Chang Tao-wen whose calligraphy graces the cover and to Mrs. Elsa Karlsmark who contributed some of the notes accompanying the articles by Hsia Chun and Liao Mo-sha.

East Asian Institute
University of Copenhagen
Copenhagen, Denmark

Robert Tung

INTRODUCTION

*Sounds of wind, rain and reading of
books all fill my ears;
Family, state and world affairs, I show
concern for them all.*

—**Ku Hsien-cheng**

It was no accident that Teng To chose to quote the above couplet by the leader of the Ming Dynasty's Tunglin Party in one of his articles. Possibly reacting against the Mandarin literati and their remoteness from everyday life, modern Chinese authors feel strongly that they must be concerned with every aspect of real life, not just with politics. Authors must write of the problems of all types of men, not solely of workers, peasants or soldiers. Chinese literature over the past 30-odd years has thus occupied itself with a wide range of subjects.

The authors have been accused of attempting to restore capitalism in China. Chinese men of letters, however, are not naive enough to believe that power grows out of the barrel of the pen or even that the pen is mightier than the sword. Their aim is purely literary——to bring fresh meaning, greater intensity and significant shape to everyday life.

Those who claim that there is no literature in China today because the Communist society admits of no freedom ignore the fact that the source of literature is life, not freedom. Chinese writers may not be as free as some others in certain other countries to write what they wish to write, or to publish what they write, some are freer than others. And almost all the authors in this collection published while they held important positions.

It may be argued that Chinese authors cannot be creatively original because Peking's rigid political "line" prevents them from thinking objectively. But this collection clearly illustrates the continuing creativity of Chinese men of letters; the political line has in no way blinkered their observation of the world. In other words, they are masters of their minds, and are as clear-sighted as any of their Western opposite numbers.

*   *   *

Wang Shih-wei joined the Communist Party in 1926 and was one of the first to write about the problems of young people under Chinese communism. For those holding out in Yenan in the Forties, according to his description in *Wild Lilies*, life hardly fulfilled youthful idealism. Young people did not eat well; nor did they enjoy the companionship of the opposite sex (there being eighteen boys to every girl). Recreational facilities were few, and life was boring. Cadres showed little concern for those who fell ill. Brought up in the old society, they were servile to their superiors and hostile to their inferiors. Young people's complaints were flippantly brushed aside as trifles. Those who objected to the hierarchical system were accused of being egalitarian. Wang Shih-wei compared those who defended the stratified heirarchy by mouthing the slogan "Learn from the Soviet Union" with those "masters who cite Greece whenever they speak" and adjured them to "keep their mouths shut". Shortly after the publication of *Wild Lilies* in March 1942, Wang was arrested as a Trotskyite. He has not been heard of since May of that year.

While Wang Shih-wei was writing about the disillusionment of the young, Ting Ling concerned herself with women's troubles. In an article *Thoughts on March 8 Day* published in the *Liberation Daily* (she was editor of the newspaper's literary page) Ting presented another aspect of life in the revolutionary cradle. It was not ethical for a woman to be friendly with men; marriage was criticised. Intellectuals alleged that a woman had eyes only for leading personalities if she married a man who rode on a horse (the horse being the symbol of a high social position). Those in authority complained that she despised uneducated veteran cadres if she married an intellectual. When she had children, she was "Nora who had returned home", meaning she had regressed politically. Applications for divorce were almost always filed by the husband. A woman's only alternative was to have an "immoral" affair, thus rendering herself worthy only of a curse. Ting Ling did not hold in high regard the way in which the political power of the proletariat had responded to the challenge of the women's liberation movement. Instead, she proposed, women should stand on their own feet. Only then could they demand equality with men.

Ting's considerable literary influence kept her out of trouble until 1957. But then she crossed swords with Chou Yang, formerly deputy director of the propaganda department of the CCP Central Committee, and was "purged"

A poet by name as well as by nature, Ai Ching was arrested by the Nationalists in 1932 for "harbouring dangerous thoughts". In 1942, he appealed to the communist authorities to give due regard to writers. In his article *Understand and Respect Writers*, he asked only for freedom for writers to publish what they write. Writers demanded no other privileges. They had fought all their lives for communist democratic politics precisely to win protection for the independent spirit of their artistic creations. Those who wished writers to describe boils as if they were flower buds, who were unable to see their own ugliness (much less change themselves) were hopeless. Those who did not, like other men, take baths, but wished the writer to scratch them where it itched were informed that writers did not regard it as their function to scratch itches.

Hsiao Chun is best-known for his novel *Village in August*. In his article *On Love and Tolerance among Comrades*, published in 1942, Hsiao quoted a passage from this novel in order to underline the importance of tolerance——or of understanding——between the leaders and their followers:

> "Anna, who had drunk some wine, now picked a quarrel with commander Chen Chu, who would not grant her request to go to Shanghai. Chen Chu did not affect pomposity as a responsible person, and refrained from punishing her. Instead, he felt somewhat sad as he looked at the child who was in love for the first time. He well understood why Anna acted as she did to-night."

Hsiao maintained that love and tolerance were inseparable. Love could only exist with tolerance, without which the great cause of Chinese revolution would suffer.

In his *Sketches of Chirping Cicadas*, published in 1957, Hsiao revealed that, like a cicada, he had been silent for some years due to the chilly climate. Now that those who preyed on insects were not after him, the change of climate allowed him to chirp on.......

His "chirpings", inspired by the greater tolerance of the "Hundred Flowers", included the observation that some Marxists were good at teaching but bad at learning themselves. They were also good at criticising what others learned. Some who had believed the theory that creative works of art involved "no conflict" rejected that idea only a year later, because the Soviet Union opposed the theory. Even more recently, they had switched their position again, advocating the idea that "poisonous weeds" should contend. A Marxist must keep two things in mind if he wanted to maintain his position, he said. One was to remember to be ultra-leftist when struggling with rightist-opportunist deviations and ultra-rightist when struggling with leftist-opportunist deviations. The second tip he gave was: always say something which the masses could not read in the newspapers, keeping them constantly wondering if the Marxist indeed boasted "confidential" sources of information.

*   *   *

After 1957 and the unhappy end to the Hundred Flowers and the Hundred

Contending Schools of Thought, Chinese writing suddenly became much more subtle and oblique in its approach. Instead of directly confronting the regime on topical issues of common interest, writers turned to nature and to historical events as their subject matters. They often quoted relevant and telling passages from Chinese classics, and by analogy produced logical and convincing reasons. Thus they forced their readers to think deeply, drawing their own parallels with modern times. The writers chose their words with great care and during this period the use of modern Chinese language reached its highest degree of excellence and readability.

From Choosing Theatrical Programmes, written by playwright Hsia Yen, uses the story from the eighteenth chapter of the *Dream of the Red Chamber* dealing with the kindness shown towards actors by Chai Yuan-chun. Thus he is able to make a telling point about the desirable relations between the man responsible for choosing theatrical programmes and those who perform them.

Meng Chao (better known as Chen Po in literary circles) wrote the unpopular historical play *Li Hui-niang*. His article *Chang Hsien-chung Kills or Kills Not?* was written during a heated debate among Chinese historians about the famous Chang, the man who revolted against the Ming Dynasty. Some historians, sympathetic with the idea of peasant uprisings, denied that Chang killed. Meng argues that Chang did kill; that is an undeniable historical fact. Whether his killings were justifiable was another matter. In the piece entitled *Secret of the Palace of White Ants*, Meng attempts, by means of a description of the discovery of the king and queen ants by Lee Shi-mei, to demonstrate the importance of flexibility in methods of study, observation, investigation and judgment.

A distinguished writer, Chin Mu published at least seven volumes of essays, the most popular of which is *Gathering Shells in the Sea of Art*. We have chosen four from this collection.

In *Chrysanthemum and Goldfish*, Chin Mu points out that in cultivating rare flowers and breeding tiny creatures to brighten an otherwise dull world, the Chinese people have specialised in chrysanthemums and gold fish. Over three thousand years, they have developed over 2,000 varieties of chrysanthemum and hundreds of different goldfish. But, in choosing a favourite type of flower or fish, one need not denigrate all other varieties. Similarly, he goes on, the lover of novels need not decry all other forms of literature.

Another essay, *To Imitate Steps from the People of Han Tan*, also elaborates the importance of artistic individuality. It retells the ancient story of a young man from the state of Yen who tried to imitate the style of walking of the people of Han Tan, the capital of Chao. But he failed to match the grace of the Han Tan people, and succeeded only in forgetting his own walking style. In great distress, he was reduced to crawling. Chin drives his point home by quoting the words of the late Chi Pai-shih, a well-known contemporary Chinese painter, who said: "He who learns from me lives; he who imitates me dies."

In *The Complication of River Branches,* Chin Mu uses the varying interpretations of minor points of Chinese folklore to illustrate the kaleidoscopic variety of life. The Yangtze flows from west to east. But in places it flows from east to west, or even northwards or southwards. Chin Mu warns that unless the unusual and extra-ordinary is tolerated in literary works, and instead a "common plot" is demanded, writers will be unable to embrace the huge variety of life.

Poison is not necessarily harmful. Some have become medicines in the hands of doctors. Such things also happen in the field of art and literature. A man went to a wine and poetry party. Those present, while drinking, were extemporising couplets. The man was not well-educated, but nevertheless scribbled a line:
    "One after another come fluttering willow catkins red."
Those round the table sneered; how could catkins be red? But one picked up a brush and added the line:
    "Over peach valleys goes shining the setting sun."
——thus transmuting a far-fetched sentence into a striking line of verse.

Similarly, a poet wrote a birthday poem for an old, rich lady surrounded by her family. The first line went:
    "This old lady is not human;"
The faces round the table ceased smiling. Undisturbed, the poet went on:
    "An Angel descending from the heaven."
The anger of the old lady's children and grand children turned to ecstasy.
    "All her children and grandchildren are thieves;"
was his third line. Anger again. But the poet skilfully softened the sharpness of his brush:
    "Stealing a heavenly peach for the dearest one."
All smiled and nodded happily in approval. Chin Mu uses these two vivid tales in *Poisons and Medicines* to push home the importance of flexibility.

A biographer and historian from Chekiang province, Wu Han's best known works are *Mirror of History, The Biography of Chu Yuan-chang,* and a series of articles on Hai Jui. These were regarded as a deliberate challenge to the Party's verdict on the purged former Defence Minister Peng Te-huai, and were some of the sparks which touched off the Cultural Revolution in 1966.

His *Hai Jui Scolds the Emperor* (included in this collection) is simply a biography of an upright government official under the Ming Emperor Chia Ching.

In *Humans and Ghosts,* Wu admits that the development of science has resulted in the lessening of superstitious beliefs in ghosts. But some of the living talk and act like ghosts, so study of the best ghost stories is still worthwhile. Living ghosts frighten people, conspire, create tensions and cause trouble. But as ghosts prey on people's fears, they can be rendered harmless by a refusal to be frightened. Wu gives a few examples.

A man named Keng moved into an abandoned, haunted house. One night, a long-haired, black-faced ghost appeared, laughing at the startled Keng. Keng started laughing himself. He smeared his own face with black ink from the desk and outstared the ghost, who shame-faced stole away

Another man, Tsao was sleeping at a friend's house. At midnight, a piece of paper slid under the door and turned into a woman. Tsao was not frightened. The ghost dishevelled her hair and stuck out her long tongue. Tsao jeered: "Your hair is like anybody's hair, only slightly dishevelled. Your tongue is like anybody's tongue, only slightly longer. What is there to fear?" The ghost then took off her head and placed it on the table. Tsao burst out laughing. Puzzled, the ghost vanished. When she re-appeared Tsao simply shouted, " How boring! Here she is again!" she left.

The third story is about a brave man named Tai, who moved into a huge house. One night, a ghost appeared:
"Is it true that you are not afraid?" said the ghost.
"It is."
The ghost then made all kinds of ghastly faces.
"Still not afraid?"
"Of course not."
"In fact, I do not intend to turn you out," the ghost said politely, "I will go if you admit that you are scared."
"This is unheard of! How can I say I am when I am honestly and truly not afraid?"
The ghost begged, but to no avail. Eventually he sighed, "I have lived here for more than thirty years but never met anyone half as stubborn. I cannot live under the same roof as such an idiot." So saying the ghost walked out.

Wu Han was disgraced in 1966 for "attacking the Party and revolution" and for portraying "our country as a world full of ghosts".

In *Stories about Bragging,* Teng To (a long-time editor of the *People's Daily*) relates historical examples of the dangers of boasting. One "should exercise caution in handling matters, should do more, talk less and, still less, court fame".

Liao Mo-sha was chairman of the departments of Education and United Front Work of the Peking Municipal Party Committee up to his purge during the Cultural Revolution. In the first of three articles selected from his collection of essays entitled *Report What Comes Handy,* he criticises the "eight-legged essay" in order to expose the equally obnoxious stereotypes in Party writing, education and leadership.*

In other articles, he deplores the fact that those who wield the greatest power and occupy the highest positions are the least criticised. The arrow of criticism should be aimed at department chiefs and above, since they are the people whose bureaucratic attitudes do the state the most harm.

Liao laments the poor quality of new poetry which, according to him, is no more than prose arranged in spaced-out lines. No matter how the written lines are arranged —— vertically or otherwise —— they still resemble an up and down escalator leading nowhere, or uneven garments hanging on a bamboo pole to dry in the sun. He questions Tu Fu's attitude to poetry —— that a poet should be "kind to the new and love the old". Liao asks whether a poet should be kind when the new is not better than the old. He advises the young to work harder if they want to compose good poems.

Liao argues in *Those Being Served by People* that the phrase "serve the people" is often interpreted as "being served by the people". If a bus driver does not treat his passengers courteously, they scold him; if a salesgirl does

---

*Stereotyped writing, or the "eight-legged essay", was the special form of essay prescribed in the imperial examinations under China's feudal dynasties from the 15th to the 19th centuries; it consisted in juggling with words, concentrated only on form and was devoid of content. Structurally the main body of the essay had eight parts – presentation, amplification, preliminary exposition, initial argument, inceptive paragraphs, middle paragraphs, rear paragraphs and concluding paragraphs, and the fifth to eighth parts each had to have two "legs", i.e., two antithetical paragraphs, hence the name "eight-legged essay". The "eight-legged essay" became a byword in China denoting formalism and triteness. Thus "stereotyped Party writing" characterizes the writings of certain people in the revolutionary ranks who piled up revolutionary phrases and terms higgledy-piggledy instead of analysing the facts. Like the "eight-legged essay", their writings were nothing but verbiage. —— *Selected Works of Mao Tse-tung,* Vol. III, Foreign Languages Press, Peking 1965, p. 50.

not smile pleasantly, they say she does not want to serve the people. Their attitude is: "As long as I pay, they will have to wait on me!" Liao writes with fine delicacy and observes with rare discernment the new intricate relations between the serving and the served in socialist China.

The last piece in this collection is Chang Pai's *Manner of Contention.* Chang Pai could be the pen name of either Wu Han or Liao Mo-sha. However, Chang Pai's style seems more closely to resemble that of Liao.

Chang says that everyone agrees that hundreds of schools should contend, but that it is not easy to practise the theory because the arguments are so irrational: "I am reasonable and you are not"; "My facts are right; yours are not"; "One talks about this, another about that".

In order to carry on healthy scholarly contention, Chang suggests that each participant should realise no one is more equal than others. Everyone is entitled to argue, but logically and scientifically.

* * *

I have thus presented typical extracts from ten authors who deal with different subjects in different styles, but who have in common the anger they aroused in official quarters and their subsequent disgrace. There is a certain pattern to their experiences. Each supported revolution in China and held important government positions. None of them opposed the dictatorship of the proletariat. They were all originally accepted by the regime but discredited later.

Mao wrote in his article *On Coalition Government:* "Provided they serve the people credibly, all intellectuals should be esteemed and regarded as valuable national and social assets". How, then, did these authors not serve the people credibly? Did they not follow the Party line? Is there no freedom in China to criticise? Or did they criticise too pointedly? Is it treason to quote the past in order to satirise the present? If these suggestions are true, then Mao himself would be most vulnerable to attack for being an anti-revolutionary.

Mao himself called stereotyped Party writing "a vehicle for filth" in *Rectify the Party's Style of Work.* In his article *Reform Our Study,* he quoted:
"The reed growing on the wall —— top-heavy, thin-stemmed and shallow of root;
The bamboo shoot in the hills —— sharp-tongued, thick-skinned and hollow inside."

Mao was describing those who lack "a scientific attitude", who "indulge in verbiage" and enjoy a reputation unwarranted by any real learning", and who are "crude and careless", behaving like "a blindfolded man catching sparrows" or "a blind man groping for fish".

His criticisms could very plausibly be applied to those who helped discredit the intellectuals —— bureaucrats like Lin Chieh, Mao Tse-min, Yen Chang-kuei, Chou Ying, Teng Wen-sheng and Chin Tien-liang, who chastised Teng To's *Evening Chats at Yenshan* as anti-Party and anti-socialist double-talk. Double-talk, maybe. But certainly not anti-Party or anti-socialist. Instead of "seeking truth from facts", the "six gentlemen" twisted the facts, creating tension and trouble, pursuing their own self-interest. By attacking others, they made themselves more important. The intellectuals were killed by "ghosts" —— the same variety of trouble maker vividly described in Wu Han's essay. They were the victims of the prejudices and the petty intrigues of bureaucrats.

It is tragic that any government, which seeks objective truth, should be fooled by the high-sounding words and benevolent facades of such petty men, who actually do more harm to the revolution than the loyal men of letters who dare to expose social injustice.

In fact, the authorities might review what Mencius once said in reply to the Emperor Chi Hsuan. Mencius warned: "When all those about you say that you should not employ this man, do not listen to them; when all your ministers say that you should not employ him, do not listen to them; when all the people say that you should not employ him, look into the matter yourself and dismiss him only when you find him unworthy. Likewise, when all those about you say that this man deserves death, do not listen to them; when all your ministers say that he deserves death, do not listen to them; when all the people say that he deserves death, examine the case carefully and put him to death only when you find him so deserving."

East Asian Institute, Robert Tung
University of Copenhagen,
Copenhagen, Denmark.

APPENDIX

TENG TO'S *EVENING CHATS AT YENSHAN* IS ANTI-PARTY AND ANTI-SOCIALIST DOUBLE-TALK

COMPILED BY LIN CHIEH, MA TSE-MIN,
YEN CHANG-KUEI, CHOU YING, TENG WEN-SHENG
AND CHIN TIEN-LIANG

FOREWORD

Since 1961 Teng To has published a series of anti-Party and anti-socialist articles in Frontline (Qianxian), *the* Peking Daily (Beijing Ribao) *and the* Peking Evening News (Beijing Wanbao), *launching fierce onslaughts on the Party and on socialism. As early as the time of their publication, these anti-Party and anti-socialist views aroused opposition among many comrades who sent in criticisms to* Frontline, *the* Peking Daily *and the* Peking Evening News. *But the latter refused to publish these contributions and suppressed them.*

As a result of the recent thorough exposure of the anti-Party and anti-socialist features of Wu Han, Liao Mo-sha and others, it was no longer possible to cover up Teng To's features either. Therefore, Frontline *and the* Peking Daily *hurriedly printed some excerpts from* Evening Chats at Yenshan *with an editorial note.*

In their editorial note, Frontline *and the* Peking Daily *kept quiet about Teng To's opposition to the Party and socialism and, with the same intention of hushing things up, arranged their extracts from* Evening Chats at Yenshan *in such a way as to hide the fundamental issue of Teng To's opposition to the Party and socialism.*

In our opinion, Teng To's Evening Chats at Yenshan *is a lot of double-talk against the Party and socialism. Therefore, we have made our own compilation of passages from the* Evening Chats *and added a number of comments. It is our hope that the readers will make a comparative study of our extracts and those compiled by* Frontline *and the* Peking Daily.

I. VENOMOUS ATTACKS ON OUR GREAT PARTY

Viciously Attacking the Scientific Thesis That "The East Wind Prevails Over the West Wind" as "Great Empty Talk" and a "Cliche"

"Some people have the gift of the gab. They can talk endlessly on any occasion, like water flowing from an undammed river. After listening to them, however, when you try to recall what they have said, you can remember nothing."

"Making long speeches without really saying anything, making confusion worse confounded by explaining, or giving explanations which are not explanatory — these are the characteristics of great empty talk."

"We cannot deny that in certain special situations such great empty talk is inevitable, and therefore in a certain sense is a necessity. Still, it will be quite awful if great empty talk should be made into a prevalent fashion indulged in on every occasion or even cultivated as a special skill. It will be still more disastrous if our children should be taught this skill and turned into hordes of experts in great empty talk."

"As chance would have it, my neighbour's child has recently often imitated the style of some great poet and put into writing a lot of 'great empty talk' . . . . Not long ago he wrote a poem entitled 'Ode to Wild Grass' which is nothing but empty talk. The poem reads as follows:

> *The Venerable Heaven is our father,*
> *The Great Earth is our mother*
> *And the Sun is our nanny;*
> **The East Wind is our benefactor**
> **And the West Wind is our enemy."**

"Although such words as heaven, earth, father, mother, sun, nanny, the East Wind, the West Wind, benefactor and enemy catch our eye, **they are used to no purpose here and have become mere cliches."**

"Recourse to even the **finest words and phrases is futile,** or rather, the more such cliches are **uttered, the worse the situation will become.** Therefore I would advise those friends **given to great empty talk** to read more, think more, say less and take **a rest when the time** comes for talking, so as to save their own as well as other **people's time and energy."**

("Great Empty Talk", *Frontline*, No. 21, 1961)

Comment: "The East Wind prevails over the West Wind" is a scientific thesis advanced by Chairman Mao Tse-tung at the Meeting of Communist and Workers' Parties on November 18, 1957. It says by way of a vivid image that the international situation has reached a new turning point and that the forces of socialism are prevailing over the forces of imperialism. The East Wind symbolizes the anti-imperialist revolutionary forces of the proletariat and of the oppressed peoples of Asia, Africa and Latin America. The West Wind symbolizes the decadent forces of imperialism and reaction in all countries. It is entirely correct to praise the East Wind and to detest the West Wind. Why then should Teng To pick up the statement, "The East Wind is our benefactor and the West Wind is our enemy", and malign it as great empty talk and a cliche? The Khrushchov revisionists have said inflammatorily that it is necessary to "oppose the dogmatic theories concerning a mythical competition between 'the West and East Winds' more boldly and more resolutely". Thus Teng To here is singing the same tune as that of Khrushchov.

Insinuating That Our Party Leadership Is "Conceited" and "Looks Down on the Masses"

"The wisdom of a man is never unlimited. Only an idiot fondly imagines that he knows everything and has an inexhaustible supply of wisdom, for that as a matter of fact is absolutely impossible. ... some people appear clever, but strictly speaking, they are only seemingly clever or only clever in a trifling way and cannot be considered really clever, let alone wise."

"Lao Tzu took an extreme position in this matter, and later the Kings of the Six Kingdoms went to the other extreme. The former wanted to obliterate all wisdom and good sense and negate everything, whereas the latter relied on their own wisdom and became blindly conceited. Naturally, neither attained good results. The root of their mistake was that they did not value the wisdom of the masses."

"The best ideas can only be produced from among the masses. During the reign of Emperor Yuan of the Han Dynasty, Prime Minister Kuang Heng memorialized the emperor, 'I have heard that one should consult and follow the multitude, as this is what Heaven wills.' ... at the time of Emperor Kuang Wu of the same dynasty, the noted scholar Cheng Hsing also counselled the emperor that he should 'seek advice from all sides and accept suggestions from below'. Fan Yao-fu, son of Fan Chung-yen of the Sung Dynasty, gave the following advice to Szuma Kuang: 'I hope that you will be modest in order to promote the discussion of state affairs among the masses. One need not plan everything oneself. When a man plans everything himself, flatterers will seize the chance to say things to please him.' The views of these ancients are all very good. Fan Yao-fu's idea that 'one need not plan everything oneself' deserves particular attention. **Some people, however, are always boastful and conceited; they look down on the masses and make all decisions themselves in the hope of achieving success with original ideas and reject good advice from below.** If such people are not aware of their short-coming and do not try to overcome it, they will eventually suffer heavy reverses."

("Is Wisdom Reliable?" *Evening Chats at Yenshan*, Vol. IV, pp. 17-19; first appeared in the *Peking Evening News*, February 22, 1962)

Comment: Why should Teng To dwell today on such old stories as that of Kuang Heng counselling Emperor Yuan to "consult and follow the multitude" and of Cheng Hsing counselling Emperor Kuang Wu to "accept suggestions from below"? He is obliquely attacking our great Party as "being conceited and looking down on the masses". This becomes clear when we compare what he says with the slanders the Khrushchov revisionists spread against us. Are not Teng To's words identical with the modern revisionists' vilifications of our Party?

Slandering Our Party as "Going Back on Its Own Word" and Being "Untrustworthy"

"There are many people afflicted with diseases . . . one of which is called 'amnesia'. This is a very troublesome ailment, and whoever suffers from it cannot be cured easily."

"Such a patient . . . often shows such symptoms as going back on his own word and failing to keep faith, and people are even inclined to suspect that he is feigning idiocy and is therefore untrustworthy."

"In *More Stories Told by Ai Tzu* by Lu Cho of the Ming Dynasty, there is a tale which presents a typical case of amnesia:

There was a man in Chi State who was so forgetful that he forgot to stop once he started walking and forgot to rise once he lay down. His wife was much worried. She said to him, 'I have heard that Ai Tzu is a witty and clever man and can treat the most baffling diseases. Why don't you go and consult him?' The man replied, 'Very good.' He rode away on horseback, bringing his bow and arrow with him. Having gone a short distance, he felt a call of nature and dismounted. He thrust his arrow into the earth and fastened his horse to a tree. Having eased himself, he looked to the left and then exclaimed on seeing his arrow, 'My God! What a narrow escape! Where is this arrow from? It nearly hit me!' He looked to the right and at the sight of his horse, cried in joy, 'Although I am badly scared, I have got a horse.' When he was about to start off again, rein in hand, he suddenly trampled on his own leavings. Stamping his feet, he complained, 'I've trodden on some dog's dung and ruined my shoes! What a pity!' He whipped the horse and rode home. Soon he reached his house and hesitated before the gate, wondering to himself, 'Who lives here? Is this Master Ai's house?' His wife saw his bewilderment and knew that he had lost his memory again and gave him a scolding. The man was puzzled, asking: 'We are not acquainted, madam. What do you swear at me for?'

Apparently this man was a bad case of amnesia. But we cannot tell how such case would be at its very worst – presumably it would result either in insanity or in idiocy.

"According to ancient Chinese medical books, . . . one of the causes of amnesia is the abnormal functioning of the so-called breath of life. In consequence, the patient not only suffers from loss of memory but gradually becomes **capricious**, has great difficulty with his speech, gets **irritable and finally goes mad and runs amuck**. Another cause is the injury to the brain. The patient feels numb at times and the blood rushes from his heart to his head, causing occasional fainting fits. Unless treated in time, he will become an idiot. Thus if anyone finds either of these symptoms present in himself, he **must promptly take a complete rest and say nothing and do nothing, and if he insists on speaking and acting, he will come to grief.**

"Are there then really no positive methods for treating this disease ? Certainly there are. For example . . . when the patient has a bad attack, you **immediately go and get a bucketful of dog's blood and pour it over his head, and then pour cold water over it so as to make him a little more clear-headed** . . . . According to modern Western medicine, one way is to **hit the patient on the head with a specially made club to induce a state of 'shock' and then restore him to consciousness.**"

("Special Treatment for 'Amnesia' ", *Frontline*, No. 14, 1962)

Comment: Obviously, this is a piece showing the bitterest hatred in its attack on our great Party. There is no medical book which says that "going back on one's own word and failing to keep faith" and being "capricious", being "mad" or "running amuck" are symptoms of amnesia, and no pharmacopoeia prescribes such treatment for amnesia as pouring dog's blood over the patient's head and clubbing him unconscious. *More Stories Told by Ai Tzu* by Lu Cho of the Ming Dynasty contains political satires and is not a medical treatise. Teng To is talking politics here, not medicine. This is an incontestable fact.

Slandering Our Party Leadership as "A Watery Chuke Liang"

" 'A Watery Chuke Liang' is a most objectionable character. This nickname appears in an anecdote headed 'Kuo Ni Compares Himself to Chuke Liang' in the 15th volume of *Bedside Table Sketches (Cheng Shih)* by Yueh Ko, grandson of Yueh Fei. The story reads in part:

When Kuo Ti was garrison commander east of the Huai River and built the walls for two cities, Kuo Ni was on his staff. ..... Kuo Ni talked boastfully and nobody dared to challenge him. One day he inscribed the following lines on his fan:

> *Three times in succession he was called on*
> *for advice about affairs of state;*
> *Under two kings the old minister gave his mind*
> *to ruling the country.*

In other words, he claimed to be like Chuke Liang. ...... I happened to visit Sze County in summer, and noticed that the two verses were indeed inscribed on a fan for guests. Thus what I had heard was not a groundless rumour. After Kuo Cho had been routed at Fuli and Kuo Chuan defeated at Yichen, Kuo Ni, in despair about mending the hopeless situation, shed tears in the presence of his guests. Peng Fa, who was fond of making jokes, was then a magistrate and witnessed the spectacle. He told people, 'We have here a watery Chuke Liang.' The joke got around and was much applauded. It reached Kuo Ni's ears and he was nettled and wanted to punish Peng, but he was dismissed from office before he could carry out his intention."

"Men like Kuo Ni, a watery Chuke Liang, simply make people laugh and also make their gorge rise. But the anecdote shows that a person who poses as Chuke Liang will never scare people, and the day is bound to come when he will be revealed in his true colours and laughed at by the whole world."

("Three Kinds of Chuke Liang", Evening Chats at Yenshan, Vol. IV, p. 12; first appeared in the Peking Evening News, March 1, 1962)

Comment: In bitterly attacking what he calls "a watery Chuke Liang", and saying "any person who poses as Chuke Liang" will be "revealed in his true colours", to whom is Teng To really referring? If he is referring to the landlord and capitalist classes, there is no need for such veiled ambiguity. The only conclusion that can be drawn is that he is maligning the leadership of our Party.

II. OPPOSING THE GENERAL LINE FOR SOCIALIST CONSTRUCTION AND THE GREAT LEAP FORWARD AND ATTACKING THE DICTATORSHIP OF THE PROLETARIAT

Vilifying Our Great Leap Forward as "Boasting" and "Bragging", and Alleging That We Have "Run Our Heads Against the Brick Wall of Reality"

"When you have time, read some foreign folk tales or fables and you will profit much from them. .... If you have **the capacity to infer three points from one**, with your discerning eye you will see through all the bogies and goblins, no matter what tricks they play."

"Suppose we look into *Aesop's Fables.* For example, there is the following fable:

A pentathlon athlete was often criticized by the people in a city state for his lack of courage. So he went abroad for a time and on his return boasted of the many feats he had performed in various city states, and especially of a long jump he had made at Rhodes, a jump unequalled by any Olympic victor. He said, 'If any of you here goes to Rhodes next time, the eye-witnesses there will testify to my feat.' At this one of the bystanders said, 'Hey! If what you say is true, my man, you don't need witnesses. The place you stand on will do as well as Rhodes. Let us see the jump!'

"Facts clearly show that **braggarts only boast and never take action.**

Even now one can always and everywhere find such braggarts. Their boastful talk may differ in degree, but is all alike in being merely boasts."

"This fable can also help people recognize the crafty braggarts for what they are and call their bluff.

"A fable by Krylov points the same moral:

A titlark flying over the sea boasted that it would boil the sea dry. .... The rumour quickly spread and those easily taken in were the first to go to the seaside with spoons to join the feast of delicious fish soup."

"Followers of Ernst Mach exaggerated the role of what they called the 'psychological factor' and talked boastfully to their heart's content. Is this not the same as the titlark's nonsense about boiling the sea dry? Nevertheless, the Machians imagined that through reliance on the role of the psychological factor they could do whatever they pleased, but the result was that they ran their heads against the brick wall of reality and went bankrupt in the end."

("Two Foreign Fables", *Evening Chats at Yenshan*, Vol. V, pp. 91-93; first appeared in the *Peking Evening News*, November 26, 1961)

Comment: Anyone with a discerning eye can see at once that this is vilification of our great leap forward, slandering us as "boasting" and as "running our heads against the brick wall of reality". Unless this was the case, Teng To would not have taken so much trouble to talk about the "subtle meaning" of these fables which, he said, afford food for "deep thought". Why does he shout even today that "one can always and everywhere find such braggarts"? If he were merely telling stories, why should he speak of the role of the "psychological factor" vaunted by the Machians? Everyone knows that the imperialists and the Khrushchov revisionists have attacked our great leap forward as "braggadocio", "an adventurist project" and "voluntarism". "The Right opportunists have likewise slandered it as "inflammation of the brain", "high fever" and "idealism". Pray, can this be mere coincidence?

"Readers of the *Romance of the Three Kingdoms* will recall the scene in which Chuke Liang shed tears on ordering the execution of Ma Su. Chuke Liang quoted what Liu Pei had said before his death about Ma Su, namely that Ma Su was given to exaggeration and therefore could not be entrusted with important missions. . . . Liu Pei had read deeply into Ma Su's character. In his eyes, Ma Su was simply a braggart. **Even in ancient times men were thoroughly acquainted with the harmfulness of bragging.** It was because of this that Kuan Tzu said, 'Words must not exceed the reality, and the reality must not exceed its name.' This is a warning to people that they must **never brag or boast, that they should use caution in handling matters, should do more, talk less and, still less, court fame.**"

"Judging by the views of Wang Chung, a thinker of the Han Dynasty, it seems that throughout the ages the men who ignored this maxim were mostly scholars or men of letters. In his book *Weighing of Views and Opinions*, Wang Chung said, 'The words of the followers of Confucius are too beautiful to be true.' Evidently he meant that literary men and their like are often fond of bragging. As a matter of fact, **literary men are by no means the only persons given to bragging, there are other people as well.**"

"Lu Cho ridiculed Chisun for bragging that, like Prince Meng Chang whom he envied, he too had three thousand retainers. But a little investigation knocked the bottom out of Chisun's boastful talk. Lu Cho's aim in this apocryphal story was to teach people not to boast."

"In history there have been many authentic cases of men who liked to boast. But these works of fiction, having a higher degree of generality and **summing up the various ways of bragging by means of typical situations, attract more attention, make people more vigilant and are, therefore, of greater educational significance.**"

("Stories About Bragging", *Evening Chats at Yenshan,* Vol. V, pp. 88-90; first appeared in the *Peking Evening News,* June 11, 1961)

"Wang An-shih was a great statesman of the reforming school in the Sung Dynasty. He had many ideas for carrying out reforms, but he lacked practical knowledge and experience. In his *Miscellaneous Notes,* Chang Lei of the Sung Dynasty said:

When Wang An-shih was Prime Minister, he talked a great deal about building water conservancy projects in the country. He wanted to drain Lake Taihu of its water so as to reclaim tens of thousands of hectares of fertile land. People laughed at the idea. Once Wang An-shih talked about the matter to his guests. Academician Liu Kung-fu who was present said quickly, 'That's easy to accomplish.' 'How?' Wang An-shih asked. **Liu Kung-fu replied, 'All you have to do is to build another lake near by to hold the water of Lake Taihu.'**

At this Wang An-shih himself burst out laughing.

During the period when Wang An-shih was at the helm of state, similar jokes were circulated, all showing up the **impractical** nature of his many ideas. In particular, he was immodest, and this can be said to be his chief defect."

("Learn More and Criticize Less", *Evening Chats at Yenshan,* Vol. II, p. 84; first appeared in the *Peking Evening News,* April 2, 1961)

Comment: Teng To again and again attacks what he calls "bragging" and "boasting" and says that "literary men are by no means the only persons" given to bragging, and that "great statesmen" have the same failing. Is he here talking about past history? No. He is satirizing the present in terms of the past, fondly hoping to incite people to oppose the Party's General Line and attack the great leap forward.

Slandering Our Party as Not Treasuring Labour Power During the Great Leap Forward

"As far back as the periods of the Spring and Autumn Annals and the Warring States and thereabout, **there were many great statesmen who understood the importance of treasuring labour power** . . . . Through the experience of their rule, they discovered the 'limits' on the 'expenditure of the people's **labour power', in fact, they discovered certain objective laws governing the increase and decrease of labour power.**"

"It is written in the 'Chapter on the Royal System' of the *Book of Rites:* 'The people's labour power should be used for no more than three days each year.' On this statement Chen Hao, a scholar of the Yuan Dynasty, glossed: 'The people's labour power was used to build city-walls, roads, lanes, ditches, palaces and temples.' **This actually refers in our present-day language to the labour power to be used in all kinds of capital construction.** According to the level of the social productive forces of their times, the ancients fixed an amount of labour power to be used in all kinds of capital construction — approximately only one per cent of the total labour power available. As we see it today, this ratio is appropriate in an old country with agricultural production as its foundation."

"Drawing up plans for Prince Chung Erh of the state of Tsin, Hu Yen advised, 'After saving your strength for a dozen years, you can go far.' He was then escorting the prince past Wulu of the state of Wei, and even predicted that 'in twelve years you will conquer this land'.... From this story, it can be seen that a man like Hu Yen well understood how to accumulate strength in the historical circumstances of ancient times. **If a man of the seventh century B.C. understood this truth, we who live in the sixties of the twentieth century should naturally understand it even better."**

"We should draw new enlightenment from the experience of the ancients."

("The Theory of Treasuring Labour Power". Evening Chats at Yenshan, Vol. I, pp. 56-58; first appeared in the Peking Evening News, April 30, 1961)

Comment: It is utter nonsense to say that the ancients discovered the "laws governing the increase and decrease of labour power". The statements that "we who live in the sixties of the twentieth century should naturally understand it even better" and that "we should draw new enlightenment from the experience of the ancients" are evidently attacks on us, meaning that we did not treasure labour power during the great leap forward and in carrying out capital construction and water conservancy projects.

Slandering Our Cause of Socialist Construction as Being "Finished"

"Indeed, **the accumulation of great wealth often begins with a very small sum,** just as a robe is the gathering together of many bits of fur or a river the confluence of many drops of water. This does not mean, however, that in all circumstances you have already amassed wealth when you possess only a single egg. Nothing is so simple and easy."

"Under Emperor Wan Li of the Ming Dynasty there lived a story writer named Chiang Ying-ko. One of his *Hsueh Tao's Tales* runs as follows:

Once there was a townsman who was so poor that he never knew where and when his next meal would be. One day by chance he found an egg. He told his wife elatedly, 'I have found our family wealth.' Asked where it was, he showed her the egg, saying, 'Here it is. But it will take ten years to build up our wealth.' Then he discussed his plan with his wife, 'I'll take the egg to the neighbour and have it hatched by his hen. When the chickens have grown up, I'll take back one of the females to lay eggs. I shall get 15 chickens a month. In two years they will multiply and make a total of 300. Then I shall sell them for ten taels of gold, with which I can buy five cows producing calves. My cows will multiply to 25 in three years and 150 in another three years. These I shall sell for 300 taels of gold. If I lend out the money at interest, I shall have amassed 500 taels of gold in three years.'

"The latter half of the story goes into rather uninteresting detail, so I would like to leave them out, except one point worth mentioning. In the end this greedy man said that he would like a concubine. At this **his wife was 'roused to great anger and smashed the egg with a blow of her fist.' Thus his family wealth consisting of a single egg was totally destroyed.**

"Don't you see that this story helps to explain a lot of things? This greedy man, too, realized that to build his family wealth would take a long time and hence in the discussion with his wife allowed himself **ten years** to do so. This seemed reasonable, but his plan was utterly lacking in any reliable basis and consisted entirely in a series of mere suppositions one piled on another. In picturing what would happen in the next ten years, he **completely substituted illusion for reality**, showing himself as one obsessed by greed for money. The result was that his wife flew into a rage and **with a blow of her fist she destroyed all his riches.**"

("The Family Wealth Consisting of a Single Egg", *Evening Chats at Yenshan,* Vol. I, pp. 76-77; first appeared in the *Peking Evening News,* June 18, 1961)

Comment: When our Party set forward its plan for socialist economic construction, the Khrushchov revisionists shouted, "We have to wait and see if there is any truth in it." When we were in temporary difficulties, they attacked our great leap forward as having "failed" and "collapsed". In the present piece Teng To also makes talk of indulging in fantasy, "substituting illusion for reality", and "the family wealth consisting of a single egg" which is "totally destroyed", etc. Are not these also attacks on our great leap forward as having "failed"? Do they not chime in with the attacks of the Khrushchov revisionists?

Maliciously Attacking the Dictatorship of the Proletariat

"Ancient historians also made numerous comments on the royal way and the tyrant's way. But how should we consider the royal way and the tyrant's way from our present-day viewpoint?"

"In the section on 'Expert Planning' in his book *Historical Anecdotes Newly Arranged*, Liu Hsiang wrote, 'The royal way is as smooth as a whetstone and stems from human sentiments and decorum.' Elsewhere in the same book he said, 'Following different ways, all the Three Dynasties established a royal rule; using different laws, the Five Tyrants established a tyrannical regime.' Apparently, Liu Hsiang praised the royal way and disapproved of the tyrant's way. He regarded the royal way as the result of combining human sentiments with law and morality. This is right, for it had been stated long before in the *Book of Rites,* 'If rites, music, punishments and administration are carried out smoothly and correctly, the royal way will reach perfection.' Therefore, the so-called royal way actually refers to certain attitudes and actions taken by people in tackling all problems in a given historical period, according to the prevailing human sentiments and social moral standards and in harmony with the current political and judicial systems. On the contrary, if in disregard of everything one relied on authority and power, used violence and coercion, ordered others about and robbed the people by force or by trick, then that would be the so-called tyrant's way."

"According to our present-day viewpoint and in our language, what then are the royal way and the tyrant's way? The royal way can be interpreted as the honest and realistic way of thinking and style of work which follow the mass line. The tyrant's way, on the other hand, can be interpreted as the arrogant subjectivist and dogmatic way of thinking and arbitrary style of work. However, we should not force such interpretations on the ancients, whom it would be unrealistic to judge from such a viewpoint."

"Nevertheless, it will not be difficult to draw a lesson from ancient history. This shows that, after all, even in ancient times the royal way was much better than the tyrant's way. In recounting the situation in the period before the Chin and Han Dynasties when the princes were contending for hegemony, Pan Ku made satirical remarks on many occasions against the tyrant's way in his *History of the Han Dynasty*. For instance, he wrote, 'King Wen of the state of Tsin decided to follow the tyrant's way. He attacked the state of Wei, captured the Earl of Tsao, defeated the state of Chu at Chengpu, and finally called a conference of the princes.' Thus people can see at a glance how those who wanted to be tyrants made enemies everywhere and became very unpopular!"

("The Royal Way and the Tyrant's Way", *Evening Chats at Yenshan*, Vol. IV, pp. 13-16; first appeared in the *Peking Evening News*, February 25, 1962)

Comment: Using the past to satirize the present, this article maliciously attacks the dictatorship of the proletariat. Teng To says slanderously that we "relied on authority and power", "used violence and coercion", and "became unpopular". We would like to ask, with whom are we unpopular? We are unpopular with the landlords, rich peasants, counter-revolutionaries, bad elements and Rightists. To these people, the dictatorship of the proletariat can apply only the "tyrant's way", not the policy of benevolence. To apply the "royal way" or the policy of benevolence to them would mean betrayal of the revolution and the people.

III. COMPLAINING ABOUT INJUSTICE TO THE RIGHT OPPORTUNISTS WHO WERE DISMISSED FROM OFFICE, PRAISING THEIR ANTI-PARTY "BACKBONE" AND ENCOURAGING THEM TO STAGE A COME-BACK

Defending Li San-tsai, Secretary of the Board of Census, Who Was Dismissed from Office

"Among the historical figures of Peking, Li San-tsai of the Ming Dynasty, a native of Tungchow, has long fallen into oblivion. **This is a regrettable thing** for students of local history.

"When I recently talked with a few friends, all historians, this man's name chanced to crop up. On returning home, I looked up some historical material and discovered that the verdict of old historians on Li San-tsai is quite questionable and **should be re-assessed.**

"Li San-tsai (courtesy name, Tao-fu, pen-name, Hsiu-wu) became a licentiate in the second year of the reign of Wan Li. He served successively as 'deputy imperial prosecutor', 'Governor of Fengyang' and 'Secretary of the Board of Census'. He opposed the prevalent methods of collecting the mining tax and was an active supporter of the Tunglin Party. He is a well-known figure in the *History of the Ming Dynasty.*

"The *History of the Ming Dynasty* compiled in the early Ching Dynasty by Chang Ting-yu and others contains a biography of Li San-tsai which concludes with the following sentences by way of summing up:

A man of great talents, San-tsai was fond of stratagems and adept at ingratiating himself with court officials. During the thirteen years he served as Governor of Fengyang, he made friends all over the country. Being unable to keep away from corruption, he was attacked by others. Those who later censured San-tsai, like Shao Fu-chung and Hsu Chao-kuei, were all followers of Wei Chung-hsien whose names were on the list of traitors, while those who recommended him, such as Ku Hsien-cheng, Tsou Yuan-piao, Chao Nan-hsing and Liu Tsung-chou, were all distinguished high officials. Therefore, the public regarded San-tsai as a wise man.

"The *History of the Ming Dynasty* characterized Li San-tsai as a man 'fond of stratagems and adept at ingratiating himself with court officials'. This is not a complimentary remark. If that had been true, **Li San-tsai would have been a political schemer and intriguer. But the facts tell another story.** According to *The Truthful Record of Emperor Shen Tsung,* in the 27th and 28th years of the reign of Wan Li (Emperor Shen Tsung) Li San-tsai time and again memorialized the emperor on the abuses perpetrated in taxing mines. He boldly exposed the crimes committed by the eunuchs in collecting such taxes, their wholesale extortions and transgressions of the law. In the 30th and 31st years of the reign, he again repeatedly memorialized the emperor, **expressing his opposition to the mining tax and proposing the prevention and control of floods and droughts by dredging rivers, digging canals and building sluice gates.** The emperor accepted none of these proposals; on the contrary, he punished Li San-tsai by 'depriving him of his salary for five months'. How could he be described as being 'fond of stratagems and adept at ingratiating himself with court officials'?"

"As he had repeatedly memorialized the emperor to no avail, Li San-tsai begged to resign from office and retire home."

"Of course, the 'Tunglin Party' also emerged at the time to attack dark feudal politics, and 'San-tsai maintained intimate connections with its members'. For this reason, **the corrupt die-hard forces** violently attacked Li San-tsai as well as members of the Tunglin Party, such as Ku Hsien-cheng and Kao Pan-lung. Small wonder that subsequently Wei Chung-hsien and his gang should have regarded Li San-tsai together with the Tunglin Party as their sworn enemies.

"It was only natural that, incited by the eunuchs, the corrupt die-hard forces represented by Shao Fu-chung and Hsu Chao-kuei should have heaped abuse on Li San-tsai. They accused him of being 'a great villain feigning loyalty and a big hypocrite feigning uprightness', and 'listed his four major crimes of corruption, deception, guile and tyranny'. Even after Li San-tsai had finally retired home, they again trumped up the charge against him of 'stealing imperial timber to build his private mansion'. Perhaps this was the factual basis of the statement in the *History of the Ming Dynasty* that he was 'unable to keep away from corruption'. But Li San-tsai repeatedly memorialized the emperor, asking that 'eunuchs be sent to conduct a trial', that 'court officials come to investigate' and that 'the emperor personally hear my case'. He seemed to be in the right and self-confident, but the court of Emperor Wan Li dared not make a thorough investigation of the facts. Isn't it clear how things really stood?"

"Judging by the facts about Li San-tsai during his lifetime and those facts which came to light after his death, we should regard him as a positive historical figure, though we cannot say that his character was entirely blameless."

("In Defence of Li San-tsai", *Evening Chats at Yenshan*, Vol. V, pp. 102-04; first appeared in the *Peking Evening News*, March 29, 1962)

Comment: Li San-tsai was an insignificant historical figure. He was a butcher who suppressed peasant uprisings. But Teng To described him as a good official who spoke out for the people and worked for their welfare. He defends him because of his dismissal from office, saying that he was "in the right and self-confident" Why? It is easy to see that Li San-tsai was a man of the type of Hai Jui. Under the guise of defending Li San-tsai, Teng To is really complaining on behalf of the Right opportunists.

> Acclaiming the "Inflexibility" of Cheng Pan-chiao Who, After
> Being Dismissed from Office on a "Framed-up Charge",
> Nursed Bitter Hatred; Calling on People to Imitate
> His Example of "Being His Own Master"
> and "Refusing to Act as a Menial"

"*In Yangchow, the land of song and music,
   he was known as an eccentric
Reading amidst the fragrance of orchids
   and shade of bamboos.*
With his brush he painted a moral like that
   of *Spring and Autumn Annals*,
His ten ballads voiced the eternal passions

> *of Heaven and Earth.*
> **He became himself only after discarding the official's hat,**
> *The splash of ink and water was his ideal.*
> *Now Pan-chiao is gone but the bridge of Hungchiao still stands,*
> *And hills without number look intensely clear and blue.*

"This is a poem in the classical pattern which I wrote during a visit to Yangchow two years ago [1961] in memory of Cheng Pan-chiao, a Ching painter and poet. . . . Tomorrow is the anniversary of his birth, and I think it is perhaps still necessary to use the opportunity to make a re-assessment of this writer."

"In the fifth year of the reign of Emperor Chien Lung, he was appointed magistrate of Fanhsien County in Shantung and in the eleventh was transferred to Weihsien County. **For several years in succession natural calamities befell Shantung; his active efforts to collect relief funds incurred the disfavour of the influential gentry and wealthy merchants. Charged with 'corruption and embezzlement', he was dismissed from office.**"

"Cheng Pan-chiao did an excellent job in his relief work in Shantung. **He stood completely on the side of the people and worked for the welfare of the masses suffering from natural calamities, and for this he aroused the anger of the feudal bureaucrats and the influential gentry and landlord class.** . . . they conspired together and trumped up the charge that Cheng Pan-chiao took advantage of relief work to practise corruption and embezzlement. In handling this case the corrupt ruling class of the Ching Dynasty lent full credence to the framed-up charge of the big landlords. Faced with this situation, Pan-chiao indignantly tendered his resignation, and his superiors were only too glad to grant it. Therefore, in late autumn and early winter of the 17th year of the reign of Emperor Chien Lung, Cheng Pan-chiao **was dismissed from office.**"

"From his **dismissal from office** to his death at the age of 73, the so-called Pan-chiao style, i.e., Pan-chiao's ideas and style, became more and more ingenuous and distinctive. It was first manifested in his poetry. Here I shall quote as an example his poem written to the melody of *Chin Yuan Chun* and simply entitled 'Hatred':

> *Flowers have no understanding, the moon provides no solace, wine gives no inspiration.*

> I would like to fell the pretty peach trees to mar the scenery and cook the parrot to enrich my broth.
> I would like to destroy my ink slab and burn my books, smash my lute and tear up my paintings,
> Scrap all my writings and blot out every trace of my name. . . . .
>
> **My character is inflexible, though I am poor, wizened, in plain garments and a straw hat.**
> I stay year after year in this shabby lane, the autumn grass growing round my thatched cottage,
> A light drizzle beating against the dilapidated window, a lone lamp burning night after night.
> Can it be that **Heaven even gags my mouth and forbids me to vent my hatred in a sigh or two?**
> **Unable to contain myself, I take up a hundred pieces of silk to paint my misery in all its detail."**

"Let me . . . . in passing show you a drawing by Pan-chiao which has never been made public before. It is entitled 'Orchids and Bamboos in Remote Mountains', and was perhaps done during his magistracy in Fanhsien County. There is a poem inscribed on the painting:

> On a remote mountain precipice lonely orchids stand,
> The sparse bamboo leaves rustle together with their cool shadows,
> I must soon doff the official's hat
> So that I may come and rest carefree in their midst."

"Evidently, he painted it when he was still a magistrate but was no longer willing to serve. The message conveyed by the painting agrees entirely with that of the poem. . . . does not the point of the painting become clear if we contrast the setting of the painting with the life of a bureaucrat the artist was then living?"

"As far as I know, there are still earnest students following the Pan-chiao style. But the most important point is, I think, to grasp the spirit of the Pan-chiao style. What is it? In my opinion, it is **to be one's own master in all respects and refuse to act as a menial!**"

"Pan-chiao said, 'Those who write should do so as masters, not as menials.' This is a very important remark. As a constant reminder to himself to carry this out, he specially made a seal on which were engraved the characters, 'Cheng the Master of the House'. In other words, in everything he did, he always was his own master and blazed the trail for himself."

("Cheng Pan-chiao and the Pan-chiao Style", the
Kuangming Daily, November 21, 1963)

Comment: It really is a curious coincidence. After Wu Han published his drama *Hai Jui Dismissed from Office,* Teng To too suddenly felt a yearning for the ancients and wrote in memory of the dismissed official Cheng Pan-chiao. First writing a poem in 1961 and then an article in 1963. Teng To vociferously complained on behalf of Cheng Pan-chiao who had been dismissed from office. And see how indignant and excited he was! If the reader compares this piece of Teng To's with Wu Han's drama, he will see immediately that they play the same tune on different instruments, i.e., airing grievances for the Right opportunists dismissed from office.

Teng To points out as a crowning touch that the spirit of the Pan-chiao style consists in "being one's own master and refusing to act as a menial". And he calls on people to grasp this spirit and seriously learn from it so as to "blaze the trail for oneself". How cunning and venomous! Isn't Teng To calling on people to oppose the leadership of the Party? The wide road of socialism lies bright before us, and yet Teng To calls on people to "blaze the trail for themselves". What is this trail if not the dark path leading to the restoration of capitalism?

Acclaiming Mi Wan-chung as One Who "Was Free from Corruption and Who Took Great Care in Dealing with Civil and Criminal Cases", and as One Who Often Criticized Current Affairs, Won the Praise of the Middle and Lower Social Strata and Was Therefore Dismissed from Office

"Mi Wan-chung was a great scholar and a man with backbone. There were many things to praise in his conduct. He was born in the fourth year of the reign of the Ming Emperor Lung Ching . . . . At 25, he passed the imperial examinations for the rank of licentiate . . . . In the following year he was appointed Governor of Kiangning. Soon afterwards, he was transferred by order to the post of Imperial Inspector of Kiangsi. He was said to be free from corruption and to take great interest in civil and criminal cases and cultural and educational affairs. Wherever he went, he won the praise of the middle and lower strata of the population and the literati."

"Mi Wan-chung was regarded by Wei Chung-hsien as a thorn in his side, because Mi always despised him and his gang and often voiced his criticism of current affairs. Ni Wen-huan, one of Wei Chung-hsien's lackeys, was particularly notorious for his incrimination of innocent people under trumped-up charges. Scores of officials were falsely accused by him; in the more serious cases, people were tortured to death, while in less serious cases they were deprived of office and their names struck off the official register. Mi Wan-chung was victimized in the latter way."

"On a piece of white silk Mi wrote a short peom entitled 'Lanko Mountain'. The calligraphy is in a flowing style completely free from academic stiffness. The poem reads:

The sun and moon vainly busy themselves revolving round the earth,
The Immortals who never grow old are to be envied.
While dynasties change in a single moment,
The human world still lasts longer than the world in the grotto.

What is the point of the poem? It obviously reflects the writer's feelings about the unpredictable political vicissitudes of the Ming Dynasty."

("The Old and Young Mi's of Wanping", *Evening Chats at Yenshan*, Vol. III, pp. 39-41; first appeared in the *Peking Evening News*, November 9, 1961)

Comment: In this piece, Teng To again takes up Mi Wan-chung, an ancient buried in oblivion, as a pretext for complaining on behalf of the Right opportunists.

Complaining About the Injustice of Li Shan's Dismissal from Office

"The life story of Li Shan is a sad one. Cheng Pan-chiao said in another poem addressed to him:

Twice deprived of your scholarly rank and once demoted,
You shiver to see your thinning grey hair in the mirror.

For a long time, Li Shan was compelled to leave the Academy of Painters at the Ching imperial court as a result of the machinations of his colleagues. He then became magistrate of Tenghsien County, Shantung Province, for a short while, **was hated by the power-wielding nobility and was therefore dismissed from office**. Afterwards, he led a vagrant life and went to Yangchow where he eked out a living by painting, thus becoming one of the eight eccentric artists of Yangchow."

"If we read Li's own poem on a scroll, we shall better understand the deep meaning of this painting. The poem says plainly:

Yellow leaves fall from the trees around the hermitage;
The cold of the frosty dawn is not to be feared.
To paint a rooster, I would show it crowing,
To awaken the conscience of man to do good deeds."

"The poem not only explains the significance of the painting but also reflects Li Shan's plight and his resentment and anger at the time."

("About Li Shan and His Paintings", the *Kuangming Daily*, February, 14, 1961)

Comment: Another case of dismissal from office! Between 1961 and 1963, Teng To complained of as many as four cases of dismissal from office and in each case sang the praises of the "rebellious spirit" of those who refused to submit despite dismissal. What "painstaking creative thinking"!

IV. ARROGANTLY SHOUTING THAT OUR PARTY SHOULD IMMEDIATELY RETIRE AND "TAKE A REST"

Demanding That Our Party "Say Nothing and Do Nothing", but Follow the "Instructions" of Teng To and Co. in Everything

"I would advise those friends given to great empty talk to read more, think more, say less and **take a rest when the time comes for talking, so as to save their own as well as other people's time and energy!**"

("Great Empty Talk", *Frontline*, No. 21, 1962)

"We cannot tell how such case [of amnesia] would be at its very worst — presumably it would result either in insanity or in idiocy."

"Thus if anyone finds either of these symptoms present in himself, he must promptly take a complete rest and say nothing and do nothing, and if he insists on speaking and acting, he will come to grief. . . . . It is imperative to follow the instructions of a competent doctor, the family of the patient must not make any decision on its own, and, in particular, the patient himself must not interfere."

("Special Treatment for 'Amnesia' ", *Frontline*, No. 14, 1962)

"It was, of course, fortunate for the titlark that it could fly away in embarrassment when its bluff was called. However, it should be borne in mind that in other circumstances those who were deceived by charlatans will certainly not let them off lightly after calling their bluff."

("Two Foreign Fables", *Evening Chats at Yenshan*, Vol. V, p. 93; first appeared in the *Peking Evening News*, November 26, 1961)

"Chia Tao came from the prefecture of Fanyang . . . . It belonged to the states of Yu and Yen in the periods of the Spring and Autumn Annals and the Warring States; it was a tradition in those places for brave and heroic men to express their chivalrous sentiments in stirring songs. As Chia Tao wrote in his short poem 'The Swordsman':

For ten years I have been whetting my sword,
Its cold blade never once put to test;
In showing it to you, I ask today:
Tell me who has been wronged.

It is obvious that the poet wrote this to voice his own feelings."

("Chia Tao's Approach to Poetic Creation", *Evening Chats at Yenshan*, Vol. I, p. 16; first appeared in the *Peking Evening News*, June 18, 1961)

Comment: These extracts help us to see the really vicious and malevolent nature of *Evening Chats* more clearly. Teng To is not just flinging abuse at our Party and socialism; he wants to overthrow them. When he says that the so-called victim of amnesia "must promptly take a complete rest", isn't it clear that he fondly hopes to oust the Communist Party from power?

Hinting That He Is Not "a Mere Intellectual Indulging in Empty Talk" but "a Stout-Hearted Man" Who "Bravely Fights the Wicked Men in Power"

"The Tunglin scholars propagated learning in the tradition of Yang Shih;
They showed concern for everything on earth and under heaven.
Don't think of them as mere intellectuals indulging in empty talk,
Fresh were the bloodstains when their heads rolled."
"Fighting the wicked men in power with unbending will,
The Tunglin scholars were a stout-hearted generation.
Kao Pan-lung's moral integrity shines forth in undying glory,
Every word of his poem written on the point of death stirs the heart."

("Singing the Praises of Lake Taihu", the *Kuang-ming Daily,* September 7, 1960)

Comment: Teng To has written much about the Tunglin Party in the past few years; he has, in particular, strongly recommended a couplet inscribed on the pillars in the Tunglin Academy, and said that the Tunglin members "had their own political objective" both in studying and in lecturing and that they all had "backbone". Obviously, there is also a "political objective" in these two poems praising the rebellious spirit of "fighting the wicked men in power with unbending will". In their anti-Party and anti-socialist activities, Teng To and his fellows try to boost the morale of their gang by invoking the Tunglin Party and playing up its rebel character.

V. *EVENING CHATS AT YENSHAN* ATTACKS THE PARTY AND SOCIALISM UNDER THE PRETEXT OF IMPARTING "KNOWLEDGE"

"Starting from the Tiniest Things Such as the Fly or Bedbug and Ending Up with Political Affairs" — One of Teng To's Tactics in Attacking the Party and Socialism

"*Evening Chats* has been serialized in this newspaper and said practically nothing about newspapers. Why? Is it because you take no interest in them?

"When reproachfully questioned by some intimate friends, I could not help breaking into laughter. What do I have to say? Well, here by chance is a letter from a reader asking me to talk about the death of Lin Pai-shui. So an opportunity finally offers itself for me to write about the press."

"After the 1911 Revolution, Lin Pai-shui founded the *New Society Daily* in Peking. In one of his articles, he wrote, 'It would indeed be fine to have democracy in China today. However, the remnant feudal forces remain intact, and it will take 15 years of effort to uproot them.' As someone noted, about 15 years elapsed between the time he wrote the article and the Great Revolution of 1925-27. This may just as well be credited to his 'foresight'. However, it was said that his articles dealt with subjects often 'casually picked up' and 'started from the tiniest things such as the fly or bedbug and ended up with political affairs' and that they showed 'much indignation laced with humour'. They therefore especially incurred the displeasure of some of those in power. The *New Society Daily* was once closed by official order, and when it resumed publication Lin Pai-shui announced, 'From now on, the word "new" is removed from the *New Society Daily*, so that the name of this paper is, so to speak, beheaded as a token of self-punishment.' This is how the *New Society Daily* became the *Society Daily*."

("The Death of Lin Pai-shui", *Evening Chats at Yenshan*, Vol. V, pp. 105-07; first appeared in the *Peking Evening News*, August 26, 1962)

Comment: Why should Teng To, a newspaperman for a long time, "break into laughter" at the very mention of newspaper? This deserves some looking into, upon which we will discover that the reason is that he was criticized when he was running a newspaper and he harbours a grudge against the Party.

Lin Pai-shui, editor-in-chief of a newspaper he founded in Peking after the 1911 Revolution, is represented as a writer whose articles dealt with subjects often "casually picked up", and "started from the tiniest things such as the fly or bedbug and ended up with political affairs". Isn't this Teng To's confession of his own methods? What if the readers fail to see the point in the articles so "painstakingly" written up by him? So he has to drop them a hint, using a dead man as his mouthpiece, to indicate that his writings about the rooftiles, bees and other such things all "end up with political affairs". Herein lies the key with which we should "unlock" the secrets contained in his *Evening Chats at Yenshan.*

Most of the Pieces in Evening Chats at Yenshan Are Full of Double Entendres and Have a "Political Purpose"

" *'Sounds of wind, rain and reading of books all fill my ears; Family, state and world affairs, I show concern for them all.'*

This is a couplet composed by Ku Hsien-cheng, leader of the Tunglin Party in the Ming Dynasty."

"Why have I suddenly recalled this couplet? Chatting with some friends of mine, I found them of the view that the ancients had no political purpose in reading books, that they read only for reading's sake and never applied their reading to anything practical. To show that this view is groundless, I quoted this couplet. Moreover, very few people are acquainted with it and there is some need to recommend it.

"The first line means that the environment of the Tunglin Academy was favourable to people's devoting themselves to reading books. The eleven characters vividly portray the scene in which the sounds made by wind and rain in nature are fused with the sound made by man in reading. The line makes us feel as though we ourselves were transported into the Academy and heard the scholars' reading and lecturing vying with all the sounds of nature.

"The second line means that all those studying at the Academy should show concern for politics. These eleven characters fully reflect the political ideals of the scholars of the Tunglin Party. They urged that one should not only be concerned with the affairs of one's own family, but also with the affairs of the state and the whole world."

"If we link up the two lines, the meaning stands out even more clearly: one should study hard and at the same time show concern for politics and the two should be closely combined. Moreover, **the sounds of wind and rain in the first line can be understood as a *double entendre* which refers both to the wind and rain as natural phenomena and to the storms of political life.** Hence, this couplet has a really **profound** significance.

"Judging by present-day views, we can see that **the scholars of the Tunglin Party obviously had a political purpose in their reading and lecturing.**"

"It becomes increasingly evident that one should study hard and at the same time show concern for politics. Even the ancients understood and propagated this truth. Can it be that we are inferior to the ancients and ignorant of this truth? At any rate, we should understand it more fully, more deeply and more thoroughly than they!"

> ("Show Concern for All Things", *Evening Chats at Yenshan*, Vol. II, pp. 60-62; first appeared in the *Peking Evening News*, October 8, 1961)

Comment: Teng To tells us that "the scholars of the Tunglin Party obviously had a political purpose in their reading and lecturing", and that what they called the sounds of wind and rain is a *double entendre* which "refers both to the wind and rain as natural phenomena and to the storms of political life" and has a "profound" significance. Here Teng To is owning up about his own methods.

Inciting People to Express "Dissatisfaction with Social Reality" by Using the "Technique of the Cartoon"

"The ancients already knew how to use drawing as a weapon to expose evil persons and evil deeds and praise good persons and good deeds. So drawings with the theme of the contrast between good and evil may be regarded as a kind of ancient Chinese cartoon."

"Generally speaking, however, the ancient cartoonists were not only unable critically to analyse the social reality of their times but fundamentally lacked the courage to expose social abuses. Hence, **some artists chose a subtly ambiguous form to express their dissatisfaction with the social reality of the time.**"

"The most noteworthy cartoons were undoubtedly those of the Eight Eccentric Artists of Yangchow. These artists were in fact scholars from **both the south and the north who were dissatisfied with social reality. They were angry and disgusted with society, full of grievances and out of tune with the times.** Therefore, people called them 'eccentrics', and they gladly acquiesced in the title. Animated by such sentiments, they were bound to be somewhat 'eccentric' in their drawings. Take Lo Liang-feng's works for example . . . . He liked most of all to draw ghosts and won great fame.

Everybody knows that his most celebrated work was 'A Picture of the Ghosts' Fun' which may be regarded as a typical ancient cartoon."

"(We) know that his **satirical portrayal of ghosts is actually a satirical portrayal of men.** In the society of that time, if the artist had used the cartoon directly to satirize living men, he would **simply have been asking for trouble;** but, on the other hand, if he only satirized a few ghosts, he would be quite safe. Probably it was after such practical considerations that the artist finally decided to adópt the method of drawing cartoons satirizing ghosts."

("Ancient Cartoons", *Evening Chats at Yenshan*, Vol. III, pp. 51-53; first appeared in the *Peking Evening News*, November 2, 1961)

Comment: Here the allusion is very clear. The "satirical portrayal of ghosts" is a "satirical portrayal of men", using the "method of drawing cartoons" to give vent to dissatisfaction with social reality. Beyond all doubt this is what *Evening Chats* does.

Beating a Temporary Retreat in an Unfavourable Situation, Decamping Being the Best of the Thirty-six Stratagems

"I have come across a mimeographed pamphlet entitled *The Thirty-six Stratagems.*"

"It enumerates the 36 stratagems and, to prove their effectiveness, also cites examples of their application by ancient strategists. **Herein lies the pamphlet's value.**"

"Did anyone in ancient times ever talk about the 36 stratagems? Who first spoke of them? As far as I know . . . perhaps the earliest mention occurs in the 'Biography of Wang Ching-tseh' in the *History of Southern Chi.*"

"In this biographical account in the *History of Southern Chi*, Vol. 26, we find the following passage:

The emperor was seriously ill. When Wang Ching-tseh suddenly revolted in the east, the court was shaken and terrified. The prince who was to be posthumously called the Muddle-headed Marquis was at that time heir apparent to the throne . . . . When he was told in the palace that Wang Ching-tseh had arrived, he hastily packed up to take flight. Told of this, Wang Ching-tseh commented, 'Of General Tan's 36 stratagems decamping is the best. The only thing the father and the son can do is to flee in haste.'

"In the 'Biography of Wang Ching-tseh' in the *History of the Southern Dynasties*, Vol. 45, there is the same sentence, 'the only thing the father and the son can do is to flee in haste.' But it is immediately followed by another sentence, 'Perhaps Wang said this to ridicule Tan Tao-chi who avoided fighting against the state of Wei.' "

"Tan Tao-chi lived a little before the period of Wang Ching-tseh. He was one of the generals who helped Liu Yu, Emperor Wu of Sung, to establish his empire during the Southern Dynasties. After Liu Yi-lung, Emperor Wen of Sung, succeeded to the throne, Tan was promoted to the post of Duke of Wuling Province and given the title of Commander-in-Chief for the Conquest of the South. Leading his army against the state of Wei, he fought more than thirty battles and won them all. Later, owing to a shortage in the supply in grains and fodder, he beat a retreat by means of skilful stratagems."

"The story is given in greater detail in the 'Biography of Tan Tao-chi' in the *History of the Southern Dynasties*, Vol. 15:

As commander of the expeditionary forces, Tan Tao-chi marched northward to seize territories and fought his way to the River Chi. He defeated a strong force of the state of Wei and took Huatai. He fought more than thirty battles against the Wei troops and won most of them. When his army arrived at Licheng, it ran short of supplies and turned back. Some surrendered to Wei and told the enemy about the Sung army's shortage of supplies. All this spread worry and fear among Tan's men and their morale became low. At night Tan Tao-chi made them weigh sand and shout out the weight as if they were measuring rice and scatter what little rice was left on the sand. After daybreak the Wei troops believed that Tan's army still had enough grain and therefore refrained from pursuit. Thinking that the men who surrendered must have told lies, they had them executed. Tan's troops were numerically inferior and had now become exhausted, and panic reigned throughout the army. Tan ordered his men to don their armour and he himself rode slowly in a chariot to the outskirts of his encampment. At the sight of this, the Wei troops suspected ambush. They dared not go near and withdrew. Although Tan Tao-chi failed to conquer the area south of the Yellow River, he returned with his army intact. This helped spread his reputation as a hero far and wide and the state of Wei feared him very much.

"Judging from this, 'decamping is the best' was not the only stratagem Tan Tao-chi employed; without employing other stratagems he could not have succeeded in getting away, much as he wanted to. Thanks to several co-ordinated stratagems, such as those of deceptive military deployment and sowing discord among the enemy, as a result of which the troops of the state of Wei dared not continue the pursuit, he succeeded in making good his retreat. Wang Ching-tseh ridiculed Tan Tao-chi for avoiding the troops of the state of Wei, but as we see it today, Wang Ching-tseh's ridicule only goes to prove that he himself was no strategist."

"After making a comprehensive study of the relevant material cited above and drawing our own conclusions, we understand the meaning of the saying: Of the thirty-six stratagems of Tan Tao-chi, decamping is the best. If we work out the implications, is it not clear what the thirty-six stratagems are?"

("The Thirty-six Stratagems", Evening Chats at Yenshan, Vol. V, pp. 84-87; first appeared in the Peking Evening News, September 2, 1962)

Comment: "The Thirty-six Stratagems" was the last item in the series of *Evening Chats at Yenshan*. It appeared on September 2, 1962, when the Party's Eighth Central Committee was about to convene its tenth plenary session. Seeing that the situation was getting unfavourable, Teng To acted on the saying "Of the thirty-six stratagems, decamping is the best" and duly made arrangements for retreat. To ensure safety in retreat, he had to use his wits and employ tactics. Unless he resorted to other stratagems, he could not get away, "much as he wanted to". Teng To listed the titles of all the 36 stratagems for the benefit of his partners. So *Evening Chats at Yenshan* was for the time "discontinued", but the Three-Family Village gangster inn carried on business as usual, conserving its strength and waiting for the opportune moment to go into action again. But whether he has 36 or 72 stratagems, Teng To will never be able to effect his get-away.

(First published in the Liberation Army Daily and the Kuangming Daily on May 8, 1966)

CONVERSION TABLE FROM PIN-YIN TO WADE-GILES TRANSCRIPTION SYSTEM

Pin-yin	Wade-Giles	Pin-yin	Wade-Giles	Pin-yin	Wade-Giles
a	a	cha	ch'a	dui	tui
ai	ai	chai	ch'ai	dun	tun
an	an	chan	ch'an	duo	to
ang	ang	chang	ch'ang	e	o,e
ao	ao	chao	ch'ao	en	en
ba	pa	che	ch'e	eng	eng
bai	pai	chen	ch'en	er (r)	erh
ban	pan	cheng	ch'eng	fa	fa
bang	pang	chi	ch'ih	fan	fan
bao	pao	chong	ch'ung	fang	fang
bei	pei	chou	ch'ou	fei	fei
ben	pen	chu	ch'u	fen	fen
beng	peng	chua	ch'ua	feng	feng
bi	pi	chuai	ch'uai	fo	fo
bian	pien	chuan	ch'uan	fou	fou
biao	piao	chuang	ch'uang	fu	fu
bie	pieh	chui	ch'ui	ga	ka
bin	pin	chun	ch'un	gai	kai
bing	ping	chuo	ch'o	gan	kan
bo	po	da	ta	gang	kang
bu	pu	dai	tai	gao	kao
ca	ts'a	dan	tan	ge	ko
cai	ts'ai	dang	tang	gei	kei
can	ts'an	dao	tao	gen	ken
cang	ts'ang	de	te	geng	keng
cao	ts'ao	dei	tei	gong	kung
ce	ts'e	deng	teng	gou	kou
cen	ts'en	di	ti	gu	ku
ceng	ts'eng	dian	tien	gua	kua
ci	tz'u	diao	tiao	guai	kuai
cong	ts'ung	die	tieh	guan	kuan
cou	ts'ou	ding	ting	guang	kuang
cu	ts'u	diu	tiu	gui	kuei
cuan	ts'uan	dong	tung	gun	kun
cui	ts'ui	dou	tou	guo	kuo
cun	ts'un	du	tu	ha	ha
cuo	ts'o	duan	tuan	hai	hai

Pin-yin	Wade-Giles	Pin-yin	Wade-Giles	Pin-yin	Wade-Giles
han	han	kuai	k'uai	mie	mieh
hang	hang	kuan	k'uan	min	min
hao	hao	kuang	k'uang	ming	ming
he	ho	kui	k'uei	miu	miu
hei	hei	kun	k'un	mo	mo
hen	hen	kuo	k'uo	mou	mou
heng	heng	la	la	mu	mu
hong	hung	lai	lai	na	na
hou	hou	lan	lan	nai	nai
hu	hu	lang	lang	nan	nan
hua	hua	lao	lao	nang	nang
huai	huai	le	le	nao	nao
huan	huan	lei	lei	nei	nei
huang	huang	leng	leng	nen	nen
hui	hui	li	li	neng	neng
hun	hun	lia	lia	ni	ni
huo	huo	lian	lien	nian	nien
ji	chi	liang	liang	niang	niang
jia	chia	liao	liao	niao	niao
jian	chien	lie	lieh	nie	nieh
jiang	chiang	lin	lin	nin	nin
jiao	chiao	ling	ling	ning	ning
jie	chieh(chiai)	liu	liu	niu	niu
jin	chin	long	lung	nong	nung
jing	ching	lou	lou	nou	nou
jiu	chiu	lu	lu	nu	nu
jiong	chiung	luan	luan	nuan	nuan
ju	chü	lun	lun	nun	nun
juan	chüan	luo	lo	nuo	no
jue	chueh	lü	lü	nü	nü
jun	chün	lüan	lüan	nüe	nüeh
ka	k'a	lüe	lüeh	(see e)	o
kai	k'ai	ma	ma	ou	ou
kan	k'an	mai	mai	pa	p'a
kang	k'ang	man	man	pai	p'ai
kao	k'ao	mang	mang	pan	p'an
ke	k'o	mao	mao	pang	p'ang
ken	k'en	mei	mei	pao	p'ao
keng	k'eng	men	men	pei	p'ei
kong	k'ung	meng	meng	pen	p'en
kou	k'ou	mi	mi	peng	p'eng
ku	k'u	mian	mien	pi	p'i
kua	k'ua	miao	miao	pian	p'ien

Pin-yin	Wade-Giles	Pin-yin	Wade-Giles	Pin-yin	Wade-Giles
piao	p'iao	sha	sha	tui	t'ui
pie	p'ieh	shai	shai	tun	t'un
pin	p'in	shan	shan	tuo	t'o
ping	p'ing	shang	shang	wa	wa
po	p'o	shao	shao	wai	wai
pou	p'ou	she	she	wan	wan
pu	p'u	shei	shei	wang	wang
qi	ch'i	shen	shen	wei	wei
qia	ch'ia	sheng	sheng	wen	wen
qian	ch'ien	shi	shih	weng	weng
qiang	ch'iang	si	ssu	wo	wo
qiao	ch'iao	shou	shou	wu	wu
qie	ch'ieh	shu	shu	xi	hsi
qin	ch'in	shua	shua	xia	hsia
qing	ch'ing	shuai	shuai	xian	hsien
qiong	ch'iung	shuan	shuan	xiang	hsiang
qiu	ch'iu	shuang	shuang	xiao	hsiao
qu	ch'ü	shui	shui	xie	hsieh
quan	ch'üan	shun	shun	xin	hsin
que	ch'üeh	shuo	shuo	xing	hsing
qun	ch'un	song	sung	xiong	hsiung
ran	jan	sou	sou	xiu	hsiu
rang	jang	su	su	xu	hsü
rao	jao	suan	suan	xuan	hsüan
re	je	sui	sui	xue	hsüeh
ren	jen	sun	sun	xun	hsün
reng	jeng	suo	so	ya	ya
ri	jih	ta	t'a	yai	yai
rong	jung	tai	t'ai	yan	yen
rou	jou	tan	t'an	yang	yang
ru	ju	tang	t'ang	yao	yao
ruan	juan	tao	t'ao	ye	yeh
rui	jui	te	t'e	yi	yi (i)
run	jun	teng	t'eng	yin	yin
ruo	jo	ti	t'i	ying	ying
sa	sa	tian	t'ien	yong	yung
sai	sai	tiao	t'iao	you	yu
san	san	tie	t'ieh	yu	yü
sang	sang	ting	t'ing	yuan	yüan
sao	sao	tong	t'ung	yue	yüeh
se	se	tou	t'ou	yun	yün
sen	sen	tu	t'u	za	tsa
seng	seng	tuan	t'uan	za	tsai

Pin-yin	Wades-Giles
zan	tsan
zang	tsang
zao	tsao
ze	tse
zei	tsei
zen	tsen
zeng	tseng
zi	tzu
zong	tsung
zou	tsou
zu	tsu
zuan	tsuan
zui	tsui
zun	tsun
zuo	tso
zha	cha
zhai	chai
zhan	chan
zhang	chang
zhao	chao
zhe	che
zhen	chen
zheng	cheng
zhi	chih
zhong	chung
zhou	chou
zhu	chu
zhua	chua
zhuai	chuai
zhuan	chuan
zhuang	chuang
zhui	chui
zhun	chun
zhuo	cho

NOTES
TO
PROSCRIBED CHINESE WRITING

野百合花　**Wild Lilies**

王實味　Wang Shih-wei (1903?–) Essayist. Wang joined the Chinese Communist Party in 1926 and wrote for the editorial department of the Marxism-Leninism Institute. In addition, he translated over 2 million words of Marxist-Leninist thought. He disappeared in 1942 after a struggle meeting in Yenan.

page 1

	野	yě	wild
	百合花	bǎihéhuā	lilies
1	前記	qiánjì	preface; foreword
2	獨步	dúbù	to go for a walk alone
	同志	tóngzhì	comrade
	舊式	jiùshì	old-styled
	棉鞋	miánxié	cotton-padded shoes
4	心臟	xīnzàng	heart
	照例	zhàolì	as usual; as a rule
	震動	zhèndòng	to quiver; to beat; to throb
	血液	xuèyè	blood
	循環	xúnhuán	to circulate
5	預科	yùkē	preparatory course
	入黨	rùdǎng	to join the Party
	犧牲	xīshēng	to sacrifice oneself for; to die for
	故鄉	gùxiāng	native town; one's birth place
6	被捕	bèibǔ	being arrested; being taken prisoner
	舅父	jiùfù	uncle on mother's side; a brother of mother
	縛	fú	to tie up with rope
	當地	dāngdì	local
	駐軍	zhùjūn	the stationed troops

7	殘忍	*cánrěn*	cruel; heartless
	赴死	*fùsǐ*	on one's way to death
	套	*tào*	a set of – measure word for clothes, books, tools, uniforms, and etc.
	襯衣褲	*chènyīkù*	underwear
8	針綫	*zhēnxiàn*	needles and threads
	密密	*mìmì*	thickly
	縫	*féng*	stitch
	槍決	*qiāngjué*	to be executed before a military squad
	縱使	*zòngshǐ*	to encourage; to allow; to tolerate
	流氓	*liúmáng*	rascals; scoundrels
9	奸屍	*jiānshī*	to rape female corpses
	血腥	*xuèxīng*	bloody
	醜惡	*chǒu'è*	ugly
	骯髒	*āngzāng*	dirty
	黑暗	*hēiàn*	dark
	噩耗	*èhào*	news of one's death
10	血管	*xuèguǎn*	veins
	猛烈	*měngliè*	strong; sudden
	熱愛	*rè'ài*	warm love
	毒恨	*dúhèn*	deep hatred
	浮	*fú*	to float; to emerge
11	聖潔	*shèngjié*	pure; sacred; divine
	殉道者	*xúndàozhě*	martyr
	影子	*yǐngz*	shadow; an image
	親	*qīn*	by blood; dear; close

12	從容就義	*cóngróngjiùyì*	calmly go to one's end for one's faith
	歌囀	*gēzhuǎn*	to warble; to sing in gentle continuous trilling manner
	玉堂春	*yùtángchūn*	spring in the palace
	舞迴	*wǔhuí*	to whirl around as in dance

page 2

1	金蓮步	*jīnliánbù*	tiny feet in graceful steps
	昇平	*shēngpíng*	peaceful
	氣象	*qìxiàng*	atmosphere; meteorology as in the study of motions and phenomena of atmosphere
	和諧	*héxié*	harmonious; in harmony
	當前	*dāngqián*	at present; at the moment; just now
	現實	*xiànshí*	reality
2	血泊	*xuèbó*	a swamp of blood
4	階級仇恨	*jiējíchóuhèn*	class hatred
	舊賬	*jiùzhàng*	old debt
	真正	*zhēnzhèng*	really
	大公無私	*dàgōngwúsī*	selfless
5	甚至	*shènzhì*	even
	拖曳	*tuōyì*	to drag along forward
	過程	*guòchéng*	process; in the process of
6	污穢	*wūhuì*	filth; dirt; impurity
	沾染	*zhānrǎn*	to get the better of; to contaminate
	散布	*sànbù*	to spread; to diffuse
	細菌	*xìjūn*	bacteria
	傳染	*chuánrǎn*	to contaminate; to infect
7	汲取	*jíqǔ*	to draw

8	偶然	ǒurán	by chance
	雜文	záwén	miscellanies
	總	zǒng	general
	標題	biāotí	subject heading
	含義	hányì	implied meanings; implications; insinuation
9	延安	yánān	Yenan, name of place. The "cradle of revolution" as the Chinese Communists call it
	山野	shānyě	wilderness; on hills and in wilderness
	野花	yěhuā	wild flowers; also unmarried females as opposed to wives
	用以	yòngyǐ	to be used as
	獻給	xiàngěi	to be dedicated to
	其次	qícì	secondly; next in order; besides
	據說	jùshuō	it is said
10	一般	yībān	common; general
	鱗狀	línzhuàng	scaly appearance; scaly
	球莖	qiújíng	bulbs of lilies
	略帶	lüèdài	slightly with
	苦澀	kǔsè	Bitter taste; a harsh flavour; an astringent taste in the mouth
	香甜可口	xiāngtiánkěkǒu	fragrant and sweet as agreeable to the taste; delicious; palatable
11	藥用價值	yàoyòngjiàzhí	medical value
13	缺少	quēshǎo	in want of; short of
14	起勁	qǐjìng	enthusiastic
	肚子	dùz	stomach; belly; abdomen
	裝	zhuāng	to fill; to cram; to be stuffed with

	不舒服	*bùshūfú*	uncomfortable; discomfort
15	營養不良	*yíngyǎngbùliáng*	under-nourished; malnutrition
	維他命	*wéitāmìng*	vitamins

page 3

1	比例	*bǐlì*	ratio; proportion
	十八比一	*shíbābǐyī*	eighteen to one
	單調	*dāndiào*	monotonous
	枯燥	*kūzào*	dull; not colourful
	娛樂	*yúlè*	entertainments; recreation
3	不是沒有	*búshìméiyǒu*	not without
	道理	*dàolǐ*	reasons; justifiability
	異性	*yìxìng*	opposite sex; another sex
	配偶	*pèiǒu*	to mate; to match; to make a pair; husband and wife
4	天經地義	*tiānjīngdìyì*	Indisputable; as of course; law of nature (Lit.)
	承認	*chéngrèn*	to admit
	犧牲精神	*xīshēngjīngshén*	spirit of sacrifice
	從事	*cóngshì*	to be engaged in
5	追求	*zhuīqiú*	in pursuit of; to go after
	食色	*shísè*	food and sex
	滿足	*mǎnzú*	satisfaction
6	圓滿	*yuánmǎn*	satisfactorily
	解決	*jiějué*	to solve (a problem); to settle (a case)
	輕于	*qīngyú*	indiscreetly; at random
	同意	*tóngyì*	to agree
7	段	*duàn*	measure word for talk, life, story, reminiscence and etc.; a short period of

	可能	kěnéng	may possibly; possible
	透露	tòulù	to reveal; to disclose
	一些	yīxiē	some; a few; a little
	消息	xiāoxī	news; information
9	凝神	níngshén	concentratedly
	諦聽	dìtīng	to listen carefully
10	動不動	dòngbùdòng	without reason; always; at any time
	小資產階級	xiǎozīchǎnjiējí	petty-bourgeoisie
	平均主義	píngjūnzhǔyì	equalitarianism; egalitarianism
	其實	qíshí	in fact
	特殊主義	tèshūzhǔyì	exceptionalism
11	漠不關心	mòbùguānxīn	not in the slightest concerned
13	烏鴉	wūyā	a crow; a rook
15	裝得	zhuāngdé	to pretend to
	如意	rúyì	as he wishes; pleased
	瞪眼	dèngyǎn	staring in anger
	搭架子	dājiàz	to put on airs
	首長	shǒuzhǎng	department heads
16	訓人	xùnrén	to lecture people

page 4

1	科長	kēzhǎng	head of a section
	畢恭畢敬	bìgōngbìjìng	very reverent
2	神氣活現	shénqìhuóxiàn	very haughty
	一下	yīxià	for a moment
3	扔	rēng	to throw
5	沉默	chénmò	silence befell

	佩服	pèifú to respect; to admire
	口齒尖利	kǒuchǐjiānlì sharpness of the tongue
	惘然	wǎngrán dimly; undecidedly
	若有所失	ruòyǒu suǒshī at a loss; as if I had lost something (Lit.)
6	害病	hàibìng to fall ill
7	添	tiān to add; to increase
	難受	nánshòu sufferings; discomfort; difficult to bear
	表情	biǎoqíng facial expressions; way of acting
12	垮台	kuǎtái to fail; to collapse
13	興奮地	xīngfèndì excitedly
	分路	fēnlù to part in opposite direction
14	偏頗	piānpō prejudice
	誇張	kuāzhāng exaggeration
	形象	xíngxiàng image
	普遍性	pǔbiànxìng generalisation
	決不能	juébùnéng by no means can
	否認	fǒurèn to deny
	鏡子	jìngz a mirror
15	作用	zuòyòng function; to function

page 5

1	碰	pèng to bump into; to come across. Here it means to contend with the author for this article *Running into Difficulties*
	碰壁	pèngbì to run into difficulties
2	不禁	bùjìn cannot help
4	抄	chāo to copy
	原文	yuánwén original texts

— 5 —

5	大後方	dàhòufāng	the rear; the big interior cities
	拂意	fúyì	undesirable; that which is opposed to one's wishes
	牢騷	láosāo	complaints; grudges
6	發泄	fāxiè	to give vent to; to exude
8	臉色	liǎnsè	facial expressions; colour of the face
10	入世未深	rùshìwèishēn	immature; inexperienced
	算	suàn	to count
	迥乎不同	jiǒnghūbùtóng	not in the least alike; quite different
	哺乳	bǔrǔ	to suckle; to be brought up
11	細語着	xìyǔzhe	to be murmuring; to be whispering
	人生	rénshēng	the meaning of life; life
	描摹	miáomó	to picture; to describe
	單純	dānchún	simple and pure
	憧憬	chōngjǐng	memory cherished
	現實	xiànshí	reality
	醜惡	chǒuè	ugliness
	冷淡	lěngdàn	nonchalance; indifference
12	陌生	mòshēng	alien to; new
	無怪乎	wúguàihū	no wonder
	風浪	fēnglàng	wind and waves – changes of situation; difficulties
	不安	bùān	uneasiness
13	知足者長樂	zhīzúzhěchánglè	blessed are those who are content
14	人生哲學	rénshēngzhéxué	philosophy of life
	可貴	kěguì	worthiness; worthy; significance
	在于	zàiyú	lies in
	敏感	mǐngǎn	sensitive; sensitiveness

page 6

2	四平八穩	sìpíngbāwěn	very safe; very firm
	不見得	bújiàndé	not necessarily
	叫嚷	jiàorǎng	brawl; to brawl
3	現象	xiànxiàng	phenomena
	探求	tànqiú	to search for; to seek
4	本質	běnzhì	essence; nature
	合理地	hélǐd	reasonably
	盲目的	mángmùd	blindly
	叫囂	jiàoxiāo	hubbub; confused yelling
	消除	xiāochú	to remove; to eliminate; to delete; to uplift
5	根源	gēnyuán	roots; sources
	教導	jiàodǎo	to instruct
	發	fā	to make (complaints)
6	絲毫	sīháo	in the least
8	表現	biǎoxiàn	appear to be
	冷靜	lěngjìng	cold-livered; dispassionate; calm
	沉着	chénzhuó	composed; steady; calm
	主題	zhǔtí	subject matter; general theme
9	少年老成	shàoniánlǎochéng	precocious
	寂寞	jímò	lonely
10	低沉	dīchén	low and heavy
	發出	fāchū	to utter
11	討厭	tǎoyàn	to dislike; to be sick of
13	主觀主義	zhǔguānzhǔyì	subjectivism
15	相反	xiāngfǎn	on the contrary

	倒是	dàoshì	but; on the contrary, a phrase commonly used to follow 相反
16	革命陣營	gémìngzhènyíng	revolutionary camp
	追求	zhuīqiú	to pursue
	依	yī	according to
	看法	kànfǎ	viewpoint
	彷彿	fǎngfú	seemingly
	嬌生慣養	jiāoshēngguànyǎng	brought up pampered and spoiled

page 7

2	正因為	zhèng yīnwèi	precisely because; just because
3	以期	yǐqī	so as to hope
	引起注意	yǐnqǐzhùyì	to call to (everybody's 大家) attention
4	減	jiǎn	to diminish; to decrease
5	曾	céng	already, a character to indicate past tense; ever
	大規模	dàguīmó	on a large scale
	檢查	jiǎnchá	to investigate
	黨中央	dǎngzhōngyāng	the central committee of the Party
	號召	hàozhào	to appeal to; to call for
	議論紛紛	yìlùnfēnfēn	a lively discussion
6	意見	yìjiàn	opinions
	不管	bùguǎn	no matter
	儘管	jǐnguǎn	without reservation; although; even if
	提	tí	to give; to express
	下層	xiàcéng	a lower unit; those at the lower unit or level
	必然性	bìránxìng	necessity; certainty
	塌	tā	to fall in ruins; to collapse; to sink down

	小事情	xiǎoshìqíng	trifle; things of slight importance
10	半截	bànjié	by half
11	宗派主義	zōngpàizhǔyì	sectarianism
	大師	dàshī	a master
12	戰鬪的	zhàndòud	fighting
	能動性	néngdòngxìng	initiative; activeness
	削減	xiāojiǎn	to reduce; to minimise
	滋長	zīzhǎng	growth
	發揮	fāhuī	to develop; to elucidate
	意識	yìshí	ideology; consciousness
13	存在	cúnzài	existence
	反作用	fǎnzuòyòng	opposite effects; reaction
	消滅	xiāomiè	to eliminate
	凈盡	jìngjìn	completely
14	必要	bìyào	necessary
	不惟	bùwéi	not only
	強調	qiángdiào	to stress; to emphasize
15	提到	tídào	to mention
	指出	zhǐchū	to point out

page 8

1	不僅	bùjǐn	not only
	而已	éryǐ	that is all; nothing more
	借口	jièkǒu	pretext
	寬容	kuānróng	forgiving; tolerant
2	溫情地	wēnqíngd	sentimentally
	靈魂	línghún	soul

4	間接	*jiànjiē*	indirectly
	助長	*zhùzhǎng*	to help grow
	直接	*zhíjiē*	directly
	製造	*zhìzào*	to manufacture; to produce
5	理論	*lǐlùn*	theory
	民族形式	*mínzúxíngshì*	national style
6	受	*shòu*	to suffer
	損失	*sǔnshī*	loss
7	層	*céng*	a layer; a tier; here it means aspect
9	與此相關	*yǔcǐxiāngguān*	relevant to
	批評	*pīpíng*	to criticise
10	有的	*yǒud*	some
	媽底個 X	*mādǐgè*	(X is not pronounced, same as 他媽的 *tāmād*) a swear phrase
	好	*hào*	to be fond of ; to love to
11	叛	*pàn*	to betray
	做人行事	*zuòrénxíngshì*	one's words and actions; one's attitude towards people and work.
12	大人物	*dàrénwù*	the VIPs
13	足以	*zúyǐ*	to suffice; to be sufficient to
	喚起	*huànqǐ*	to arouse; to excite
	引起	*yǐnqǐ*	to induce; to cause
15	聽說	*tīngshuō*	it is said; people said
	曾有	*céngyǒu*	there was
	某同志	*mǒutóngzhì*	a certain comrade
	本	*běn*	local; our
	機關	*jīguān*	office; organisation; institution

	墻報	qiángbào	a hand-written periodical on walls
	該	gāi	that

page 9

1	首長	shǒuzhǎng	heads; leaders
	打擊	dǎjī	to hurt; to strike; to attack
	致	zhì	so as to; so that; so much so that
	陷于	xiànyú	to fall into; to sink
	傳聞	chuánwén	rumours
	失實	shīshí	not true to fact
	小鬼	xiǎoguǐ	lad; an endearment addressed to the young in Yenan
	確鑿	quèzuó	indeed; actually
2	神經	shénjīng	nerves
3	自信	zìxìn	to be confident
4	等級制度	děngjízhìdù	grading system
6	做	zuò	to compose; to write
	八股	bāgǔ	old style of essay writing
	保証	bǎozhèng	to guarantee
	伙伕	huǒfū	a cook
	炊事員	chuīshìyuán	a respectful term for cook in Yenan
7	諷刺	fěngcì	satirical
	意味	yìwèi	meaning; a touch of; to mean as verb transitive
	理性	lǐxìng	reason; intellect
	良心	liángxīn	conscience
	溫和	wēnhé	gentle
	語調	yǔdiào	tone
	稱呼	chēnghū	to call; to address

8	妄想	*wàngxiǎng*	wishful thinking; wild ideas
9	麻煩	*máfán*	to trouble; troublesome
10	實際	*shíjì*	in fact
11	合理	*hélǐ*	reasonable
12	各盡所能	*gèjìnsuǒnéng*	from each according to his ability
	各取所值	*gèqǔsuǒzhí*	to each according to his worth
13	原則	*yuánzé*	principle
	享受	*xiǎngshòu*	to enjoy
	三三制	*sānsānzhì*	the "three-thirds" government work system – one third of cadres to take part in production at the lower unit, one third to investigate work as government inspectors and one third to do administration work in the office
	實行	*shíxíng*	to put into effect; to carry out; to enforce
	薪給制	*xīnjǐzhì*	salary system
14	待遇	*dàiyù*	salary; wages
	等差	*děngchā*	difference in grade
15	商量餘地	*shāngliángyúdì*	room for discussion
16	拖着	*tuōzhe*	to be dragging. 着 a participle indicating progressive tense
	困憊	*kùnbèi*	tired; exhausted; worn out
	軀體	*qūtǐ*	the body
	支撐	*zhīchēng*	to prop up; to support; to endure
	煎熬	*jiān'áo*	long endured sufferings
	寶貴	*bǎoguì*	precious
	無論誰	*wúlùnshuí*	no matter who

page 10

2	同甘苦	*tónggānkǔ*	to share joys and sorrows; through thick and thin

	發揚	fāyáng	to develop; to foster; to extend
	美德	měidé	virtue
	衷心	zhōngxīn	sincere; heart-felt
3	特殊	tèshū	special; exceptional
	優待	yōudài	preferential treatment; special care for
6	傳統	chuántǒng	tradition
	感動	gǎndòng	to move; to touch
	合作	hézuò	to co-operate
	恕	shù	to forgive; to pardon
	冒昧	màomèi	ignorance; impertinence; to take the liberty of
9	所謂	suǒwèi	so-called
	幹部服	gànbùfú	to be better clothed as cadre
	小廚房	xiǎochúfáng	to be better fed as cadre
	階層	jiēcéng	social strata
	葡萄	pútáo	grapes
	酸	suān	sour
10	麵湯	miàntāng	noodle soup
11	粥	zhōu	rice boiled to gruel; congee
12	異類	yìlèi	of different kind
14	聽候	tīnghòu	to look forward to; to await
	批判	pīpàn	repudiation; to repudiate; criticism; to criticise

三八節有感　Thoughts on March 8 Day

丁　玲　Ting Ling (1907–　　　) Pen name for Chiang Ping-chih; novelist and short story writer; born in Liling, Hunan. In 1924, she went to Peking where she met and later married Hu Yeh-pin. Two years later, she began to write for *The Short Story Magazine* (小說月報). In 1928, the couple went to Shanghai and together with Shen Tsung-wen launched two short-lived monthly magazines, *Jen Chien* (人間月刊) and *Red & Black* (紅黑月刊).

In 1930, the pair joined the China League of Leftist Writers. A year later, Hu was arrested and executed by the Nationalist secret police for being a member of the Communist Party. Ting Ling joined the Communist Party in protest, but was also arrested in 1933. After being freed in 1936, she managed to get to Peking, Sian and finally to the Communists in Yenan, where she worked as editor of the literary page of the *Liberation Daily.*

In 1949 she published her famous *Sun over the Sangkan River*, the novel which won her the second Stalin Literary Award in 1951. Before she was dismissed from the Party and finally disgraced in 1957, she held important positions as editor of the *People's Literature*, editor of the *Literary Gazette* (文藝報), head of the Central Literary Research Institute, and vice-president of the All-China Literary Association.

page 11

	三八節	sānbājié	March 8th, Women's Day
1	重視	zhòngshì	to pay attention to
	特別的	tèbiéd	particularly; specially
2	檢閱	jiǎnyuè	to review
3	隊伍	duìwǔ	troops; assembled company
	延安	yánān	Yenan
	熱鬧	rènào	lively; busy; bustling
4	大會	dàhuì	big assembly; a meeting with a good number of people taking part
	演說	yǎnshuō	to make a speech; speeches

— 11 —

	通電	tōngdiàn	a circular telegram
5	嫉羨	jíxiàn	to envy and admire
6	小米	xiǎomǐ	millet; yellow millet
	醫院	yīyuàn	a hospital
	休養所	xiūyǎngsuǒ	sanatorium
	門診部	ménzhěnbù	out-patient department
	佔	zhàn	to take up; to occupy
	比例	bǐlì	proportion
7	驚奇	jīngqí	taken by surprise; surprise
	免除	miǎnchú	to exempt from; free from
	幸運	xìngyùn	fortune
	不管	bùguǎn	no matter
	場合	chǎnghé	an occasion
8	應得的	yīngdéd	deserving; worthy of
	誹議	fěiyì	slanderous talk; gossip
9	責難	zénàn	reproach; reproval
	嚴重	yánzhòng	serious
	確當	quèdàng	correct; proper
10	結婚	jiéhūn	to marry; marriage
	接近	jiējìn	to be close; to have a close relationship
11	畫家	huàjiā	a painter; an artist
	諷刺	fěngcì	to satirise; satire; irony
	科長	kēzhǎng	head of a department
	嫁	jià	to marry a husband
12	詩人	shīrén	a poet
	騎馬	qímǎ	to ride a horse

	首長	shǒuzhǎng	boss; head; leader; leading members
	藝術家	yìshùjiā	an artist
	漂亮的	piàoliàngd	handsome; pretty
	情人	qíngrén	a lover
13	聆聽	língtīng	to hear; to listen
	訓詞	xùncí	instructions
	他媽的	tāmād	a swear expression
	瞧不起	qiáobùqǐ	to look down upon
	幹部	gànbù	cadres; a cadre
	土包子	tǔbāoz	a rustic; a country bumpkin

page 12

1	罪惡	zuìè	sin; crime
2	製造	zhìzào	to manufacture; to fabricate
	謠言	yáoyán	rumours
	對象	duìxiàng	object; target
	污衊	wūmiè	to desecrate; to pollute; to tarnish
	草鞋	cǎoxié	straw-sandals
3	總務科長	zǒngwùkēzhǎng	head of the department of general affairs
	命運	mìngyùn	fate; destiny
	細	xì	fine; thin
	羊毛線	yángmáoxiàn	sheep's woollen yarn
	花絨布	huāróngbù	flowery flannels
4	包	bāo	to wrap up
	抱	bào	to carry in the arms
	保姆	bǎomǔ	nurse
	懷	huái	the bosom

	洗淨	xǐjìng	washed clean
	布片	bùpiàn	a piece of cloth
	扔	rēng	to throw
	牀頭	chuángtóu	the head of a bed
	啼哭	tíkū	to weep
5	大嚼	dàjiáo	to chew with relish; to eat greedily
	津貼	jīntiē	subsidy
	價值	jiàzhí	worth
	要是	yàoshi	if
	也許	yěxǔ	perhaps; maybe
6	根本……不	gēnběn...bù	by no means can
	就	jiù	then
	嘗	cháng	same as 嚐, to taste
	然而	ránér	however
	究竟	jiūjìng	after all
	迫	pò	to force; to compel
	帶孩子	dàiháiz	to baby sit
7	公開的	gōngkāid	open; public; in the open; in public
	譏諷	jīfěng	sneer
	娜拉	nálā	Nora, heroine of Ibsen's play *A Doll's House*
8	衛生的	wèishēngd	hygienic, healthy
	交際舞	jiāojìwǔ	social dance, same as 交誼舞 jiāoyìwǔ
	雖說	suīshuō	although; although (we can safely) say
	在背地裏	zàibèidìlǐ	secretly; covertly; behind one's back
	會有	huìyǒu	would be; would have
	難聽的	nántīngd	unpleasant to the ear

	誹語	*fěiyǔ*	slanderous words
	悄聲的	*qiǎoshēngd*	whisperingly; to converse privately
	傳播	*chuánbō*	to broadcast; to transmit
10	無關	*wúguān*	having nothing to do with; without connection
	主義	*zhǔyì*	– isms
	思想	*sīxiǎng*	ideology
12	大抵	*dàdǐ*	generally; on the whole
	條件	*tiáojiàn*	conditions
	注意	*zhùyì*	to note
	政治上	*zhèngzhìshàng*	politically
13	純潔	*chúnjié*	pure; not tarnished; clean
	相貌	*xiàngmào*	appearance; looks
	差不多	*chàbuduō*	not far off; near enough; almost as good
	彼此	*bǐcǐ*	one and another; each other
14	具備	*jùbèi*	ready; available; to have acquired
	漢奸	*hànjiān*	traitor
	所謂	*suǒwèi*	so-called
	縫補	*féngbǔ*	to sew and mend (lit.); to patch
	安慰	*ānwèi*	consolation; comfort
15	堂皇的	*tánghuángd*	grandly; without feeling ashamed
	考慮	*kǎolǜ*	to consider
	離婚	*líhūn*	divorce
	口實	*kǒushí*	excuses
	落後	*luòhoù*	politically backward; backwardness; to regress
16	進步	*jìnbù*	politically progressive
	拖	*tuō*	to drag along
	可恥的	*kěchǐd*	shameful

1	凌雲的	língyúnd	to reach the clouds (lit.); pre-eminent
	志向	zhìxiàng	ambition; aspiration
	克苦的	kèkǔd	same as 刻苦的, assiduous
	鬥爭	dòuzhēng	struggle
	生理的	shēnglǐd	biological; physiological
	要求	yāoqiú	needs; to demand; to ask for
2	蜜語	mìyǔ	sweet words
	操勞的	cāoláod	painstaking; industrious
	唯恐	wéikǒng	only fear that; for fear lest
3	危險	wēixiǎn	danger
	厚顏的	hòuyánd	shamelessly; without sense of shame
	托兒所	tuōérsuǒ	nursery
	收留	shōuliú	to take; to admit; to take and keep (lit.)
	刮	guā	to scrape; to brush away
	子宮	zǐgōng	uterus; womb
	刮子宮	guā zǐgōng	abortion
	寧肯	níngkěn	would rather
4	受處分	shòuchǔfèn	to be punished administratively
	不得不	bùdébù	have to; must
	冒……險	mào . . . xiǎn	to take the risk of
	悄悄的	qiǎoqiǎod	silently; quietly
	墮胎	zhuìtāi	abortion; to abort
5	貪圖	tāntú	to covet; to desire eagerly
	舒服	shūfú	comfort
	好高鶩遠	hàogāowùyuǎn	apt to plan much too big; unrealistic

	到底	*dàodǐ*	after all; actually
	了不起	*liǎobùqǐ*	extraordinary; superb; remarkable
6	既然	*jìrán*	since
	不肯	*bùkěn*	not willing; reluctant
	負責	*fùzé*	to be responsible
7	犧牲	*xīshēng*	to sacrifice
	事業	*shìyè*	cause; undertaking
	賢妻良母	*xiánqīliángmǔ*	virtuous wife and good mother
8	未始	*wèishǐ*	may not necessarily
	歌頌	*gēsòng*	to sing praises
	悲劇	*bēijù*	tragedy
9	實在	*shízài*	indeed
	可愛的	*kěaid*	lovely; lovable
10	摺皺	*zhézhòu*	a wrinkle or crease
	疲憊	*píbèi*	utterly exhausted; worn out
	奪取	*duóqǔ*	to take away; to snatch; to wrest from
	愛嬌	*àijiāo*	coquetry
	處於	*chùyú*	to be in (a state or situation)
11	悲運	*bēiyùn*	lamentable turn of fate; misfortune
	可憐	*kělián*	pitiable
	薄命	*báomìng*	unfortunate in life
12	自作孽	*zìzuòniè*	willingly allow oneself to degenerate; to throw oneself away; retribution
	活該	*huógāi*	served you right
	法律上	*fǎlùshàng*	legally
	爭論	*zhēnglùn*	to argue

	一方	*yīfāng*	one party
13	不道德	*búdàodé*	immoral
14	詛咒	*zǔzhòu*	to curse; curse
15	缺點	*quēdiǎn*	weakness; shortcoming
	痛苦	*tòngkǔ*	bitter suffering
16	超時代的	*chāoshídàid*	transcendent of the era
	鐵打的	*tiědǎd*	made of iron
	抵抗	*dǐkàng*	to resist
	誘惑	*yòuhuò*	temptations

page 14

	壓迫	*yāpò*	oppression
1	崇高的	*chónggāod*	lofty
2	奮鬥	*fèndòu*	to make strenuous efforts; to advance in spite of difficulties and opposition
	捲入	*juǎnrù*	to be carried away; to be swept into; to be engulfed
	庸俗	*yōngsú*	vulgarity
3	冤枉	*yuānwǎng*	a wrong; an injustice; a false accusation
	寬容	*kuānróng*	toleration; leniency
	淪為	*lúnwéi*	to sink into; to fall to be
4	地位	*dìwèi*	social status; position
	過錯	*guòcuò*	mistake; error; fault
	聯繫	*liánxì*	affiliated relationship. association; connection
	發	*fā*	to pass (an opinion); to speak; to utter
5	議論	*yìlùn*	opinions; talks; criticisms
	實際的	*shíjìd*	practical
	脫節	*tuōjié*	to disjoint; to dislocate; to lose contact

	修身	xiūshēn to cultivate oneself
7	企望	qǐwàng eager expectation
	勉勵	miǎnlì to encourage; to urge
8	友好	yǒuhǎo friendly; friends
9	資格	zīgé qualification; entitled to
	平等	píngděng equality
10	政權	zhèngquán political power
11	陣線	zhènxiàn front, ex.: united front (線 is also written as 缐)
	一員	yīyuán a member
	也好	yěhǎo be it; no matter it be
12	事項	shìxiàng items; things; a series of things
13	節制	jiézhì moderation; control; economy
	浪漫	làngmàn romantic
14	環境	huánjìng circumstances; environment
	適宜	shìyí suitable; fit
16	青春	qīngchūn youth
	活力	huólì vigour
	飽滿	bǎomǎn full

page 15

1	擔受	dānshòu to undertake
	磨難	mónàn sufferings; tribulations
	前途	qiántú the future; the road ahead
	享受	xiǎngshòu enjoyment
2	進取	jìnqǔ to make progress; to advance in personal attainments; progress
	游惰	yóuduò idleness and laziness; to be idle and lazy

3	空白	kōngbái	blank
	疲頓	píruǎn	fatigued and weak
	枯萎	kūwěi	withered; decayed; to fail in vigour
4	養成	yǎngchéng	to form
	習慣	xíguàn	habit
	改正	gǎizhèng	to correct; to set right; to amend
	思索	sīsuǒ	to meditate on; to think over
	隨波逐流	suíbōzhúliú	to follow the current – to do as others; to live aimlessly
	毛病	máobìng	disease; defect; fault
5	處理	chǔlǐ	to treat; to manage; to handle; to conduct
	得當	dédàng	properly; rightly
	違背	wéibèi	to go against; to run counter to
	原則	yuánzé	principle
6	後悔	hòuhuǐ	regrets; to regret
	理性	lǐxìng	sense of reason
	上當	shàngdàng	to be taken in; to be fooled; to be swindled
7	蒙蔽	méngbì	to befuddle; to deceive; to fool
	小利	xiǎolì	small favours
	誘	yòu	to tempt; to allure
	浪費	làngfèi	to waste
	熱情	rèqíng	warm affection; enthusiasm
	煩惱	fánnǎo	worries; vexation; annoyance
8	下決心	xià jué xīn	to make a firm decision
	吃苦	chīkǔ	to suffer hardship
	堅持到底	jiānchídàodǐ	to hold on to the very end

	覺悟	juéwù	conscious; enlightened; awareness
	認定	rèndìng	firmly believe; to recognise for sure
	薔薇色	qiángwéisè	the colour of a red rose; rosy
9	溫柔	wēnróu	tender; soft; meek
	夢幻	mènghuàn	dream; illusion
	暴風雨	bàofēngyǔ	storms
	搏鬥	bódòu	to wrestle; to fight recklessly
	吟詩	yínshī	to hum poetry; to recite poems
10	停歇下來	tíngxiēxiàlái	to stop and take a rest
	悲苦	bēikǔ	misery
	墮落	duòluò	degradation; degeneration
11	有恒	yǒuhéng	perseverance; constancy
	抱負	bàofù	ambition; aspiration
	便宜	piányí	small advantage; cheap
	堅忍	jiānrěn	to persist in; persistency
12	眞正	zhēnzhèng	really
	附及	fùjí	Postscript
	重	chóng	again; once more
15	發稿	fāgǎo	to send in the manuscript
	限	xiàn	to limit; to restrict
	整理	zhěnglǐ	to arrange; to put in order
	不過	búguò	however; yet

page 16

1	痛快	tòngkuài	satisfying; outspoken; having duly let out one's having a share in the opinion; having the same feelings
	取消	qǔxiāo	to cancel; to cross out; to make void

2 仍舊   *réngjiù*   still; as before

    同感   *tónggǎn*   having a share in the opinion; having the same feelings

了解作家，尊重作家   **Understand and Respect Writers**

艾青　Ai Ching (1910–　　　) Pen name for Chiang Hai-cheng; poet; born in Chekiang. After graduating from high school, he studied medicine for a while, but gave it up when he went to France and began designing porcelain figures.

He returned to China in 1932, but was arrested shortly afterwards for "harbouring dangerous thoughts" and not released until October 1935. Thereafter he became a teacher and writer, editing magazines and later teaching at Lu Hsun Institute of Arts in Yenan.

He is one of the great living Chinese poets, and at one time the leading literary figure in China. But in one of the literary purges of 1957, he was downgraded and branded a rightist. He has lived in obscurity ever since.

page 17

	了解	liǎojiě	to understand
1	作家	zuòjiā	writer; men of letters
	尊重	zūnzhòng	to respect
	民族	mínzú	nation
	階級	jiējí	class
	器官	qìguān	organ
	神經	shénjīng	nerves
	智慧	zhìhuì	wisdom
	瞳孔	tóngkǒng	pupil of the eye
2	情感	qínggǎn	sentiments; feelings; affection
	心理	xīnlǐ	psychology
	守衞	shǒuwèi	to guard; to watch
	忠實的	zhōngshíd	faithful
4	凝結	níngjié	to congeal; to curdle
	形象的	xíngxiàngd	symbolic; figurative

7	省察	xǐngchá	scrutiny
	提高	tígāo	to increase; to heighten; to enhance
	自尊	zìzūn	self-respect
8	文藝	wényì	literature and art
9	的確	díquè	indeed; really
	板凳	bǎndèng	stool; bench
10	六〇六	liùlíngliù	salvarsan
	治	zhì	to cure; to treat
	梅毒	méidú	syphilis
11	反	fǎn	anti; to oppose; to be against
	功利主義	gōnglìzhǔyì	utilitarianism
	唯美論者	wéiměilùnzhě	estheticist
	滿懷憤慨	mǎnhuáifènkài	in great anger; full of righteous anger
	物喻	wùyù	the illustration of a thing
12	拖鞋	tuōxié	a pair of slippers
	比喻	bǐyù	parable
	對偶法	duìǒufǎ	contraposition; opposite theorem (logic)
	雨傘	yǔsǎn	umbrella
	音韻	yīnyùn	rhyme
13	背心	bèixīn	vest

page 18

1	人類	rénlèi	mankind
	思索	sīsuǒ	to think hard; to reflect; to ponder
	恥辱	chǐrǔ	shame; disgrace
	光榮	guāngróng	honour
	嫉妒	jídù	to be jealous

	同情	tóngqíng	sympathy
2	空漠	kōngmò	in a state of emptiness and abstraction
	因而	yīnér	therefore; so as to be
	悲哀	bēiāi	sad
	孤獨	gūdú	lonesome; lonely
	深沉地	shēnchéndì	deeply; profoundly; abstrusely
	發問	fāwèn	to pose a question; to put forward a question
	究竟	jiūjìng	after all
5	發生	fāshēng	to take place; to occur
	物質憂慮	wùzhíyōulǜ	materialistic worries
6	就連	jiùlián	even; including even
	原始的	yuánshǐdì	primitive
	不開化的	bùkāihuàdì	uncivilised
8	水仙	shuǐxiān	narcissus
	辭	cí	a form of poetical composition; phrases; expressions
	出版	chūbǎn	to publish
	批評家	pīpíngjiā	critics; a critic
9	頌揚	sòngyáng	to laud; to praise
	作品	zuòpǐn	works of art; literary works
	近年來	jìnniánlái	in recent years
11	爛熟了的	lànshóuledì	rotten to the core; too ripe; overcooked
12	提出	tíchū	to put forward
	內心	nèixīn	heart
	顫慄不安	chànlìbùān	shaking and uneasy with fear
	審視	shěnshì	scrutiny; a close investigation
	從哲學上	cóngzhéxuéshàng	philosophically

	引起	yǐnqǐ	to induce; to lead to; to cause to happen
13	具體	jùtǐ	concrete; concretely; specific
	懷疑	huáiyí	doubt; to harbour doubts
14	寧可	níngkě	would rather
15	商業	shāngyè	commerce; commercial
	抬頭	táitóu	to get the upper hand
	代言人	dàiyánrén	spokesman
16	擴展	kuòzhǎn	to expand
	勢力	shìlì	power
	鼓吹者	gǔchuīzhě	advocator

page 19

4	百靈鳥	bǎilíngniǎo	lark
	專門	zhuānmén	specially; particularly
	娛樂	yúlè	to amuse; to entertain; amusement
	歌妓	gējì	geisha; a sing-song girl
	竭盡	jiéjìn	to exhaust; to drain
	心血	xīnxuè	mental power; energy; blood of the heart (lit.)
5	搏動	bódòng	to throb; to beat (pulse, heart)
	欺騙	qīpiàn	to hoodwink; to mislead by concealing facts
	根據	gēnjù	according to; on the basis of
	世界觀	shìjièguān	world outlook
6	描寫	miáoxiě	to describe; to depict
	批評	pīpíng	to criticise
	創作	chuàngzuò	creative works; to write creatively
7	虛偽的	xūwěid	hypocritical

	癬疥	xiǎnjiè	itch and ringworm
	膿包	nóngbāo	pustules filled with pus. 包 is also written as 疱 or 胞
	蓓蕾	bèilěi	flower buds
	沒有出息	méiyǒuchūxī	without being able to stand out from one's fellows; without being able to achieve anything; unpromising; hopeless
9	醜陋	chǒulòu	ugliness
	勇氣	yǒngqì	courage; guts
	更何況	gènghékuàng	not to mention; not to say
10	愈……愈	yù....yù	the more ... the better
	搔癢	sāoyǎng	to scratch to relieve itching
11	洗一個澡	xǐyigèzǎo	to take a bath
	盲腸炎	mángchángyán	appendicitis
	割	gē	to cut
	痧眼	shāyǎn	trachoma. 痧 is also written as 砂 or 沙
	硫酸銅	liúsuāntóng	sulphate of copper
	刮	guā	to scrape; to brush away
12	生病	shēngbìng	to take ill; to fall sick
	開刀	kāidāo	to operate; operation
	患	huàn	to suffer from
	傷寒	shānghán	typhoid
	症	zhēng	illness; case
	貪吃	tānchī	gluttonous; gluttonise
	不行的	bùxíngd	do not work; will not do
	菌	jǔn	bacteria; bacilli
14	保衞	bǎowèi	to safeguard; to guard; to protect

	健康	jiànkāng	health
	後者	hòuzhě	the latter
	普遍	pǔbiàn	universal; wide-spread; general
	持久	chíjiǔ	protracted; enduring; that which lasts long
	深刻	shēnkè	profound; deep
15	特權	tèquán	privileges
	擁護	yōnghù	to support; to uphold
	民主政治	mínzhǔzhèngzhì	democratic politics
16	保障	bǎozhàng	to ensure
	藝術創作	yìshùchuàngzuò	artistic creations

page 20

1	獨立的	dúlìd	independent
	社會改革	shèhuìgǎigé	social reforms
	事業	shìyè	a cause; undertaking
	起……作用	qǐ . . . zuòyòng	to play the role of; to play the part of
	推進	tuījìn	to push ahead with
3	適如其份地	shìrúqífènd	properly; duly
	不恰當的	búqiàdàngd	improper; inopportune
	等於	děngyú	equal to
	諷刺	fěngcì	irony; sarcasm
	稍有	shāoyǒu	slightly with
	損抑	sǔnyì	to depreciate
	評價	píngjià	appraisal; estimation
4	侮辱	wǔrǔ	insult; disgrace
5	情操	qíngcāo	sentiments
6	封	fēng	to confer; to designate; to appoint; to bestow (title of honour)

蟬噪居漫筆　　Sketches of Chirping Cicadas

蕭軍　Hsiao Chun (1908—　　　　) Pen name for Tien Chun; novelist, short story writer and essayist; born and educated in Liaoning, Northeast China. In 1932, he met Hsiao Hung, also a famous writer, and later married her. They collaborated in his first book *To Travel* in 1933. During the following three years, he published two novels *(Village in August* and *The Third Generation)*, two collections of short stories *(Sheep and On the River)* and two collections of essays *(A Tale of Green Leaves* and *October the Fifteenth)*. *Village in August*, a best-seller for many years, was later translated into English and Russian.

From 1938 to 1940, he edited the literary page of *Hsin Min Pao* in Chengtu. In 1942 he worked for the *Liberation Daily* in Yenan, in collaboration with Ting Ling, the well-known authoress. In 1946, he became the editor of the *Cultural Gazette* (文化報) in Harbin. In 1948 he was criticised for his articles about the arrogance of the Russian advisers and the cruelty of civil war and disappeared until November 1954, when he emerged with his new book *Coal Mines in May*. Although initially well-received, the book lost popularity within the year. In 1957, he went to Peking where his article, *Sketches of Chirping Cicadas*, in the *Literary Gazette* (文藝報) brought him under severe attack during the anti-rightist movement of 1958. Since then, nothing has been heard of him.

page 21

	蟬噪	chánzào	chirping of cicadas
1	氣候	qìhòu	climate
	噤若寒蟬	jìnruòhánchán	as silent as a cicada in winter
2	百家爭鳴	bǎijiāzhēngmíng	hundreds of schools contend
	空間	kōngjiān	space
	散播	sànbō	to spread; to scatter
	擾人午夢	rǎorénwǔmèng	disturbing other people's nap
	噪音	zàoyīn	noises
	不識趣的	bùshíqùd	unwise; imprudent; foolish
3	欲罷而不能	yùbà'érbùnéng	wishing to stop but unable to do so

	螳螂	tángláng	mantis
	追捕	zhuībǔ	to pursue and catch
5	畢竟	bìjìng	after all
	才略	cáilüè	ability; talents
	非凡的	fēifánd	outstanding; remarkable; uncommon
7	結論	jiélùn	conclusion
9	主張	zhǔzhāng	to advocate; to propose; to support
10	無衝突論	wúchōngtūlùn	theory of no conflict
	大張旗鼓	dàzhāngqígǔ	with great fanfare
11	體無完膚	tǐwúwánfū	there is not one piece of skin intact on the whole body — damaged to the utmost extent; thoroughly refuted
	暴露陰面	bàolùyīnmiàn	exposure of the dark side
12	毒草	dúcǎo	poisonous weeds
	無關緊要	wúguānjǐnyào	unimportant; insignificant
13	英明的	yīngmíngd	talented; clever

page 22

2	慣於	guànyú	to be accustomed to; used to
3	資料	zīliào	material; literature
	文件	wénjiàn	document
	處理	chǔlǐ	to treat; to handle
4	徹底	chèdǐ	thoroughly
	極端	jíduān	extremely
5	黨性	dǎngxìng	Party principles
	貫澈	guànchè	to carry out; to implement
6	秘本	mìběn	secret record
	秘聞	mìwén	confidential information

	威信	wēixìn	prestige
7	胡蘆	húlú	a gourd; a bottle, cup or bowl made from the hard skin of such fruit
8	靈丹妙藥	língdānmiàoyào	effective drug and excellent medicine
9	千方百計	qiānfāngbǎijì	thousand methods and hundred plans; full of plans
	捕風捉影	bǔfēngzhuōyǐng	to seize wind and grasp the shadow; using bits of information to exaggerate
	發動	fādòng	to rally; to mobilise
10	嚴迫	yánpò	to coerce; to force
	承認	chéngrèn	to confess to (a crime); to acknowledge; to admit
	罪名	zuìmíng	crime
	肅反運動	sùfǎnyùndòng	campaign to liquidate counter-revolutionaries
11	定義	dìngyì	definition
	經典著作	jīngdiǎnzhùzuò	classical works
12	成立	chénglì	to establish
	偏偏	piānpiān	on the contrary; instead; nevertheless; all the same
	創造性	chuàngzàoxìng	creativeness
13	在哲學上	zàizhéxuéshàng	philosophically
	目的論	mùdìlùn	theory of purpose
14	同類相殘	tónglèixiāngcán	mutual destruction
16	本質	běnzhì	nature
	奴才	núcái	slave; stooge; vassal

page 23

1	特性的	tèxìngd	characteristic
	虛偽	xūwěi	hypocritical; hypocrisy
2	痛惡	tòng'wù	to hate; to dislike

3	無可奈何	wúkěnàihé	It cannot be helped; there is nothing one can do; resignedly
	依從	yīcóng	to obey; to be agreeable
	制服	zhìfú	to overpower; to master over
4	表現	biǎoxiàn	to display; to manifest; to show
	眞誠	zhēnchéng	sincere; faithful; loyal
	一旦	yīdàn	once
	猢猻	húsūn	monkey
5	堪	kān	enough reason for; suitable for; may well
	優伶	yōulíng	actress; actor
	緣	yuán	the pre-ordained or inevitable course of events; one's fate; lot; luck
	感嘆	gǎntàn	to lament; to deplore
6	百般順從	bǎibānshùncóng	to obey in every way

論同志之〔愛〕與〔耐〕
On Love and Tolerance among Comrades

page 24

2	鄉村	xiāngcūn	a village
	疙瘩	gēdā	trouble, used here as a nickname
3	情婦	qíngfù	a mistress; a sweetheart
	日本	rìběn	Japan
	污辱	wūrǔ	to insult; to violate (a woman)
	傷害	shānghài	to hurt; to injure
	厲害	lìhài	severely; badly
4	馬上	mǎshàng	immediately; in no time
	避免	bìmiǎn	to avoid
	隊伍	duìwǔ	rank; troop
	損害	sǔnhài	harm; damage; injury
	勸	quàn	to advise; to persuade
	情人	qíngrén	a sweetheart; a lover
5	耍起脾氣	shuǎqǐpíqì	to show one's temper
	扔	rēng	to throw
	革命	gémìng	revolution
6	共存亡	gòngcúnwáng	to live or die together
	若不	ruòbù	otherwise; if not
	隊長	duìzhǎng	commanding officer
	槍斃	qiāngbì	shoot to death
	一道	yīdào	together
	外號	wàihào	nickname
	鐵鷹	tiěyīng	iron eagle
7	紅鬍子	hónghúz	lit. red beard, a name for Manchurian bandits

	眨眼	zhǎyǎn	to wink
	敵人	dírén	enemy
8	紀律	jìlǜ	discipline
	躊躇	chóuchú	to hesitate
	一番	yīfān	for a while
	終于	zhōngyú	finally; at last; in the end
	提起	tíqǐ	to pick up; to lift
	手槍	shǒuqiāng	pistol; revolver
9	處理	chǔlǐ	to handle; to deal with
	場面	chǎngmiàn	the scene
	青島	qīngdǎo	Tsingtao, city and port in Shantung Province
10	足足	zúzú	exactly; fully; good
	思索	sīsuǒ	to think deeply; to contemplate
	近乎	jìnhū	nearly; almost
	流彈	liúdàn	a stray bullet
11	心情	xīnqíng	state of mind
	難受	nánshòu	sad; wretched; miserable; lit. hard to take
12	如今	rújīn	now; at the present moment
	記憶起來	jìyìqǐlái	in retrospect
	愉快	yúkuài	happy

page 25

1	另外	lìngwài	another
	戀愛	liàn'ài	to fall in love
	引起不滿	yǐnqǐbùmǎn	to cause dissatisfaction
	司令	sīlìng	a commander
	顧慮	gùlǜ	to take into consideration; to bear in mind

	影响	yǐngxiǎng	influence; effect
2	暫時	zhànshí	temporarily; for the time being
	看不起	kànbùqǐ	to look down upon; to have contempt for
3	冷嘲	lěngcháo	freezing irony; to jeer at; to mock at
	照常	zhàocháng	as usual
	出發	chūfā	to set forth
	目送	mùsòng	to see off; to follow with eyes
4	描寫	miáoxiě	description
5	腰間	yāojiān	at the waist
	出現	chūxiàn	to appear; to show
	懇切的	kěnqièd	earnestly
	沉重的	chénzhòngd	seriously; gravely
6	當心	dāngxīn	to take care
	鬥爭	dòuzhēng	struggle
	以外的	yǐwàid	beyond; besides
	忘掉	wàngdiào	to forget
7	不久	bùjiǔ	before long; shortly
8	戀戀地	liànliànd	unwillingly
	撒開	sākāi	to let go
	似乎	sìhū	to seem; as though; as if
9	敬重	jìngzhòng	to respect; to esteem; to honour
	直	yīzhí	until; till
10	子彈	zǐdàn	a bullet
	打進	dǎjìn	to shoot into
	胸膛	xiōngtáng	breast; chest
11	隨落	duòluò	to degenerate; to degrade

	結束	jiéshù	to end
12	圍攻	wéigōng	to encircle and attack
	誤解	wùjiě	to misunderstand
13	眞誠的	zhēnchéngd	sincere; genuine
	溫暖	wēnnuǎn	warmth; warm; to warm
14	和着	hézhe	to mix with
	悲痛的	bēitòngd	grievous; sad; anguished
	迸出來	bèngchūlái	to utter with difficulty

page 26

1	年來	niánlái	for the past few years
	接觸	jiēchù	contact; to get in touch with
	越來越	yuèláiyuè	more and more
2	稀薄	xībó	thin; watery
	悲愴	bēicàng	sadness; sorrow; grief
4	竟	jìng	actually; in fact
	牢騷	láosāo	complaints; discontent; dissatisfaction
5	倦怠	juàndài	tired; remiss
6	申訴	shēnsù	to appeal; to complain
7	擺架子	bǎijiàz	to put on airs
	資格	zīgé	qualification
8	狗皮膏藥	gǒupígāoyào	fakes and rubbish
	樂意	lèyì	to be glad to
9	意見	yìjiàn	opinions; views
	算做	suànzuò	regarded as; taken for
10	七十二難	qīshí'èrnàn	seventy two difficulties or hardships

	出生入死	*chūshēngrùsǐ*	going through many dangers; through thick and thin
	經	*jīng*	the Buddhist Canon
11	福樓拜爾	*fúlóubài'ěr*	Gustav Flaubert, French novelist (1821–1880)
12	撒旦	*sādàn*	satan; devil
	上帝	*shàngdì*	God
	宗教情操	*zōngjiàoqíngcāo*	religious sentiments
13	具備	*jùbèi*	to possess; to have
14	試煉	*shìliàn*	to try; to test; to put to trial
	九妖十八洞	*jiǔyāoshíbādòng*	the nine demons and eighteen caves
	搗亂	*dǎoluàn*	to cause disturbance or trouble
15	過程	*guòchéng*	course; process

page 27

1	現代化	*xiàndàihuà*	to modernise; modernisation
	稍一	*shāoyī*	to be slightly; to be somewhat
	馬虎	*mǎhǔ*	careless; negligent
	細菌	*xìjūn*	germs; bacteria
	閃擊戰	*shǎn jī zhàn*	lightning ambush; a surprise attack
2	反攻	*fǎngōng*	counter-attack; to launch a counter-attack
3	被冤屈	*bèiyuānqū*	to be wronged; to be falsely accused
4	履行	*lǚxíng*	to exercise; to implement; to fulfill
	組織	*zǔzhí*	organisation
	黨員	*dǎngyuán*	party member
5	懷抱	*huáibào*	to embrace; to cherish (hopes); to carry in the arms

	登淨土	dēngjìngtǔ	a Buddhist expression – to ascend to the pure region, a grade of Buddhist priesthood
	入地獄	rùdìyù	to go to hell
	不安	bùān	having no peace; ill at ease; restless
6	任務	rènwù	a task; an assigned job
	隨時隨地	suíshísuídì	at all times and in all places
	醜惡	chǒu'è	ugliness; ugly
	不義	búyì	injustice; unrighteousness
	開路	kāilù	to make way; to do the pioneering work
	退敗的	tuìbàid	being defeated
7	想頭	xiǎngtóu	idea, thought
	攢進	zuānjìn	to worm into; to penetrate
8	瞳孔	tóngkǒng	the pupil of the eye
	引伸出	yǐnshēnchū	to amplify; to infer
9	交會點	jiāohuìdiǎn	the focus point
	蹲	dūn	to squat
	權威	quánwēi	authority
10	混不下去	hùnbúxiàqù	cannot make it pay; unable to muddle along
	色盲	sèmáng	colour blindness; the colour blind
11	品行	pǐnxíng	moral conduct; virtue and behaviour
	賽跑員	sàipǎoyuán	a competitor in a race; a runner
12	釘子鞋	dīngzxié	track shoes
	何況	hékuàng	moreover; besides; not to say
	保証	bǎozhèng	to guarantee; to ensure
13	弄	nòng	to manage to get
	算爲	suànwéi	can (or may) be counted as

14　難道　　　　nándào　Is it possible that . . . ? Is it conceivable that . . . ?

15　既然　　　　jìrán　since; this being the case

page 28

1　說服　　　　shuōfú　persuasion; to talk into; convince

　　韌帶　　　　rèndài　ligaments

2　缺乏　　　　quēfá　to. lack; to be in want

8　反過來說　　fǎnguòláishuō　conversely; on the other hand

　　不管　　　　bùguǎn　no matter; regardless of

　　題外　　　　tíwài　beside the point

10　堅決的　　　jiānjuéd　determined; firm; resolute

　　結了契約　　jiéleqìyuē　to be bound in contract; to be tied with

11　滾爬出來　　gǔnpáchūlái　to come out rolling and creeping

　　賺得　　　　zhuànde　to have earned; to have reaped

　　遍體瘡疤　　biàntǐchuāngbā　scabs and scars over the entire body

　　不倦地　　　bújuànd　untiringly; indefatigably

12　尊嚴　　　　zūnyán　dignity

13　看法　　　　kànfǎ　opinion; viewpoint

14　保險箱　　　bǎoxiǎnxiāng　fire-proof money box, safe deposit box

　　逞英雄　　　chěngyīngxióng　to presume an air of a hero; to show off one's ability

15　終究　　　　zhōngjiū　after all; finally

16　浪子　　　　làngzǐ　wastrel; bum; beachcomber

從點戲說起　From Choosing Theatrical Programmes

夏衍　Hsia Yen (1900–　　　) Pen name for Shen Tuan-hsien; playwright; born of a small family of landowners in Hangchow, Chekiang. Graduated from Hangchow Technical School. In 1919, he went to Japan to study electrical engineering, passing out of the Kyushu Engineering School in 1925. He joined the Northern Expedition of the Revolutionary Army in 1927, and from then on dedicated himself solely to writing. He became active in the China League of Leftist Writers in 1930 and by 1932 was virtually the man in charge of the Chinese Communist film industry. During the Sino-Japanese War, he was responsible for the left-wing circle of journalists in Kweilin, Hongkong and Chungking. After the war, he travelled throughout Shanghai, Singapore and Hongkong promoting the Chinese Communist cause by writing for various newspapers. After the foundation of the People's Republic in 1949, he held important posts as director of the Asian Department in the Ministry of Foreign Affairs, deputy director of the Propaganda Department of the CCP East China Bureau, and director of the Cultural Department of Shanghai. From 1954 to 1965, he was Vice-Minister of Culture. First criticised when his film *Lin's Store* was re-shown in 1965, he was eventually purged at the beginning of the Cultural Revolution in 1966.

His important literary works include: *Under the Shanghai Eaves*, *Sai Chin Hua* (賽金花), *Chiu Chin's Biography* (秋瑾傳), *A Tale of the City of Sorrows*, *Within a Year*, *The Fascist Germs*, *The Protection of Heart* (心防), *The Realm of Fragrant Grass* (芳草天涯), *The Extending Grass* (離離草), etc.

page 29

	點戲	diǎnxì	to tick off or select what one desires to see on a list of performances; to order to have one's favourite plays performed
1	廣播	guǎngbó	broadcast; to broadcast
	相聲	xiàngshēng	comic dialogue; mimicry
	出	chū	originated from
2	回	huí	chapter
3	風格	fēnggé	style
4	急	jí	in a hurry; hurriedly

	將	*jiāng* same as 把 or 拿, meaning to take or get, used as a helping verb
	錦冊	*jǐncè* an embroidered volume; an embroidered playbill
	呈上	*chéngshàng* to hand in; to present
	並	*bìng* together with; as well as; and also
	花名	*huāmíng* nickname; alias
	單子	*dānzǐ* list; programme
	少時	*shǎoshí* for a short while; in a minute
	太監	*tàijiàn* eunuch
	齣	*chū* measure for plays
5	執	*zhí* to hold; to carry
	金盤	*jīnpán* golden plate
	糕點	*gāodiǎn* pastry; cakes
	屬	*shǔ* kind; sort; to belong
	賜	*cì* to bestow; to confer upon
6	叩頭	*kòutóu* kowtow; to knock the head on the ground in reverence
	貴妃	*guìfēi* imperial concubines
	諭	*yù* an order; to order; an official notice
	不拘	*bùjū* no matter; no matter which
8	本角之戲	*běnjiǎozhīxì* plays familiar to a role in a drama
	執意	*zhíyì* to insist on one's opinion
	扭她不過	*niǔtābúguò* unable to turn her round — to change her mind
9	依	*yī* to comply with
	難爲	*nánwéi* to give trouble to; to censure
	好生	*hǎoshēng* carefully; well; kindly
	教習	*jiāoxí* to teach and train

	額外	éwài	beyond the fixed amount; additionally
	賞	shǎng	to reward; to grant; to bestow a reward
10	錁子	kèzǐ	small ingots of gold or silver
11	寵	chǒng	favourite; beloved
	地位	dìwèi	position; social position or status
12	戲提調	xìtídiào	one who is in charge of stage affairs; stage manager; stage director
	也算	yěsuàn	can also be counted or regarded as
	子弟	zǐdì	children; offsprings; juniors
	只不過	zhǐbúguò	no more than; only
	蘇州	sūzhōu	Soochow
	採買	cǎimǎi	to buy up, to pick up
13	女伶	nǚlíng	actress
	論	lùn	to speak of
	身份	shēnfen	social status; rank; position
	連	lián	even
	人身自由	rénshēnzìyóu	personal freedom
	奴隸	núlì	slave
	表現	biǎoxiàn	to act; to show
	特點	tèdiǎn	characteristics

page 30

1	強人之難	qiǎngrénzhīnán	to force what is difficult upon another
2	內行	nèiháng	in the know; expert; in the field
	主觀主義	zhǔguānzhǔyì	subjectivism
3	藝術家	yìshùjiā	artist
	脾氣	píqì	temperament

	解釋	jiěshì	to explain; to take as; to regard as
4	拿腔作勢	náqiāngzuòshì	same as 裝腔作勢, artificial behaviour designed to impress others
	堅持	jiānchí	to insist on
5	一朝	yīzhāo	once
	副官	fùguān	aide de camp
	通情達理	tōngqíngdálǐ	reasonable
	有主見地	yǒuzhǔjiàndì	resolutely; decidedly; wisely
6	對工戲	duìgōngxì	same as 拿手戲, favourite play
	不僅	bùjǐn	not only
7	鼓勵	gǔlì	encouragement
8	演戲者	yǎnxìzhě	performers
	矛盾	máodùn	contradiction; conflict; collision
	避免	bìmiǎn	to avoid
	在於	zàiyú	to depend on; to rest with; to lie in
	妥善地	tuǒshàndì	properly; well
9	處理	chǔlǐ	to arrange; to manage; to deal with
	順利	shùnlì	smoothly; successfully; well
	任務	rènwù	task
	得罪	dézuì	to offend
10	正如	zhèngrú	just as
	受罪	shòuzuì	to suffer distress
11	為難	wéinán	in difficulty; in a spot
	適	shì	just
	足以	zúyǐ	sufficient to
	暴露	bàolù	to reveal; to expose

	狹窄	xiázhǎi	narrow-mindedness
	專橫	zhuānhéng	despotism
	無知	wúzhī	ignorance
	而已	éryǐ	that is all; no more than that; merely
12	性格	xìnggé	disposition; trait; character
	欣賞	xīnshǎng	to appreciate; to enjoy
	藝術	yìshù	art
13	特別	tèbié	particularly; specially
	指出	zhǐchū	to point out; to make clear
14	愛護	àihù	to love and protect
	尊重	zūnzhòng	to respect; to hold in esteem
	意思	yìsī	idea; meaning; significance
	氣度	qìdù	tolerance; capacity for tolerance
15	教養	jiàoyǎng	breeding
	賣好	màihǎo	same as 討好 meaning to toady, to ingratiate oneself with
	露一手	lùyīshǒu	to show off; to show what is one's best
16	這一下	zhèyīxià	for what one did; for all that
	主觀	zhǔguān	subjectivity
	了解	liǎojiě	to understand
	特長	tècháng	specialities; a strong point
	至於	zhìyú	as for; as to
	刻劃	kèhuà	to describe; to depict

page 31

1	可愛	kěài	lovely; lovable
	敢於	gǎnyú	to dare to

2	難能可貴	*nánnéngkěguì*	extremely invaluable; indescribably worthy
3	插曲	*chāqǔ*	episode
	值得	*zhídé*	worthy of; worth
	深思	*shēnsī*	contemplation; deep thought

白蟻宮的秘密　　Secret of the Palace of White Ants

陳波　Chen Po (1904?-　　) Pen name for Meng Chao; born in Shantung; poet and essayist. A member of the Chinese Communist Party, he was one of the most important writers in the Sun Society, a revolutionary literary group of 1928. His poems and stories in the *Sun Monthly* and his collections of essays, *Chang Yeh Chi* (長夜集) and *Wei Yen Chi* (未偃集) were both well-received at the time. But his historical play *Li Hui-niang* (李慧娘), first published in 1961, is now "a poisonous arrow shooting at the Party and the people". At the time of his disgrace in 1966, he was a director on the board of the All-China Dramatists' Association.

page 32

	白蟻	báiyǐ	white ants
	宮	gōng	palace
	秘密	mìmì	secrets
1	最近	zuìjìn	recently
	登載	dēngzài	to publish; to carry (news)
	帶領	dàilǐng	to take and lead
	研究	yánjiū	research
	人員	rényuán	personnel; staff
	深入	shēnrù	to go deep into; closely
	探索	tànsuǒ	to search; to seek
2	引起	yǐnqǐ	to cause; to bring about; to arouse (interest)
	足供	zúgōng	to provide sufficiently; to offer sufficiently
	著	zhù	famous; prominent; obvious
	喻	yù	to illustrate
3	開動	kāidòng	to set in motion
	鎖匙	suǒshí	key
	啟示	qǐshì	to reveal and show

	認識	rènshí	to know
	複雜	fùzá	complicated
	事理	shìlǐ	principles of action; rules of action
	解決	jiějué	to solve
	縈繁	yíngfán	intricate; complicated; mixed-up
	規律	guīlǜ	the law; the rule
4	意義	yìyì	significance
5	描述	miáoshù	to describe; to state
	爲害	wéihài	harm done; ability to do harm
	蠹蝕	dùshí	to eat away; to corrode
6	木材	mùcái	timber
	甚至	shènzhì	even
	屋宇	wūyǔ	a house; a cottage
	船舶	chuánbó	ships and boats
	橋樑	qiáoliáng	the beams of a bridge; a bridge
	內部	nèibù	(from) within; inner part
	蛀嚙	zhùniè	to eat and gnaw as insects
	侵害	qīnhài	to encroach and harm
	以至於	yǐzhìyú	the result of which is; which ends in ...
	朽枯	xiǔkū	loss of life due to decay
7	重複地	chóngfùd	repeatedly
	讚許	zànxǔ	to praise and commend
	科學家	kēxuéjiā	scientist
	事跡	shìjī	facts of a case; deeds
8	詳細	xiángxì	detailed
	介紹	jièshào	introduction

	奧秘	àomì	mystery; secrets
	着重	zhāozhòng	to lay stress on; to attach importance to
10	且說	qiěshuō	to resume; let us now come back to
	湛江市	zhànjiāngshì	a city in Kwangtung Province
	防治	fángzhì	to prevent and deal with
11	巢	cháo	a nest
	外形	wàixíng	outward appearance
	特徵	tèzhēng	characteristics
	判斷	pànduàn	to judge and decide
12	解剖	jiěpō	to dissect; to cut open; anatomy
	果然	guǒrán	as was expected
	發現	fāxiàn	to discover; to find out
	指揮	zhǐhuī	to command; to lead; to guide
13	專司	zhuānsī	to take responsibility for one duty only; in charge of
	繁殖	fánzhí	to multiply; to propagate in abundance
	由於	yóuyú	due to; owing to

page 33

1	音響	yīnxiǎng	the sound of noises; noises
	烟熏	yānxūn	fumes; smokes
2	情節	qíngjié	details of a matter
	仔細地	zǐxìd	carefully
	追究	zhuījiū	to investigate; to search into
	一番	yīfān	measure word for more than once; over and over again
3	竟而	jìngér	unexpectedly
	結論	jiélùn	conclusion
4	證實	zhèngshí	to confirm; to verify

	耐人尋味	nàirénxúnwèi	subtly interesting; that which induces deep thinking
5	研究員	yánjiūyuán	researcher
	觀察	guānchá	to observe; observation
6	符合	fúhé	to fit; to correspond to; in keeping with; in harmony with
	實際	shíjì	fact; reality
	僅僅	jǐnjǐn	merely
	局限	júxiàn	limited; confined; restricted
7	表面	biǎomiàn	surface; outward; superficial
	測斷	cèduàn	to estimate; to assume; to decide by assuming
	內在的	nèizàid	inner; internal
	實質	shízhí	essence; nature; substance
	孤立地	gūlìd	alone; isolatedly
	一般	yībān	general; ordinary; usual
	現象	xiànxiàng	phenomenon; phenomena
8	周圍環境	zhōuwéihuánjìng	surroundings
	具體條件	jùtǐtiáojiàn	actual conditions; specific conditions
	物象	wùxiàng	impressions; objective things
	因而	yīnér	thus; therefore; and hence
	便	biàn	then
	某種的	mǒuzhòngd	a certain kind of; a sort of
	片面性	piànmiànxìng	one-sidedness
9	一定的	yīdìngd	certain
	經驗	jīngyàn	experience
	客觀	kèguān	objective
10	已往的	yǐwǎngd	past
	跳脫	tiàotuō	to jump out of; to rid oneself of

	固有的	*gùyǒud*	fixed; given; inherent
	看法	*kànfǎ*	viewpoint; way of looking at things
	放開	*fàngkāi*	to broaden
	眼光	*yǎnguāng*	vision; foresight; insight
11	習性	*xíxìng*	habit; nature; usual disposition
	到家	*dàojiā*	fully; thoroughly; duly
12	脚步	*jiǎobù*	steps
	驚擾	*jīngrǎo*	to frighten and disturb
	足以	*zúyǐ*	enough to
	安然	*ānrán*	at ease
	靜處	*jìngchǔ*	to live peacefully
	火炙	*huǒzhì*	to broil
13	適合	*shìhé*	suitable; fit
	絕不會	*juébúhuì*	by no means will
	鑄造	*zhùzào*	to mould
	隨着	*suízhe*	to follow; along with; under (condition)
14	簡單化地	*jiǎndānhuàd*	in an over-simplified way
15	剛剛相反	*gānggāngxiāngfǎn*	just the opposite; quite on the contrary
	有素	*yǒusù*	for quite a while; experienced
	調查	*diàochá*	to investigate
16	一整套	*yīzhěngtào*	a whole set of
	依據	*yījù*	in accordance with; in terms of; in the light of; on (prep.); basis
	主觀	*zhǔguān*	subjectivity
	代替	*dàitì*	to replace

page 34

1	弊病	*bìbìng*	demerits; corrupt practices
	揣測	*chuǎicè*	to guess; to conjecture
2	迷惑	*míhuò*	to deceive; to confuse
	估計	*gūjì*	to estimate; estimation
	對頭	*duìtóu*	correct
3	存在	*cúnzài*	to exist
	學問	*xuéwèn*	knowledge
	推而廣之	*tuīérguǎngzhī*	to extend it to all
4	具	*jù*	to possess
	理	*lǐ*	principle
5	苛求	*kēqiú*	to demand without mercy; unreasonable demand
	專門	*zhuānmén*	specially; particularly; specialised in
6	得失	*déshī*	gains and losses
	關鍵	*guānjiàn*	keys; crucial point
	所系	*suǒxì*	wherein lies
	獲	*huò*	to obtain
	智珠	*zhìzhū*	pearl of wisdom

張獻忠不殺人辨　　Chang Hsien-chung Kills or Kills Not?

page 35

	張獻忠	zhāngxiànzhōng	a well-known rebel in Ming Dynasty
	辨	biàn	to distinguish right from wrong; to clarify; discussion on
1	殺星下界	shāxīngxiàjiè	the Destroying Star descending into this world
	殺人如麻	shārénrúmá	to kill ruthlessly
	說法	shuōfǎ	talk
	顯然	xiǎnrán	obviously
	封建	fēngjiàn	feudal
2	詆誣	dǐwū	to accuse falsely; to calumniate
	毀謗	huǐbàng	to slander; to libel
	反動	fǎndòng	reactionary
	宣傳	xuānchuán	propaganda
	毫無	háowú	without the slightest
	歷史	lìshǐ	historical; history
	眞實	zhēnshí	real
	價値	jiàzhí	value; worth
	另一方面	lìngyīfāngmiàn	on the other hand
	同情	tóngqíng	to sympathise; to have sympathy for
3	一反其道	yīfǎnqídào	to go to the other extreme
	偏說	piānshuō	to insist stubbornly
	根據	gēnjù	on the basis of; according to
4	筆記	bǐjì	to take notes; notes taken
	記載	jìzǎi	to record; what is on record
	得出結論	déchū .... jiélùn	to draw or to come to a conclusion

	不合	*bùhé*	does not tally with; does not agree with
	實際	*shíjì*	actuality; practice; what actually happened
5	有害的	*yǒuhàid*	harmful
	論斷	*lùnduàn*	assertions; conclusion; judgement
6	誇張的	*kuāzhāngd*	exaggerated; exaggeratedly
	描繪	*miáohuì*	to describe; to depict
	事實	*shìshí*	facts
	官書	*guānshū*	a book concerning official duties
	半官書	*bànguānshū*	a semi-official book concerning the duties of officials
	所謂	*suǒwèi*	the so-called
	私家史乘	*sījiāshǐchéng*	private history
7	真也	*zhēnyě*	could well be said of; could surely be described as
	成篇累牘	*chéngpiānléidú*	innumerable articles and documents (covering it)
	難於勝計	*nányúshèngjì*	difficult to count; uncountable (number)
	製造	*zhìzào*	to manufacture; to fabricate
	誑言	*kuángyán*	wild talks
	尚	*shàng*	still; yet
	解……恨	*jiě...hèn*	to give vent to anger or animosity
	起義	*qǐyì*	uprising
	心頭	*xīntóu*	the heart
8	從而	*cóng'ér*	therefore; thus
	歸之於	*guīzhīyú*	to put (the blame) one; to attribute to
	因果報應	*yīnguǒbàoyìng*	a cause-and-effect retribution
	甚至	*shènzhì*	even
	假以	*jiǎyǐ*	to borrow; to use

	神話	*shénhuà*	fairy tales
	迷惑	*míhuò*	to deceive; to confuse
	立碑	*lìbēi*	to set up a monument
9	鐫	*juān*	to engrave or carve
	以	*yǐ*	to; so as to; in order to; to use
	養	*yǎng*	to bring up, to breed; to rear
	何以	*héyǐ*	to use what; by what
	對	*duì*	to face; to answer for; to repay
	接連著	*jiēliánzhe*	followed by
	刻上	*kèshàng*	to carve or engrave
10	碑文	*bēiwén*	inscription on a tablet
	索解	*suǒjiě*	to find an answer
	憤世嫉俗	*fènshìjísú*	misanthropy
	流	*liú*	a kind; a class; a set of persons
	指	*zhǐ*	to reproach; to accuse; to point at
	代天行刑	*dàitiānxíngxíng*	to execute on behalf of the Heaven
11	擔當	*dāndāng*	to take up; to undertake; in charge of
	使命	*shǐmìng*	mission
	隨	*suí*	to follow; with (prep.)
	販棗	*fànzǎo*	to deal in dates; to carry about dates for sale
	誤將	*wùjiāng*	to take or use by mistake; to use mistakenly
	驢糞	*lǘfèn*	dung of a donkey
	玷污	*diànwū*	to debauch; to disgrace
	石坊	*shífāng*	a stone gateway
	不但……且	*búdàn...qiě*	not only....but
12	迫	*pò*	to force; to compel

	擦淨	cājìng	to wipe clean
	埋下……種子	máixià...zhǒngz	to sow the seed of
	深刻的	shēnkèd	profound; deep
	階級仇恨	jiējí-chóuhèn	class hatred
	出發	chūfā	to start off with; (as) a starting-point
13	引伸	yǐnshēn	to extend; to infer
	石碑	shíbēi	a stone monument
	因而	yīnér	thus; thereby; and hence
	傳說	chuánshuō	rumours; legend
	不管……如何	bùguǎn...rúhé	no matter how; no matter what
	動因	dòngyīn	motive

page 36

1	增加	zēngjiā	to increase; to add to
	添油加醬	tiānyóujiājiàng	to add oil and soy to; additional; that which was not there; to exaggerate
	材料	cáiliào	material
	正中了	zhèngzhòngle	to hit right on; highly acceptable to
	上懷	shànghuái	best of wishes; top-most intents of the heart
2	樂於	lèyú	gladly to; glad to
	廣爲傳播	guǎngwéichuánbō	to spread or broadcast far and wide
3	殺人成性	shārénchéngxìng	to kill has become one's nature
4	卷二	juànèr	Book II
	載	zài	to have the record; to print; to say
	余聞	yúwén	I heard that
	衡州	héngzhōu	a prefecture or county, of Hunan Province
	戮	lù	to kill in war

	以問	yǐwèn	to ask ... of (it); to put (the question) to (a person)
	則	zé	a particle indicating consequence or result; then; and so; consequently
	果然	guǒrán	it turns out as was expected or said
5	究竟	jiūjìng	just how
	詳情	xiángqíng	minute details; exact conditions; just how true was the record　這一記載究竟詳情如何
	考查	kǎochá	to examine and investigate
6	官吏	guānlì	officials
	望風	wàngfēng	on hearing it
	壓迫	yāpò	to oppress
7	剝削	bōxuē	to exploit
	歸附	guīfù	to subordinate oneself to
	對象	duìxiàng	object; target
	歷史學家	lìshǐxuéjiā	historians
	大做文章	dàzuòwénzhāng	to make a great fuss
	翻案	fānàn	to reverse the verdict
8	證明	zhèngmíng	to prove
	違反	wéifǎn	to violate; to act contrarily
9	自然	zìrán	of course; naturally; nature
	好心	hǎoxīn	good will; good intentions; kind-heartedness
10	誣蔑	wūmiè	to slander
	屠殺	túshā	to slaughter
	盈野	yíngyě	the field is filled with
	恰恰的	qiàqiàd	just; exactly
11	翻個個兒	fāngègèr	to turn heels over head; to turn a somersault; quite the contrary

	看來	kànlái	it seems; it looks
	鮮明	xiānmíng	striking
	强烈的	qiánglièd	sharp
	對比	duìbǐ	contrast
	現實	xiànshí	reality
	事理	shìlǐ	facts and principles of action
12	民衆性的	mínzhòngxìngd	mass; popular
	武裝革命	wǔzhuānggémìng	armed revolution
	既已	jìyǐ	since (it) has already
	訴之於	sùzhīyú	to resort to
	刀兵	dāobīng	arms
	就	jiù	then
	想像	xiǎngxiàng	to imagine
13	而況	érkuàng	besides; moreover
	自動的	zìdòngd	automatically; automatic; on one's own; willingly
	滚下	gǔnxià	to step down in disgrace (term of abuse)
	統治的	tǒngzhìd	ruling
	寶座	bǎozuò	precious seat; throne
	加以	jiāyǐ	in addition; besides; to inflict
	兇殘的	xiōngcánd	cruelly
14	鎭壓	zhènyā	to suppress; suppression
	撲滅	pūmiè	to put out
	則已	zéyǐ	then it is all very well
	遏止	èzhǐ	to stop; to check
15	主觀上	zhǔguānshàng	subjectively
	不欲	búyù	do not wish to

	誅殺	zhūshā	to kill; to put to death
	對付	duìfù	to deal with
	勢難由己	shìnànyóujǐ	in spite of oneself due to the (critical) situation
16	不在於	búzàiyú	does not lie in; does not rest on
	敵對的	díduìd	opposing; hostile; antagonistic

page 37

1	難免	nánmiǎn	difficult to avoid; unavoidably
	誤傷	wùshāng	wounds or injuries inflicted by mistake
	誤殺	wùshā	manslaughter; unintentional homicide
	鬥爭	dòuzhēng	struggle
2	最高形式	zuìgāoxíngshì	the highest form
	絕不是	juébushì	by no means
	吃素念佛者	chīsùniànfózhě	those who do not eat meat of any sort and pray all day long; the merciful
	幹	gàn	to do; to act
3	反過來	fǎnguòlái	on the other hand
	不許	bùxǔ	do not allow
	動刀槍	dòngdāoqiāng	to brandish a sword or a rifle; to use arms; to resort to violence
	進行	jìnxíng	to make
	提倡	tíchàng	to promote; to bring forward; to recommend
4	主張	zhǔzhāng	to advocate; to stand for
	意	yì	idea
	還以	huányǐ	to restore . . . .to; to return
	本來面目	běnláimiànmù	original features; what (he) was like
5	斤斤	jīnjīn	to count catty by catty; narrow-mindedly; scrupulously; fastidiously; stingily

沾	*zhān*	to taint with; to be infected by
倒是	*dàoshì*	on the contrary
趙太爺	*zhàotàiyé*	a minor character in "The True Story of Ah Q" by Lu Hsun
准不准	*zhǔnbùzhǔn*	to allow or not to allow
阿 Q	*ākiū*	the hero of "The True Story of Ah Q" by Lu Hsun

菊花與金魚　　Chrysanthemum and Goldfish

秦牧　Chin Mu (1902?—　　　　) Pen name for Lin Chueh-fu; essayist; born in Singapore, parents originally from Chenghai, Kwangtung. He began writing in 1937 for the literary page of the *Kuomin Daily* (國民日報) in Canton. In the early 1940's he was active in the literary movement of the left-wing writers in Kweilin. Following the reorganisation of the Leftist Labour Association in 1946, he went to Hongkong and stayed there until the communists occupied Canton.

In 1949 he went to Canton to work for the department of literature and art, and a year later for the culture bureau of the Kwangtung Provincial Government, editing its publication *Education and Culture in Kwangtung*. At the time when he was purged in 1966, he was deputy editor of the *Yangcheng Wan Pao* (羊城晚報) in Canton and vice-chairman of the Canton branch of the All-China Writers' Association. He has published at least 7 collections of essays and 2 novels. According to his critics, his main crime was that in his collection of essays, published in 1962, he failed to write about workers, peasants or soldiers.

page 38

1	菊花	júhuā	chrysanthemum
	金魚	jīnyú	goldfish
	培育	péiyù	to cultivate; to cherish
	絕妙	juémiào	most excellent
	藝術品	yìshùpǐn	work of art
2	植物性	zhíwùxìng	botanical
	動物性	dòngwùxìng	zoological
	歷代	lìdài	successive generations
	巧匠	qiǎojiàng	a skilled workman; an ingenious artisan
	苦心	kǔxīn	to take great pains in; to spare no efforts
3	繁衍	fányǎn	to multiply; to propagate in abundance
	品種	pǐnzhǒng	classes; varieties; species

4	天才	*tiāncái*	natural genius; talented people
	文明	*wénmíng*	civilisation; culture
	創造	*chuàngzào*	to create
5	提供	*tígōng*	to supply; to furnish; to offer
	相當	*xiāngdāng*	rather
	乏味的	*fáwèid*	monotonous; lacking in variety; wearisome through sameness
	地球	*dìqiú*	the globe
	光華璀燦	*guānghuácuīcàn*	glorious and glittering
	大千世界	*dàqiānshìjiè*	macrocosm (Budd.)
6	奇花異卉	*qíhuāyìhuì*	rare flowers and curious plants
	人工	*réngōng*	artificial
	選擇	*xuǎnzé*	to select; to choose
	有趣的	*yǒuqùd*	interesting
	小生物	*xiǎoshēngwù*	tiny little creatures
	方面	*fāngmiàn*	aspect; as far as ... concerned
	馴養	*xúnyǎng*	to tame and bring up
	金絲雀	*jīnsīqiāo*	canary
7	紛繁	*fēnfán*	various
	蘭花	*lánhuā*	orchid
	鴿子	*gēz*	pigeon
	長尾雞	*chángwěijī*	pintail
	歷史悠久	*lìshǐyōujiǔ*	a history of long standing
8	端	*duān*	to bring out
	鯽魚	*jìyú*	crucian
9	千年以上	*qiānniányǐshàng*	more than a thousand years

	郵局	yóujú	post office
	曾經	céngjīng	ever; in the past
	發行	fāxíng	to circulate; to put out
	一套	yītào	a set of
	郵票	yóupiào	stamps
10	彩畫	cǎihuà	coloured pictures
	令	lìng	to cause; to induce
	愛不釋手	àibúshìshǒu	to like (a thing) so much that one would not let go one's hand
	藝菊	yìjú	to cultivate chrysanthemum, as an art
	能手	néngshǒu	capable hands; good workers
11	無數	wúshù	numerous
	功參造化	gōngcānzàohuà	the excellence (of work) has reached that of the Creator
	能工巧匠	nénggōngqiǎojiàng	capable and skilled workmen
	祖國	zǔguó	fatherland
	深厚的	shēnhòud	profound
	文化	wénhuà	culture
12	舉辦	jǔbàn	to conduct; to hold; to initiate
	展覽	zhǎnlǎn	exhibition
13	深深地	shēnshēnd	deeply
	體會	tǐhuì	to realise; to appreciate; to understand
	含義	hányì	implication; inference; implied meaning

page 39

| 1 | 場面 | chǎngmiàn | an occasion |
| | 多姿多彩 | duōzīduōcǎi | full of beauty and colours |

	儀態萬千	*yítàiwànqiān*	myriads of postures; boundless charms and graces
2	荒郊	*huāngjiāo*	a wilderness
	寒傖的	*háncāngd*	cold and haggard; in poor circumstances
	野菊	*yějú*	parthemum
	人類	*rénlèi*	mankind
	加意	*jiāyì*	meaningfully; intentionally; with special caution
	選種	*xuǎnzhǒng*	to select the finest species
	歷時	*lìshí*	for a period of
	終於	*zhōngyú*	in the end; at last; eventually
	異采	*yìcǎi*	unusual brilliance
3	光說	*guāngshuō*	to speak only of; to mention only; for . . . only
	花瓣	*huābàn*	petal of a flower; petals
	就有	*jiùyǒu*	there are no less than
	分	*fēn*	distinction; difference
	瓣端	*bànduān*	tip of a flower petal
	鈎	*gōu*	a hook; a sickle
	捲	*juǎn*	to roll up
4	球形	*qiúxíng*	spherical; globular
	談到	*tándào*	to talk about; to speak of
	墨菊	*mòjú*	black daisy
5	別	*bié*	distinction; difference
	至於	*zhìyú*	as for
	花型	*huāxíng*	flower pattern; shape of a flower
6	牡丹	*mǔdān*	peony
	端雅大方	*duānyǎdàfāng*	fine; elegant and dignified
	龍飛鳳舞	*lóngfēifèngwǔ*	free and vigorous

7	瑰麗	*guīlì*	gorgeous beauty; captivating beauty
	彩虹	*cǎihóng*	rainbows
	潔白	*jiébái*	whiteness
	賽	*sài*	to compete; to rival
	霜雪	*shuāngxuě*	frost and snow
	火燄	*huǒyàn*	flames
	熱烈	*rèliè*	fiery; red-hot
	羽毛	*yǔmáo*	feather
	輕柔	*qīngróu*	light and gentle
8	簡直	*jiǎnzhí*	simply
	羣芳競艷	*qúnfāngjìngyàn*	beauties competing at a beauty contest
	江南	*jiāngnán*	south of the Yangtze River
	花朝	*huāzhāo*	the birthday of flowers, generally dated on the 12th of the 2nd lunar month
9	游動	*yóudòng*	to swim and move about
	什麼	*shénme*	what with
	珍珠鱗	*zhēnzhūlín*	pearl scale
	獅頭	*shītóu*	lion head
	鶴頂紅	*hèdǐnghóng*	crane-top red goldfish
10	水泡眼	*shuǐpàoyǎn*	bubble-eyed (goldfish)
	朝天眼	*cháotiānyǎn*	telescope (goldfish)
	吃驚	*chījīng*	to be frightened; taken by surprise
	妙處	*miàochù*	beauty; subtlety
11	才	*cái*	then; only
12	魚類	*yúlèi*	pisces
	丑角	*chǒujiǎo*	clown

	竟	jìng	actually; really
13	試想	shìxiǎng	just imagine
	光	guāng	only for
	叫得出	jiàodechū	that can be named
14	欣賞	xīnshǎng	to appreciate
	無窮無盡	wúqióngwújìn	endless; infinite
15	栽培	zāipéi	to tend; to care for
	養殖	yǎngzhí	to nurture; to bring up; to breed
	老行尊	lǎohángzūn	an expert; one being respected by those in the same line
	心願	xīnyuàn	wish
16	豪情勝慨	háoqíngshēngkǎi	full of a fine spirit of vigour and fearlessness
	結果	jiéguǒ	consequently; as a result
	圍觀	wéiguān	to look on in a crowd

page 40

1	投以	tóuyǐ	to eye with; to throw a look at
	激賞	jīshǎng	admiration; great appreciation
	眼光	yǎnguāng	a look
	多行呀！	duōxíngyā	how capable (they are)!
	自然	zìrán	nature
2	增添	zēngtiān	to add to
	花樣	huāyàng	patterns of a flower; forms; content (colloq.)
3	不妨	bùfáng	might as well; harmless to
	花盆	huāpén	flower-pot
	魚缸	yúgāng	fish-globe
	徜徉	chángyáng	to amuse; to entertain (oneself); to make excursions; to wander

	不禁	bùjīn	cannot help feeling
4	感觸	gǎnchù	stirrings of emotion; emotionally stirred
5	人工	réngōng	human labour; the work of man
	可貴	kěguì	valuable
	巧奪天工	qiǎoduótiāngōng	(its) excellence surpassing that of Heaven; work excels that of Heaven
6	人為的	rénwéid	man-made
	作用	zuòyòng	function; work
	還不是	háibúshì	would it yet (still) not be ....?; it would still be ....
	野外	yěwài	desert; open country
	平平常常	píngpíngchángcháng	common; ordinary
	貌不驚人	màobùjīngrén	without surprising features; features that do not surprise people
7	配	pèi	good for
	餚饌	xiáozhuàn	table delicacies
	貫注	guànzhù	to concentrate on
8	奇跡	qíjī	miracles
	加工	jiāgōng	to process; extra work
	放棄	fàngqì	to give up; to abandon; to forsake
	原始的	yuánshǐd	primitive
9	自然崇拜的	zìránchóngbàid	adoring nature
	觀點	guāndiǎn	a point of view; viewpoint
10	繁多	fánduō	multitudinous
	不斷地	búduànd	incessantly
11	更深地	gèngshēnd	more deeply
	多樣性	duōyàngxìng	multiplicity; manifold variety
	飄逸洒脫	piāoyìsǎtuō	graceful and free

	雅緻大方	yǎzhìdàfāng	elegant and dignified
12	固然	gùrán	as expected; really; unquestionably
	異常	yìcháng	rarely
	珍貴	zhēnguì	valuable
	滿天星	mǎntiānxīng	a kind of chrysanthemum, like a clear sky full of stars
13	萬壽菊	wànshòujú	Australian chrysanthemum
	不失為	bùshīwéi	worth the name or credit; as good as
	值得	zhíde	worthy of
	重視	zhòngshì	great attention
	各式各樣	gèshìgèyàng	manifold; various
15	吸引	xīyǐn	to attract the attention of
	廣大的	guǎngdàd	broad
	羣衆	qúnzhòng	messes
16	情趣	qíngqù	taste; relish

page 41

1	包括	bāokuò	to include
	夠味	gòuwèi	interesting; delicious
	道理	dàolǐ	principle; reason
	單一	dānyī	monotony
	必然	bìrán	inevitably
2	導致	dǎozhì	to lead to
	枯燥	kūzào	dryness; dullness
	目不暇接	mùbùxiájiē	so fully occupied that the eyes cannot take more
3	偏愛	piānài	personal liking; prejudice for
	切忌	qiējì	to avoid absolutely
4	自然	zìrán	of course; by all means; naturally

	悉聽尊便	xītīngzūnbiàn	do as your Highness please
	決不應該	juébùyīnggāi	by no means should
5	一文不值	yīwénbùzhí	not worth a farthing
6	長篇小說	chángpiānxiǎoshuō	long novels
	就	jiù	then; therefore
	貶低	biǎndī	to devalute; to under-estimate
	樣式	yàngshì	forms
	樸素	púsù	simple and plain
	風格	fēnggé	style
	認爲	rènwéi	to deem; to believe; to count; to think
	華麗的	huálìd	splendid and fine
	纖巧的	xiānqiǎod	delicate and fine
7	價值	jiàzhí	value; worth; quality
	方向	fāngxiàng	direction; orientation; general line
	一致性	yīzhìxìng	unanimity
8	提倡	tíchàng	to promote; to develop; to initiate
	多樣化	duōyànghuà	multiplicity
	揚此抑彼	yángcǐyìbǐ	to wilfully raise high the value of one and keep low that of another
	主張	zhǔzhāng	to advocate
	定於一尊	dìngyúyīzūn	to be restricted to only one authority
	論調	lùndiào	tone of agrument
9	妨碍	fáng'ài	to hinder
	百花齊放	bǎihuāqífàng	"Hundred Flowers Blossom", a campaign in 1957 to encourage diversity of literary styles
	即使	jíshǐ	even if
	觀賞	guānshǎng	to enjoy seeing

	領略	*lǐnglüè*	to apprehend
	稍加	*shāojiā*	a little more than originally intended
11	思索	*sīsuǒ*	to think deeply; to think and find out
	大胆	*dàdǎn*	brave; bravely; bold; boldly
	發揚	*fāyáng*	to enhance ; to extend the glory or virtue of
	特點	*tèdiǎn*	special characteristics; special features
12	形成	*xíngchéng*	to form
	獨特的	*dútèd*	unique
13	失掉	*shīdiào*	to miss; to lose
14	巨大	*jùdà*	enormous; tremendous
	特色	*tèsè*	unique features; distinctive features
15	就	*jiù*	then
	談不上	*tánbúshàng*	not to mention; not to say; out of question
	不僅	*bùjǐn*	not only
16	恐怕	*kǒngpà*	perhaps

page 42

1	藏	*cáng*	to hide; to conceal

邯鄲學步　**To Imitate Steps at Han Tan**

	邯鄲學步	hándānxuébù	to imitate steps at Han Tan, capital of the State of Chao
1	乘坐	chéngzuò	to board (a train) to travel by
	京漢列車	jīnghànlièchē	train from Peking to Hankow
	月台	yuètái	platform
2	往事	wǎngshì	past incidents; vista
	陳迹	chénjì	remains; relic; historical traces; vestiges;
	名將	míngjiàng	famous generals
	策士	cèshì	counsellor; strategist
	俠客	xiákè	knight-errant
	美人	měirén	beauty
	尤其是	yóuqíshì	particularly for
	慷慨	kāngkǎi	generous; disinterested; chivalrous
3	禁不住	jīnbúzhù	cannot help
4	可笑的	kěxiàod	laughable
	典故	diǎngù	old story
5	傳說	chuánshuō	rumour had it that
	大邑	dàyì	a big city
	所在	suǒzài	location; that where it is located
	講究	jiǎngjiū	particular about; dainty about; go for
	姿勢	zīshì	posture; bearing; style
	風度	fēngdù	manners; demeanour; style
6	決不能	juébùnéng	can in no way
	容許	róngxǔ	to allow; to permit

	鵝步	ébù	goose steps; to walk like a goose
	八字脚	bāzìjiǎo	steps in the form of the character 八
	總之	zǒngzhī	in a word; to be brief; to sum up
	美妙	měimiào	gracefully; graceful
	名氣	míngqì	reputation; fame
7	特地	tèdì	on purpose; specially
	學樣	xuéyàng	to learn the ways; to imitate; to follow exactly the same style as
8	全力	quánlì	to spare no effort
	模仿	mófǎng	to imitate, same as 摹仿
	拋掉	pāodiào	to throw away; to leave behind
	最後	zuìhòu	in the end; finally
	簡直	jiǎnzhí	simply
9	狼狽	lángbèi	ill at ease; disorderly; in great distress
10	掌故	zhǎnggù	story
	風格	fēnggé	style
	一味	yīwèi	entirely; solely
	諷刺	fěngcì	to satirise
	頗	pō	rather
	歷代	lìdài	successive generations
11	文人	wénrén	literary men; intellectuals
	重視	zhòngshì	to give attention to; great attention
	莊子	zhuāngzǐ	Chuang Tzu, a famous Taoist philosopher
	著作	zhùzuò	literary works
	敘述	xùshù	to state; to narrate
	失步	shībù	to lose steps; to lose one's own way of walking

	成語	chéngyǔ	proverb
12	常常	chángcháng	now and then
	引用	yǐnyòng	to quote
	李白	lǐbái	a famous poet of Tang dynasty
	古風	gǔfēng	old style; tradition; customs of the old days
	醜女	chǒunǚ	an ugly girl
	效顰	xiàopín	to imitate the frowning of a beauty
13	還家	huánjiā	on returning home
	驚	jīng	to take by surprise; to frighten
	四鄰	sìlín	the neighbourhood; neighbours on the four sides
	笑殺	xiàoshā	to greatly amuse; to be badly mocked at by

page 44

1	必不如	bìbùrú	inevitably not as good as
	蓋	gài	for; because
	意中	yìzhōng	in the mind of
	既恐失之	jìkǒngshīzhī	since one is afraid of losing it
2	筆力	bǐlì	the strength of a pen
	復	fù	again
	自遂	zìsuí	to follow one's inclinations; freely
	可知	kězhī	thus; understandably
3	典故	diǎngù	story; anecdote; a precedent
	包含	bāohán	to imply
	令人	lìngrén	to cause people
	警惕	jǐngtì	to be vigilant
	意義	yìyì	meaning
	大師	dàshī	great masters

	深爲	shēnwéi	greatly
	讚許	zànxǔ	to praise and approve
4	拋棄	pāoqì	to forsake; to give up; to abandon
	既然	jìrán	since
	理論上	lǐlùnshàng	theoretically
	事實上	shìshíshàng	in reality; as a matter of fact
	完全	wánquán	fully; wholly
	證明	zhèngmíng	to prove; to testify; to certify
5	死胡同	sǐhútòng	a blind alley
	醉心於	zuìxīnyú	intoxicated with; greatly interested in
	初學者	chūxuézhě	beginners
6	往往	wǎngwǎng	very often
	少年	shàonián	a lad; teenagers
	成人	chéngrén	a grown-up; grown-ups
	不便	búbiàn	not convenient
	加以	jiāyǐ	to give . . . to; to crown with
	責難	zénàn	repirimand; reproof
	達到	dádào	to reach
	一定的	yīdìngd	certain
7	水平	shuǐpíng	level
	階段	jiēduàn	phase
	推陳出新	tuīchénchūxīn	to weed out the old and to let the new emerge
	發揚	fāyáng	to foster; to develop; to promote
8	談不上	tánbúshàng	out of question
	創造	chuàngzào	to create; creation
	倍	bèi	a fold

	唯	wéi	only
9	貪圖	tāntú	to seek after; to scheme for; greedy for
	方便	fāngbiàn	convenience
	鑽進	zuānjìn	to bore or creep into; to enter deeply into
10	糟糕	zāogāo	too bad; an awful mess
	存在	cúnzài	to exist; existence
	又來	yūlái	firstly; on the one hand
	反映	fǎnyìng	to reflect
11	變動	biàndòng	to change; to move; to alter
	不居	bùjū	not to stay or to remain; not stagnant
	表現	biǎoxiàn	to express; expression
	形式	xíngshì	a form; forms
	不斷地	búduànd	incessantly
	隨着	suízhe	to follow; accordingly
	發展	fāzhǎn	to develop
	僵硬了的	jiāngyìngled	stiffened
	殼	ké	shell
	不管	bùguǎn	No matter
12	美好	měihǎo	beautiful and fine
	總不能	zǒngbùnéng	can in no way
	新鮮的	xīnxiānd	fresh
	內容	nèiróng	content
	適應	shìyìng	to adjust; to adapt to
	強烈的	qiánglièd	violent; vigorous; strong and powerful
	新鮮感	xīnxiāngǎn	feeling of freshness
	離開	líkāi	to divorce; to depart from

	個性	gèxìng	individuality
	獨特	dútè	unique
	味兒	wèir	flavour
	大大地	dàdàd	greatly
	打個折扣	dǎgèzhékòu	to make or give a discount; to decrease
14	閹割	yāngē	to castrate
15	廣泛的	guǎngfànd	extensive
	繼承	jìchéng	inheritance; to inherit
16	諸家	zhūjiā	all schools of philosophers

page 45

1	發揮	fāhuī	to bring into play; to give free scope to
	創造性	chuàngzàoxìng	creativeness
	形成	xíngchéng	to form
	源流	yuánliú	the source and history of
	光會	guānghuì	can only
2	密切	mùqiè	close; closely
	關係	guānxì	related; relationship
	這就	zhèjiù	thus; consequently
	範圍	fànwéi	sphere; field
	狹隘	xiá'ài	to narrow; to restrict; to limit
3	取法於上 僅得其中	qǔfǎyúshàng-jǐndéqízhōng	to imitate the first class, one gets only the second class (of quality)
	取法於中 僅得其下	qǔfǎyúzhōng-jǐndéqíxià	to imitate the second class, one gets only the third class (of quality)
	十全十美	shíquánshíměi	perfect

4	就是	*jiùshì*	even; even if
	維妙維肖	*wéimiàowéixiào*	life-like
5	可貴	*kěguì*	valuable
	優秀的	*yōuxiùd*	excellent
	臨摹之作	*línmózhīzuò*	copy; reproduction
	何況	*hékuàng*	besides; what is more
	境界	*jìngjiè*	state; stage
6	足見	*zújiàn*	sufficient to see; can well perceive
	一般	*yībān*	generally; in general; usually; commonly
8	部門	*bùmén*	a section; a department; a division
	經驗	*jīngyàn*	experience
	師承	*shīchéng*	inheritance from masters
9	齊白石	*qíbáishí*	a well-known contemporary Chinese painter, 1862-1957
	風趣	*fēngqù*	interesting as well as humourous
	學我者生 似我者死	*xuéwǒzhěshēng-sìwǒzhěsǐ*	he who learns from me lives; he who imitates me dies
	實際上	*shíjìshàng*	in reality
11	超越	*chāoyuè*	to excel; to surpass; to transcend
12	代代	*yīdàidài*	generation after generation
13	整體	*zhěngtǐ*	as a whole
	到頭來	*dàotóulái*	in the end; eventually
	終於	*zhōngyú*	after all; in the end
	關鍵	*guānjiàn*	key to a situation; crux of the matter
	怪不得	*guàibùdé*	no wonder
	釀取	*niàngqǔ*	to brew
	蜜	*mì*	honey

14	蜜成花不見	*mìchénghuābújiàn*	flowers are no longer seen when honey is made
	蜜蜂	*mìfēng*	bees
	世代	*shìdài*	generations
	受到	*shòudào*	to have received
	思想家	*sīxiǎngjiā*	thinkers
	藝術家	*yìshùjiā*	artists
	寓意深長	*yùyìshēncháng*	that entertains a deep thought
	讚美	*zànměi*	praises

河汉错综　The Complication of River Branches

	河汉	héchà	river branches
	错综	cuòzōng	complication
1	剧本	jùběn	a play
	演出	yǎnchū	to perform; performance
	地区	dìqū	region
	长期	chángqī	long-term
	衍变	yǎnbiàn	change in due succession; evolution
	结果	jiéguǒ	result; consequence
	骨干	gǔgàn	skeleton
2	基础	jīchǔ	basis; foundation
	出现	chūxiàn	to emerge; to appear
	悬殊	xuánshū	far different; greatly different
	小节	xiǎojié	minor matters; unimportant points
	差别	chàbié	difference; dissimilarity
	发人深思	fārénshēnsī	to induce one's deep thought
3	白蛇传	báishézhuàn	*Story of the White Snake*, name of a traditional play and opera
	剧种	jùzhǒng	variety of plays
	白娘娘	báiniángniáng	heroine in the *Story of the White Snake*
	女侍	nǚshì	maid
	小青	xiǎoqīng	name of the heroine's maid, another snake
	唯独	wéidú	only
	川剧	chuānjù	Szechuan opera
	遭到	zāodào	to have suffered; to have met with; to have encountered

5	追逐	zhuīzhú	to chase after; to run after
	被擊敗	bèijībài	to suffer defeat; to be defeated
	俯首貼耳	fǔshǒutiēěr	to surrender tamely; subservient
	心悅誠服	xīnyuèchéngfú	to yield willingly
	化成	huàchéng	to turn into
	服侍	fúshì	to wait on
6	異心	yìxīn	disagreement; disloyalty
7	奇特	qítè	specially strange
	細想	xìxiǎng	careful thought
	一下	yīxià	measure word for careful deliberation
8	表現	biǎoxiàn	to show; to express
	義氣	yìqì	loyalty; faithfulness
	何損於	hésǔnyú	Where-at does it harm . . . ? used to expect an answer in the affirmative
	神話	shénhuà	fairy tales
	發展	fāzhǎn	development; to develop
9	描述	miáoshù	to depict; to describe
	拋棄	pāoqì	to abandon; to forsake
	逼害	bīhài	to persecute; to force to die
10	死裏逃生	sǐlǐtáoshēng	to escape narrowly; to make a narrow escape
	包公	bāogōng	a provincial governor known for his justice
	投訴	tóusù	to fire an accusation; to make a complaint
	鍘	zhá	a lever-knife for beheading—a special instrument used to punish evil criminals
	伸冤	shēnyuān	to redress one's wrongs inflicted by others
	淮劇	huáijù	Anhwei opera
	番	fān	measure word for details and plot; a kind of

11	情節	qíngjié	details; content; plot
	刺客	cìkè	assasinator
	義釋	yìshì	to justly release
	道行深厚	dàoxíngshēnhòu	profound moral attainments
	搭救	dājiù	to save; to rescue
	練	liàn	to train
12	武藝	wǔyì	feats of strength; art of fighting
	終於	zhōngyú	in the end; eventually
	女扮男裝	nǚbànnánzhuāng	a female in disguise of a male
	改姓換名	gǎixìnghuànmíng	to change one's name
	邊關	biānguān	a frontier pass
	立	lì	to establish
	戰功	zhàngōng	military merits; meritorious military services
	逐漸	zhújiàn	gradually; step by step
	升為	shēngwéi	to be promoted to be
	統帥	tǒngshuài	commander-in-chief
	回京	huíjīng	to return to the capital
13	親自	qīnzì	in person; personally
	違旨	wéizhǐ	disobeying orders of the emperor

page 47

1	仔細	zǐxì	carefully; meticulously
	吟味	yínwèi	to chant in order to feel the gusto of; to feel; to sense
	何嘗不是	hécángbúshì	Where is the lack of . . . . ?
	言之成理	yánzhīchénglǐ	reasoning; right in reasoning
2	曲折	qǔzhé	ins and outs; zigzag
	經過	jīngguò	to run through

	河床	héchuāng	river bed
	未嘗不可	wèichángbùkě	not without possibility; not unlikely
3	十八相送	shíbāxiāngsòng	to say goodbye for the eighteenth time; unwilling to part
	折	zhé	a scene in a play
	由於	yóuyú	due to; as a result of
4	師母	shīmǔ	wife of the teacher
	做媒	zuòméi	to make the match
	恍然大悟	huǎngrándàwù	to realise suddenly; unintelligible
	路程	lùchéng	journey
	迷離惝恍	mílíchǎnghuǎng	indistinct and confusing
	原來	yuánlái	no other than
5	廣東	guǎngdōng	the province of Kwangtung
	潮州戲	cháozhōuxì	Chaochow opera
	面貌	miànmào	outlook; outward appearance
6	歸程	guīchéng	on one's way home; return journey
	已極	yǐjí	to the extreme; extremely
	入睡	rùshuì	to fall asleep
	夢境	mèngjìng	in dream
	着上	zhuóshàng	to be dressed in
7	重説一遍	chóngshuōyībiàn	to say it again; to repeat
	驚覺	jīngjué	to awake in surprise
	推敲	tuīqiāo	to consider
	不待	búdài	without waiting
8	提醒	tíxǐng	to remind
	就	jiù	then; at once; forthwith
	斷定	duàndìng	to ensure; to make sure

9	細節	*xìjié*	minute details
	充分的	*chōngfèn de*	sufficient
	心理科學	*xīnlǐkēxué*	psychology
	根據	*gēnjù*	basis; grounds; on the ground of
	擺脫	*bǎituō*	to get rid of; to remove
10	習慣觀念	*xíguànguānniàn*	habitual views; views formulated by habits
	羈絆	*jībàn*	fetters; shackles; impediments
	隱約	*yǐnyuē*	indistinctly
	突然	*tūrán*	all of a sudden
	清晰	*qīngxī*	to become distinct; to clear up
	起來	*qǐlái*	gradually; increasingly
11	充滿	*chōngmǎn*	to be filled with; teeming with
	抒情	*shūqíng*	lyrical
	優美	*yōuměi*	excellent; beautiful
	氣氛	*qìfēn*	atmosphere
12	傳說	*chuánshuō*	hearsay; rumours; folk-lore
	民間故事	*mínjiāngùshì*	folk-story; folk-tale
	舞台	*wǔtái*	a stage
	差異	*chàyì*	difference
13	千變萬化	*qiānbiànwànhuà*	ever-changeable
	一成不變	*yīchéngbúbiàn*	unchangeable; invariable; inflexible
14	登高	*dēnggāo*	to ascend heights
	水網	*shuǐwǎng*	the net of water
	地帶	*dìdài*	region; area
	景象	*jǐngxiàng*	sight
15	俯瞰	*fǔkàn*	to look down and watch from above

	溪流	xīliú	brooks and streams
	葉脈	yèmài	veinlet
	複雜	fùzá	complicated; tangesome
	熠熠發亮	yìyìfāliàng	brightly shining; sparkly bright
	放射	fàngshè	to radiate; to shine; to glisten
16	乍看	zhàkān	to see for the first time; to glance
	糾纏	jiūchán	entangled; tanglesome
	條理	tiáolǐ	order; regularity; sequence
	辨認	biànrèn	to distinguish and recognise; to identify
	覺察	juéchá	to discover and realise
	氣勢萬千	qìshìwànqiān	magnificent; majestic; grand

page 48

1	支脈	zhīmài	a branch veinlet
	歸根到底	guīgēndàodǐ	in the end; to revert to the original root
	滙集	huìjí	to gather into one place
	主脈	zhǔmài	main vein
	流向	liúxiàng	flowing direction
3	社會生活	shèhuìshēnghuó	social life
	事象	shìxiàng	phenomena
	道理上	dàolǐshàng	in principle
	一脈相通	yīmàixiāngtōng	to communicate with each other through one and the same vein; in communication
	反映	fǎnyìng	to reflect
4	千差萬殊	qiānchàwànshū	greatly different
5	不管	bùguǎn	no matter (how, what, when, where, who . . .)
	形式上	xíngshìshàng	in form
	詭奇	guǐqí	odd; strange; uncommon

	實際上	*shíjìshàng*	in reality
	基本的	*jīběnd*	fundamental; basic
	貫串	*guànchuàn*	to thread together
7	體現	*tǐxiàn*	to embody
	盡有	*jìnyǒu*	each of them can by any means have
8	長江	*chángjiāng*	The Yangtze River
	黃河	*huánghé*	The Yellow River
	整體	*zhěngtǐ*	as a whole
10	反常曲折	*fǎnchángqūzhé*	reversion out of the usual way; to change the course
14	隨身	*suíshēn*	personal; accompanying
	認定	*rèndìng*	to make sure of; to ensure
15	冤抑	*yuānyì*	grievances; wrongs
	總是要	*zǒngshìyào*	will in the end
	設法	*shèfǎ*	to manage
	伸雪	*shēnxuě*	to redress and wipe out (a grievance)
16	報仇	*bàochóu*	to avenge
	結局	*jiéjú*	the result; the outcome; the endings of a drama

page 49

1	親密	*qīnmì*	close; endeared; beloved
	同窗	*tóngchuāng*	classmate
	說穿	*shuōchuān*	to divulge; to reveal; to speak out
	始終	*shǐzhōng*	from beginning to end; throughout
2	觀念上	*guānniànshàng*	conceptually; of mental conception
	固定	*gùdìng*	fixed
	狠狠地	*hěnhěnd*	fiercely; heavily; hard
3	當頭一棒	*dāngtóuyībàng*	a knock right on the head (by a cudgel)

4	了解	liǎojiě	to understand
	簡單化	jiǎndānhuà	simplified; over-simplified
	劃一化	huàyīhuà	unified; uniformed
	碰壁	pèngbì	to meet with a refusal, difficulty
6	批評	pīpíng	to criticise
	文章	wénzhāng	an article
	指責	zhǐzé	to reprimand; to reprove
	文學作品	wénxuézuòpǐn	literary works
	眞實	zhēnshí	real; true (to life)
	所持的	suǒchíd	that one adheres to
7	社會科學	shèhuìkēxué	social sciences; sociology
	結論	jiélùn	conclusion; results; end results
	套	tào	to fit
	符合	fúhé	to correspond to; to be in harmony
8	心目	xīnmù	the mind
	批准	pīzhǔn	to approve
9	浪花	lànghuā	waves
10	飛濺	fēijiàn	to splash
	無窮無盡	wúqióngwújìn	endless; infinite
	樣式	yàngshì	forms; patterns
	容忍	róngrěn	to tolerate; to permit
	獨特	dútè	unique; uncommon
11	勢必	shìbì	inevitably; unavoidably
	影響	yǐngxiǎng	to affect; to influence
	創造性地	chuàngzàoxìngd	creatively
	處理	chǔlǐ	to treat; to deal with; to tackle; to arrange

	豐富多采	*fēngfùduōcǎi*	abundant and colourful
	題材	*tícái*	subject material
	滿足	*mǎnzú*	content; well-pleased with; satisfied with
	一般的	*yībānd*	general; ordinary; common; usual
12	減少	*jiǎnshǎo*	to decrease; to diminish; to reduce
	光輝	*guānghuī*	splendour; dazzling brightness
14	隨意	*suíyì*	to act as one pleases; to do as one's mind directs
	規定	*guīdìng*	to stipulate; to lay down as a rule
	海洋	*hǎiyáng*	ocean
	多采多姿	*duōcǎiduōzī*	full of colours and beauty
15	貝類	*bèilèi*	conch
	水藻	*shuǐzǎo*	algae

毒物和藥　Poisons and Medicines

	毒物	dúwù	poisonous stuffs
	藥	yào	medicines
1	公認	gōngrèn	universally acknowledged
	良醫	liángyī	a skilful doctor
	妙藥	miàoyào	good medicines
2	砒霜	pīshuāng	arsenic
	皮膚病	pífūbìng	skin diseases
3	克	kè	a gramme
	整百	zhěngbǎi	the whole lot of a hundred
	專門	zhuānmén	specially; solely; devoted to one thing alone
	採	cǎi	to pick; to pluck; to gather; to extract
4	眼鏡蛇	yǎnjīngshé	cobra
	響尾蛇	xiǎngwěishé	rattlesnake
	飼養	sìyǎng	to feed and keep; to rear
5	蝎子	xiēz	scorpion
	中醫	zhōngyī	a Chinese doctor; a herbalist doctor
	主治	zhǔzhì	to cure mainly
	驚風	jīngfēng	eclampsia
	抽搐	chōuchù	convulsion
	瘡	chuāng	ulcer
	症	zhēng	a disease; diseases; ailments
6	西醫	xīyī	a Western medical doctor
	還	hái	in addition; besides; also
	證實	zhèngshí	to prove and confirm

	醫療	yīliáo	to heal; to cure diseases
	大腦炎	dànǎoyán	cerebritis
	地區	dìqū	region
	人民公社	rénmíngōngshè	people's communes
	建築	jiànzhù	to build; to erect; architecture
7	針劑	zhēnjì	injections
	關節炎	guānjiéyán	arthritis
8	塗抹	túmǒ	to smear
	箭鏃	jiànzù	the barb of an arrow; the head of a javelin
	蟾酥	shànsū	juice from the warts of a toad, used for medicine
	癩蛤蟆	làigémá	the toad, same as 癩蝦蟆 làihámá
	分泌物	fēnmìwù	secretions
9	劇毒	jùdú	a powerful poison; extremely poisonous
	鴉片	yāpiàn	opium
	嗎啡	mǎfēi	morphine
	施用	shīyòng	to put to use
	份量	fènliàng	a dose; a portion
11	場合	chǎnghé	an occasion
	適當	shìdàng	properly; proper
	運用	yùnyòng	to apply; to put to use; to use
12	僅僅	jǐnjǐn	merely
	認識	rènshí	knowledge; to know; to realise
	跨	kuà	to stride
13	類似	lèisì	similar

page 51

1	傳說	chuánshuō	rumour had it that

	軼事	yìshì	anecdotes; tales
	詩酒之會	shījiǔzhīhuì	a party of wine and poetry
	聯句	liánjù	to compose either the first or second line of verse to form a couplet; couplets
	吟詩	yínshī	to hum poetry; to chant to the rhymes of poetry
	根底	gēndǐ	a foundation; basic knowledge
2	下筆	xiàbǐ	to put pen to paper; to put brush to paper
	竟	jìng	actually; in fact
	柳絮	liǔxù	willow catkins
3	四座	sìzuò	all seated
	嘩然	huārán	clamour; hubbub; in a confused din
	忍受不了	rěnshòubùliǎo	cannot stand any longer
	提筆	tíbǐ	to pick up the pen (brush)
	夕陽	xīyáng	the setting sun; the afternoon sun
	方	fāng	just now; a moment ago
	桃花	táohuā	peach blossoms
	塢	wù	a valley; a village
4	這一來	zhèyīlái	in this way; thus; by so doing
	動人的	dòngrénd	moving; touching
6	同類的	tónglèid	similar; of the same nature; of the same kind
	富貴人家	fùguìrénjiā	a well-to-do and decent family; lit., a family of riches and honour
	老太婆	lǎotàipó	an old lady; an old woman; an elderly woman
	題詩	tíshī	to write impromptu verses in honour of a person or in memory of an occasion
	賀壽	hèshòu	to greet one's birthday with presents
7	婆娘	póniáng	an old woman

	舉座	jǔzuò	all seated; those present
	失色	shīsè	to change colour; to change countenance
	接着	jiēzhe	to follow by; to continue to
	九天	jiǔtiān	the highest heavens
	仙女	xiānnǚ	a fairy; an angel
	下	xià	to descend
	凡塵	fánchén	this world; earthly world; human world; mortal life
	人家	rénjiā	a family; sometimes it means "other people", "I"
	兒孫	érsūn	children & grand children
8	轉怒爲喜	zhuǎnnùwéixǐ	to turn anger into joys
	個個	gègè	each; every one; all of them
	不禁	bùjīn	cannot help being
	勃然震怒	bóránzhènnù	suddenly (all at once) in a towering rage
9	筆鋒	bǐfēng	the tip of a brush or a pen; sharpness
	輕輕	qīngqīng	lightly
	一轉	yīzhuǎn	one turn; to make a turn; to turn quickly
	偷得	tōudé	having stolen; having secretly taken
	蟠桃	pántáo	the flat peach; the heavenly peach
	奉	fèng	to offer; to serve; to present
	至親	zhìqīn	a very near relative; closest relatives; the dearest
	改顏	gǎiyán	to change countenance
10	贊許	zànxǔ	to praise and approve; to approve in praise
11	思想性	sīxiǎngxìng	ideological merits; ideological quality
12	啟示	qǐshì	to reveal; revelation; enlightenment
	一成不變	yīchénbúbiàn	once completed, it cannot be altered; unalterable; inflexible

14	法則	fǎzé	law; rules; methods
	粉碎	fěnsuì	to smash; to shatter; to crush
	道理	dàolǐ	principle; reason
	軼談	yìtán	that which is talked about in tales
15	如出一轍	rúchūyīzhé	to originate from the same source; one and the same; identical
	共通的	gòngtōngd	concurrent; agreeing; common; of the same nature

page 52

1	相對	xiāngduì	relative; comparative
2	參考	cānkǎo	for reference; to compare; to collate
	絕對化	juéduìhuà	to "absolutise"; to dogmatise
	條條	tiáotiáo	provisions of a law – one kind of restrictions
	框框	kuàngkuàng	frames – another kind of restrictions
3	舉例	jǔlì	to illustrate with an example (lit.); to cite an instance; for example
	描繪	miáohuì	to describe; to depict; to portray
	生動的	shēngdòngd	vivid
4	一般而論	yībān-érlùn	generally speaking
	直接的	zhíjiēd	direct
5	栩栩如生	xǔxǔrúshēng	pleasantly life-like; vividly
6	精彩	jīngcǎi	grandificent; colourful
	刻劃	kèhuà	lit. to carve and paint; to describe graphically
7	場面	chǎngmiàn	an occasion; stage-setting
	超越	chāoyuè	to overtake and surpass
8	材料	cáiliào	material
	架空	jiàkōng	lit. that which is propped up on nothing; fictitious; hovering in the air; unrealistic

9	真實感	zhēnshígǎn	reality; sense of reality
	名家	míngjiā	famous writers or artists
	耶穌	yēsū	Jesus
	伊索	yīsuǒ	Æsop
	蘇格拉底	sūgélādǐ	Socrates
10	馬克吐溫	mǎkètùwēn	Mark Twain
	魯迅	lǔxùn	Lu Hsun
	親切	qīnqiè	having intimate connections; being close
	感動	gǎndòng	moved; touched
12	荒誕不經	huāngdànbùjīng	grotesquely ridiculous
13	牛虻	niúmáng	gadfly
14	範例	fànlì	model examples
	志士	zhìshì	a determined man; a strong-willed person

page 53

1	險阻道路	xiǎnzǔdàolù	a difficult and treacherous path
	陽關大道	yángguāndàdào	shiny and bright road
2	事跡	shìjì	facts of a historical case
	水平	shuǐpíng	level
	對象	duìxiàng	objects
3	病況	bìngkuàng	conditions of disease
	劑量	jìliàng	a dose; an amount of medicine
	轉化	zhuǎnhuà	to invert; to mutate; to turn into
4	根本	gēnběn	fundamental; basic
	規律	guīlù	regulation; law (of nature)
	認爲	rènwéi	to deem; to believe
5	自然	zìrán	naturally; nature

	荒唐	huāngtáng	ridiculous
	透頂	tòudǐng	to the extreme; extremely; highly
	否認	fǒurèn	to deny
	瘋子	fēngz	maniac; madman
	揪住	qiūzhù	to hold fast by the hand; to seize fast
	提	tí	to lift up; to uplift
6	大體	dàtǐ	as a whole; a general principle; in the main
	定體	dìngtǐ	a fixed principle
	具備	jùbèi	furnished with
7	知識	zhīshí	knowledge; learning
	淵博	yuānbó	profound
	園地	yuándì	garden
	縱橫馳騁	zònghéngchíchěng	to ride freely, as on a horse
8	劃地爲牢	huàdìwéiláo	lit. to draw a circle and be imprisoned in it; to be restricted by artificial means
9	該不致於	gāibúzhìyú	should not go so far as to ....
	誤認	wùrèn	to be misunderstood
	宣傳	xuānchuán	to propagate
	當飯吃	dàngfànchī	to take it as food; to regard it as absolutely necessary
	培植	péizhí	to cultivate
10	譬喻	pìyù	simile; parable
	尙且	shàngqiě	still; for all that

人和鬼　　Humans and Ghosts

吳晗　Wu Han (1909–) Historian; born of a poor family in Yiwu, Chekiang. After graduating from Tsinghua University in 1934, he taught Chinese history at the Southwest Associated University in Kunming and the Tsinghua University in Peking. He joined the China Democratic League in 1944 and became vice-chairman in 1958. He was the head of the Department of History of the Tsinghua University and deputy mayor of Peking when he became a target of the Cultural Revolution of 1966.

He is the author of many historical essays, the best known being *Mirror of History* and *The Biography of Chu Yuan-chang* (朱元璋傳). His series of articles and his historical play about Hai Jui, the upright official, incurred the regime's criticism and caused his downfall. His crime was "using the past to satirise the present".

Published in connection with Hai Jui are: *Hai Jui Scolds the Emperor* (海瑞罵皇帝 ; June 1959, *People's Daily*), *On Hai Jui* (論海瑞 ; September 1959, *People's Daily*), *Tales of Hai Jui* (海瑞的故事 ; November 1959, *Pocket Book of Chinese History*), *Hai Jui* (海瑞 ; October 1960, *New Construction*), *Hai Jui Dismissed from Office* (海瑞罷官 ; January 1961, *Peking Literature and Art*).

page 54

1	鬼	*guǐ*	ghost; evil spirits; demons
	講	*jiǎng*	to be interested in; to believe in
	迷信	*míxìn*	superstition; superstitious
	相信	*xiāngxìn*	to believe in; to believe
2	據說	*jùshuō*	it is said that
	難看的	*nánkànd*	unpleasant to look at; ugly
3	總之	*zǒngzhī*	in a word
9	形形色色	*xíngxíng-sèsè*	various and sundry; all forms
	脾氣	*píqì*	temperament; disposition
	實在	*shízài*	indeed; really; truly
10	諷刺	*fěngcì*	to satirise; to ridicule

	教育	jiàoyù	to educate; education; to bring up
	其實	qíshí	in fact; actually
	大體上說來	dàtǐshàng-shuōlái	on the whole; generally speaking

page 55

1	投生	tóushēng	to be reborn into another state of existence
	屈死	qūsǐ	to have died through injustice
	替身	tìshēn	a scapegoat; a substitute
2	以此	yǐcǐ	because of this
	倒過來	dàoguòlái	on the other hand
	到底	dàodǐ	after all
3	關係	guānxì	relationship; connection
	經驗	jīngyàn	experience; to experience
	大概	dàgài	probably; for the most part
	借鑒	jièjiàn	to take (it) as a warning or an example
5	科學	kēxué	science; scientific
	知識	zhīshí	knowledge
	唯物主義	wéiwù-zhǔyì	materialism
	不再	búzài	no longer
6	研究	yánjiū	to study; to make a research
	若干	ruògān	several; a certain number of
	了解	liǎojiě	to understand; to perceive
	社會相	shèhuìxiàng	social aspects
	畢竟	bìjìng	after all; finally
8	何況	hékuàng	besides; moreover
	存在	cúnzài	to exist; existence
	確實	quèshí	really; actually

	成天	chéngtiān	all day long; from early till late
	張牙舞爪	zhāngyáwǔzhǎo	with wild threatening gestures
	青面獠牙	qīngmiànliáoyá	with a green face and long projecting teeth
	嚇唬	xiàhǔ	to scare; to frighten
	鬼頭鬼腦	guǐtóuguǐnǎo	sneaky; shifty; clandestine; secretive
	擺弄	bǎinòng	to ill use (a person); to make fun of
	心思	xīnsī	thoughts
	主意	zhǔyì	ideas; opinions; views; decisions
	行當	hángdàng	acts; business
	伙伴	huǒbàn	companions
	一小撮	yīxiǎocuō	a handful of
10	興風作浪	xīngfēngzuòlàng	to cause disturbances
	造謠生事	zàoyáoshēngshì	to fabricate rumours and cause trouble
	搬弄是非	bōnòngshìfēi	to carry tales, same as 搬 (bān) 弄是非
	造成	zàochéng	to create; to make; to finish
	緊張局勢	jǐnzhāngjúshì	tense situation; state of tension
	擺架子	bǎijiàz	to put on airs
	威風	wēifēng	pomposity; dignity; majesty
	愈……愈	yù	the more . . . the more
11	狠	hěn	fierce; cruel; relentless
	非……不可	fēi . . . bùkě	would not feel satisfied until; would not do or stop until; must
12	對付	duìfù	to deal with
	辦法	bànfǎ	ways; methods; measures
	揭穿	jiēchuān	to unmask; to expose; to disclose
	揪	qiū	to drag; to grasp with the hand

13	戳穿	chuōchuān	to lay bare; to uncover; to poke a hole in
	把戲	bǎxì	juggling; tricks
	伎倆	jìliǎng	tricks; cheating device
	認識	rènshí	to recognise; to know
	親眷	qīnjuàn	relatives; dependants; family members
14	孤立	gūlì	to isolate; to be isolated; isolation
	搞	gǎo	to do; to make; to deal with; to play
	玩意	wányì	game; toy
	倒不妨	dàobùfáng	it would be better to; might as well; it does not do more harm to
	隨便	suíbiàn	as (one) pleases; as (you) like it; at will
15	首先	shǒuxiān	first of all; firstly
	道理	dàolǐ	reason; secret; essence of the matter
	有意思	yǒuyìsī	interesting; meaningful; intentional

page 56

1	狂生	kuángshēng	profligate; arrogant person
	荒廢的	huāngfèid	dilapidated; decayed; neglected
	宅子	zháizi	mansion; residence; private dwelling
	鬧鬼	nàoguǐ	to have devils about
2	堂門	tángmén	door of a hall
	鋪蓋	pūgài	beddings
	用功	yònggōng	to work hard; to study diligently
3	披髮	pīfǎ	dishevelled hair; with long hair hanging down; to let their down
	漆	qī	lacquer; paint; varnish
	對	duì	to face
	順手	shùnshǒu	while convenient; in passing

4	硯台	yàntái	ink slab
	墨汁	mòzhī	Chinese black ink
	塗	tú	to smear; to daub; to cross out
	瞪眼	dèngyǎn	staring in anger; gazing at fixedly
	不對頭	búduìtóu	uncongenial; ill-mated; disadvantageous
	羞慚	xiūcán	shame; ashamed
	溜	liū	to sneak away
6	門縫	ménfèng	opening or slit of a door
	吐舌	tùshé	to put out the tongue
7	模樣	móyàng	appearance; look
	亂	luàn	in disorder; disorderly; dishevelled
8	摘下來	zhāixiàlái	to take off
	一下	yīxià	in a moment; at once
9	剛一	gāngyī	as soon as; no sooner than
	露頭	lùtóu	to show the head; to appear; conduct of a secret peeper
	嚷	rǎng	to shout; to bawl out; to yell
	討厭	tǎoyàn	tiresome; annoying; irritating; to dislike
10	只好	zhǐhǎo	can only; cannot but; the only thing would be
11	族祖	zúzǔ	ancestors
	膽大	dǎndà	daring; fearless; courageous
	陰風慘慘	yīnfēngcǎncǎn	awe-inspiring wind from Hades
13	客氣地	kèqid	politely
	不一定	bùyīdìng	not necessarily; do not have to
	趕走	gǎnzǒu	to drive (one) away
14	豈有此理	qǐyǒu-cǐlǐ	This is unheard of! Never heard! How can there be such a thing! Ridiculous!

	再三	zàisān	repeatedly; again and again
	央告	yānggào	to implore; to beseech; to entreat
15	不理	bùlǐ	to disregard; to neglect
	嘆氣	tànqì	to sigh
	這號	zhèhào	of this size; of the kind; to such an extent
	頑固	wángù	stubborn; obstinate; conservative
	蠢才	chǔncái	a stupid person; idiot

page 57

1	和尚	héshàng	monk
	廟	miào	temple
2	正說好	zhèngshuōhǎo	I was just saying to myself, same as 正說呢 or 正說着
	蠟燭	làzhú	candle
3	朗誦	lǎngsòng	to recite; to read aloud
	念不了	niànbùliǎo	to have not yet read
	扣壁	kòubì	to knock at the wall
4	厠所	cèsuǒ	toilet
5	檢起	jiǎnqǐ	to pick up
	燈台	dēngtái	lamp stand
	正好	zhènghǎo	just in time; just enough
	仰頭	yǎngtóu	to look up; to raise the head
6	偏要	piānyào	bent on having or doing
	趕	gǎn	to follow; to catch up with; to pursue
7	萬不可以	wànbùkěyǐ	by no means should; should not in any way
	對不起	duìbùqǐ	to do injustice to; to be unfair; to mistreat
	隨手	suíshǒu	while convenient; freely; without a second thought; in passing

	用過的	*yòngguòd*	used
	手紙	*shǒuzhǐ*	toilet paper; toilet tissue
	抹	*mò*	to wipe; to rub over; to smear
	嘔吐	*oǔtù*	to vomit; to throw up
8	狂吼	*kuánghǒu*	to make an uproar; to roar
	從此	*cóngcǐ*	from then on; from now on
9	蔑視	*mièshì*	to despise; to look down upon
	鄙視	*bǐshì*	to disdain; to belittle; to scorn
	仇視	*chóushì*	to hate; to look with hatred
	合理	*hélǐ*	reasonable; justifiable
	盛	*shèng*	abundant; flourishing; full; strong
10	衰	*shuāi*	weak; feeble; failing; impotent
12	尊重	*zūnzhòng*	to respect; to esteem
13	以爲	*yǐwéi*	to think; to believe; as one sees it

海瑞罵皇帝　Hai Jui Scolds the Emperor

page 58

1. 封建時代　*fēngjiànshídài*　age of feudalism
   不可侵犯　*bùkěqīnfàn*　inviolable
   連　*lián*　even
   避諱　*bìhuì*　to avoid the use of certain words which have similar sound or meaning to others' natural defects so as not to offend them
   御諱　*yùhuì*　Imperial taboos of the same
   就得　*jiùdé*　would have to
   缺筆　*quēbǐ*　a Chinese character short of a stroke
   鬧殘廢　*nàocánfèi*　to suffer from deformity or being a cripple
   胳膊　*gēbò*　the arms
   成爲　*chéngwéi*　to have become
   不全的　*bùquánd*　incomplete; unfinished; imperfect

3. 正字　*zhèngzì*　a perfect character, with no strokes missing; a right word
   就算　*jiùsuàn*　might even be regarded as; might be counted as
   犯法　*fànfǎ*　to commit a crime; to violate the law
   吃官司　*chīguānsī*　to suffer legal punishment; to suffer imprisonment; to be sued
   判　*pàn*　to pass sentence; to pronounce a verdict
   徒刑　*túxíng*　term of imprisonment

4. 痛快　*tòngkuài*　to heart's content; satisfactorily; with great pleasur
   厲害　*lìhài*　severe

5. 賦役　*fùyì*　taxes and levies of service
   平常　*píngcháng*　as usual; at normal times
   化　*huà*　to spend; to squander
   用在　*yòngzài*　to spend on

	宗教	zōngjiào	religion; religious
	迷信	míxìn	superstition
6	弄得	nòngde	to have caused or made
	老百姓	lǎobǎixìng	the people
	光光的	guāngguāngd	extremely; without anything left
	極點	jídiǎn	to the extreme end; terminal point
	天下	tiānxià	under the heaven; all over; in the world
	改元	gǎiyuán	to change the year-title of a reigning monarch
7	年號	niánhào	the style of an emperor's region; government designation of a Chinese Emperor
	取	qǔ	to adopt; to take
	皆淨	jiējìng	all clean
	乾乾淨淨	gāngānjìngjìng	all gone; with absolutely nothing left; clean; pure
8	大胆	dàdǎn	brave(ly)
	直接	zhíjiē	direct(ly)
	不僅...就是	bùjǐn...jiùshì	not only...but also
	朝代	cháodài	dynasty; generation
9	句句	jùjù	each and every sentence
	刺痛	cìtòng	to hurt deeply
	要害	yàohài	tender point
	氣惱	qìnǎo	angry as well as annoyed
	十分	shífēn	greatly; hundred percent
	冒火	màohuǒ	indignant; cross; to take offence; to become furious
10	原來	yuánlái	as a matter of fact; actually
	管事	guǎnshì	to manage (state) affairs
	上朝	shàngcháo	to discharge regular Imperial duties

	西苑	xīyuàn	a garden on the western side in the Imperial Palace
	成天	chéngtiān	all day long; from morning till night
	齋醮	zhāijiào	Buddhist and Taoist sacrifices — fasting and prayers to avert calamity
11	儀式	yíshì	ceremonies
	上	shàng	to send up; to present to superiors; to go to; to present in writing, etc.
	講究	jiǎngjiū	refined; particular about; to be choosy
	宰相	zǎixiàng	prime minister
12	得寵	déchǒng	to get favour; to be in favour
	政治	zhèngzhì	politics
	腐敗	fǔbài	corrupt; rotten
	朝臣	cháochén	ministers of state
	提意見	tíyìjiàn	to express opinions; to criticise
	不是...便是	búshì...biànshì	either ... or
	殺頭	shātóu	to behead
	革職	gézhí	to depose; to remove (one) from office
	監禁	jiānjìn	to imprison; to jail
	充軍	chōngjūn	to transport for a term of years; to be banished
13	便是	biànshì	precisely
	針對	zhēnduì	directly towards; to be directed towards

page 59

1	當時	dāngshí	prevailing; existing; then
	提出	tíchū	to put forward; to request
	質問	zhíwèn	to question; a questionnaire
	要求	yāoqiú	to demand; a demand
	改革	gǎigé	reforms; to reform

2	倒	dào	however
	還	hái	nevertheless; still
	講	jiǎng	to believe in; to be interested in; to seek
	修道	xiūdào	to cultivate Tao — to strive for virtue, to seek by culture and asceticism, etc., so as to become an immortal
	大興	dàxīng	to revive greatly; to greatly promote
	土木	tǔmù	building operations
3	濫派	lànpài	to give out or distribute at random; to appoint at random
	以為	yǐwéi	to think; to believe
	薄於	bóyú	to slight; to disregard; to treat badly
	猜疑	cāiyí	suspicion
4	誹謗	fěibàng	slander; to slander; to libel
	殺戮	shālù	to kill; to massacre
	臣下	chénxià	officials of the rank of minister and below
	盡	jìn	entirely; wholly; altogether; to exhaust
5	吏	lì	officer; civil servant
	貪	tān	greedy; covetous
	暴動	bàodòng	riots; uprising; unrest
	即位	jíwèi	to ascend the throne; to succeed
	嚴重	yánzhòng	serious
6	罷相	bàxiàng	to be dismissed as a prime minister; to resign as a prime minister
	清明	qīngmíng	bright and promising
	遠不如	yuǎnbùrú	far more unworthy than
7	自比	zìbǐ	to compare oneself with; to style oneself as
	號	hào	a name or style

10	一意	yīyì	with one mind; bent on
	長生不老	chángshēngbùlǎo	immortality
	迷惑	míhuò	confused
	過於	guòyú	excessively; overly; far too
	苛斷	kēduàn	harsh and despotic
	性情	xìngqíng	temperament; character
	偏	piān	to follow wrong courses; partial; prejudiced; to insist on; to persist
	自以爲是	zìyǐwéishì	to insist on one's own way; obstinate; to believe oneself to be in the right
11	拒絕	jùjué	to refuse; to reject
	批評	pīpíng	criticisms; to criticise
	一心	yīxīn	to devote solely to; to think entirely of
	成仙	chéngxiān	to become immortal
	得道	dédào	to attain Tao (the Way)
13	上天	shàngtiān	Heaven above; God
	賜	cì	to bestow; to grant
	仙桃	xiāntáo	the flat peach; the heavenly peach
	藥丸	yàowán	pills; tablets
	那就更	nàjiùgèng	that is even more
	怪	guài	ridiculous; strange
15	立即	lìjí	right now; at once
	醒悟過來	xǐngwùguòlái	to begin to realise the error of one's ways
	研究	yánjiū	to study closely
	國計民生	guójìmínshēng	national economy and people's livelihood
16	痛改	tònggǎi	to correct (one's mistakes) drastically
	謀	móu	to plan; to strive for; to seek; to do

		福利	fúlì	welfare; social care

page 60

1	目前的	mùqiánd	existing; prevailing
3	奏本	zòuběn	a memorial to the throne
	丟	diū	to throw away; to lose
	左右	zuǒyòu	attendants (on the right and left)
	逮捕	dàibǔ	to arrest; to nab
	宦官	huànguān	eunuch
4	聽說	tīngshuō	I heard people say; it is said
	活不了	huóbùliǎo	would not live for long
	臨死告別	línsǐgàobié	to say goodbye at the point of death
	托人	tuōrén	to entrust to somebody
	準備	zhǔnbèi	to prepare for
	後事	hòushì	affairs after death; funeral
	佣人	yòngrén	servants
5	光	guāng	all; totally
	素性	sùxìng	one's usual disposition; character; nature
	剛直	gāngzhí	upright; unyielding; firm in principle; frank
	名聲	míngshēng	reputation; fame
	居官	jūguān	in office; while holding a government post
	清廉	qīnglián	honest; incorruptible
	取	qǔ	to take; to get
6	一聽	yītīng	on hearing
	愣住了	lèngzhùle	to be stunned
	一面	yīmiàn	while
7	下不了	xiàbùliǎo	unable to make (a decision)

	決心	juéxīn	decision; firm will
	發脾氣	fāpíqì	to fly into a temper
	發怒	fānù	to get angry
	宮婢	gōngbèi	a maid-servant in imperial palace
8	私下	sīxià	secretly; in private
	挨罵	āimà	to get a scolding
	出氣	chūqì	to give vent to; to vent one's spleen on
	派	pài	to send; to despatch
	查訪	cháfǎng	to investigate on the spot
9	商量	shāngliáng	to consult; to discuss
	出主意	chūzhǔyì	to suggest; to give ideas
	連累	liánlèi	to implicate; to be involved in trouble
	不以為意	bùyǐwéiyì	do not mind; do not take offence
10	坐牢	zuòláo	to be imprisoned
11	比干	bǐgān	uncle of Shang Chou, last ruler of the Shang Dynasty, B.C. 1122
	不過	búguò	however
	紂王	zhòuwáng	Shang Chou, the notorious ruler who caused downfall of the Shang Dynasty
	畜物	chùwù	beast; brute, term of abuse
12	口頭上	kǒutóushàng	verbally
	批處	pīchǔ	to officially comment on and deal with a case in writing
	案件	ànjiàn	a case at court
	文件	wénjiàn	documents; dossier
	氣	qì	anger; spleen
13	傳位	chuánwèi	to transmit the throne

14	愛惜	àixī	to love and pity; to care for; to take care of
	鬧病	nàobìng	to fall ill
	場	cháng	measure word for illness
	要是	yàoshì	if
15	下令	xiàlìng	to give order
	下獄	xiàyù	to throw into prison
	追查	zhuīchá	to investigate and look for
	主使	zhǔshǐ	to instigate; the chief instigator
	刑部	xíngbù	the former Board of Punishments
	論處	lùnchǔ	to pass judgement on a court case; to sentence; to pass sentence
	死刑	sǐxíng	death sentence
	批復	pīfù	to give an official reply in writing
16	戶部	hùbù	the former Board of Revenue and Population
	主事	zhǔshì	to be in charge; the head of (a board)

page 61

1	同情	tóngqíng	to have sympathy for; sympathy
	支持	zhīchí	to support; to stand up for
	越來越	yuèláiyuè	same as 愈來愈, more and more
	萬曆	wànlì	the title of reign of Emperor 神宗 (A.D. 1573) in the Ming Dynasty
2	公元	gōngyuán	Anno Domini
	誣告	wūgào	to accuse falsely
	進士	jìnshì	third degree graduate under the old system, reckoned as equivalent to Ph. D.
	辯誣	biànwū	to defend a case of false accusation
3	申救	shēnjiù	to redress a grievance and deliver; to rescue by petitioning

	認爲	rènwéi	to regard as; to believe
	當代的	dāngdàid	contemporary
4	瞻仰	zhānyǎng	to look up to someone with reverence; to regard with respect
	趕得上	gǎndéshàng	able to reach; able to catch up with
	評價	píngjià	appraisal; estimation; valuation
5	愛戴	àidài	to love with special respect
	歌頌	gēsòng	to sing praises
6	反對	fǎnduì	to be opposed to; to be against
	貪污	tānwū	corruption
	奢侈	shēchǐ	luxury
	浪費	làngfèi	waste
	主張	zhǔzhāng	to advocate; to stand for
	節儉	jiéjiǎn	frugality
	打擊	dǎjī	to check; to attack; to hurt
	豪強	háoqiáng	those who are overbearing
	主持	zhǔchí	to direct; to sponsor
	貫徹	guànchè	to carry out completely
7	一條鞭法	yītiáobiānfǎ	levies of service and native products in the form of silver dollars according to the acres of land one possesses
	裁革常例	cáigéchánglì	to cut and abolish usual procedures
	興修水利	xīngxiūshuǐlì	to construct water conservation projects
	作爲	zuòwéi	doings; activities; workings
8	商戶	shānghù	commercial households
	裁減	cáijiǎn	to cut and reduce
	派差派捐	pàichāipàijuān	the alloted services and contributions
	禁止	jìnzhǐ	to forbid; to prohibit

	無償	wúcháng	without making restitution; without consideration
	供應	gōngyìng	to supply; to provide
	措施	cuòshī	measures
	減輕	jiǎnqīng	to ease; to lessen
9	工商業者	gōngshāngyèzhě	industrialists and commercialists
	負担	fùdān	burden
	此外	cǐwài	moreover; besides
	注意	zhùyì	to pay attention to
	刑獄	xíngyù	punishment for criminals
10	着重	zhāozhòng	to stress; to lay emphasis on
	調查研究	diàochá yánjiū	to investigate and study
	知縣	zhīxiàn	a district magistrate
	巡撫	xúnfǔ	former title of the governor of a province
	任上	rènshàng	while in office; while on duty
	親自	qīnzì	in person; personally
	審案	shěnàn	to try a case in court
	處理	chǔlǐ	to treat; to deal with (a case)
	積案	jīàn	delayed cases; unsolved criminal cases
11	判清	pànqīng	to judge correctly; to treat justly
	冤獄	yuānyù	those unjustly imprisoned
	都堂	dūtáng	former title of a Censor of the Court of Censors
	壓抑	yàyì	to suppress
	欺侮	qīwǔ	to take advantage of; to treat badly
	冤屈	yuānqū	a grievance; a wrong; a false charge
	救星	jiùxīng	saviour
12	廣大	guǎngdà	broad; wide; large

	稱譽	chēngyù	to commend
	贊揚	zànyáng	to praise
	被畫像禮拜	bèihuàxiànglǐbài	to be portrayed and worshipped
	被謳歌傳頌	bèiōugēchuánsòng	to be sung and acclaimed
	罷市	bàshì	to shut up shops in protest against authorities
	喪船	sāngchuán	funeral ship
13	送葬	sòngzàng	to take part in a funeral procession
	奠祭拜哭的	diànjìbàikūd	to offer sacrifices with condolences
	百里不絕	bǎilǐbùjué	do not see the end (of a procession) even for a hundred miles
	事迹	shìjì	deeds
	主要	zhǔyào	chiefly; in the main
	方面	fāngmiàn	field (in the field of)
14	流傳	liúchuán	to circulate
15	正直的	zhēngzhíd	upright

page 62

1	堅決	jiānjué	resolutely
	反動	fǎndòng	reactionary
	勢力	shìlì	forces
	鬥爭	dòuzhēng	to struggle (with)
	百折不撓	bǎizhébùnáo	unyieldingly
	值得	zhídé	worthy of
	明辨是非	míngbiànshìfēi	to clearly distinguish right from wrong
2	到底	dàodǐ	to the finish; to the end
	精神	jīngshén	spirit

3	觀點	*guāndiǎn*	viewpoint
	立場	*lìchǎng*	(political) stand
	鮮明	*xiānmíng*	bright
	戰鬥精神	*zhàndòujīngshén*	fighting spirit
4	旺盛	*wàngshèng*	vigorous
	效法	*xiàofǎ*	to imitate; to follow the example; to follow suit

說大話的故事　　**Stories about Bragging**

鄧拓　Teng To (1910?–　　) Historian and essayist. Born in Shantung. During the Sino-Japanese War, he worked for the *Hsinhua Daily* in Chungking and later became president of the *Shansi-Chahar-Hopei Daily*.

In 1950 he became vice-president of the *People's Daily* (1950-57), served as editor from 1953-59 and as president from 1957-59. From 1959-66 he was a member of the Peking Municipal Party Committee Secretariat and editor of the fortnightly *Frontline* (前綫). At the same time, he was a member of the Department of Philosophy and Social Sciences, Chinese Academy of Sciences (1955-66) and an alternate member of the CCP North China Bureau (1965-66).

Under his pen-name Ma Nan-tsun, he published 152 essays within eighteen months -- from 1961 to September 1962 -- in the *Peking Daily*. These essays were later collected in the well-known book *Evening Chats at Yenshan* (燕山夜話). Since the beginnings of the Cultural Revolution in 1966, he has been pilloried for his "anti-Party and anti-socialist double talk".

page 63

	說大話	shuōdàhuà	to boast; to lie; to brag
1	三國演義	sānguóyǎnyì	a popular version of the Romance of the Three Kingdoms
	諸葛亮	zhūgěliàng	the master mind
	揮淚	huīlèi	to shed tears; to wipe away tears
	斬	zhǎn	to behead
	提到	tídào	to mention; to talk about; to speak of
	劉備	liúbèi	the emperor of the Minor Han Dynasty, one of the Three Kingdoms
	生前	shēngqián	while living; before one's death
2	言過其實	yánguòqíshí	to exaggerate; exaggerations
	不可大用	bùkědàyòng	should not be employed for important tasks
	根據	gēnjù	basis
	誌	zhì	annals

3	先主	*xiānzhǔ*	the late master
	謂...曰	*wèi...yuē*	said to; spoke to (one) saying
	看來	*kànlái*	it seems
4	了解	*liǎojiě*	to understand; understanding
	實在	*shízài*	indeed; actually
	深刻的	*shēnkèd*	deep; profound
5	管子	*guǎnz*	管仲 Kuan Chung (died 645 B.C.), a statesman of Ch'i
	告誡	*gàojiè*	to warn; to enjoin
6	千萬不要	*qiānwànbúyào*	should in no way; by no means should
	吹牛	*chuīniú*	to boast; to brag
	採取	*cǎiqǔ*	to adopt; to take
	慎重	*shènzòng*	discreet; careful
	態度	*tàidù*	attitude
7	名聲	*míngshēng*	fame; reputation
8	歷來	*lìlái*	historically; for successive generations
	名流	*míngliú*	notables; very famous persons
	學者	*xuézhě*	scholars; learned men
	常常	*chángcháng*	very often; usually
	引用	*yǐnyòng*	to quote
	座右銘	*zuòyòumíng*	to make a note of instructions or cautions on the sides of one's seat, as a reminder; a motto
	然而	*rán,'ér*	however
9	理會	*lǐhuì*	to rceive; to understand
	道理	*dàolǐ*	principle; reason
	據	*jù*	in accordance with
	意見	*yìjiàn*	opinion

	忽視	hūshì	to disregard; to neglect
	書生	shūshēng	students; scholars
	文人	wénrén	literary men; intellectuals
10	儒者	rúzhě	scholars of the Confucian school
	溢美過實	yìměiguòshí	undue praise; to overstate the merit of; praise that rings more than what is due
	顯然	xiǎnrán	apparently; obviously; to all appearances
	認為	rènwéi	to think; to believe; to deem
11	流	liú	... and his ilk; and his like; kind
	往往	wǎngwǎng	very often; usually
	其實	qíshí	in fact; in reality; in actual fact
	各色人	gèsèrén	all and sundry; all kinds of men
	而已	éryǐ	merely; only; that is all
13	筆記	bǐjì	notes taken; to take a note
	小說	xiǎoshuō	a novel

page 64

1	有意思	yǒuyìsī	interesting; meaningful
	居	jū	to live; to dwell
	禮	lǐ	politeness; courtesy; to honour (one) as
	上客	shàngkè	guest of honour
2	既而	jì'ér	since; then
	賢者	xiánzhě	a man of virtues
	無如	wúrú	none other than; none as
3	德	dé	virtue; goodness
	食客	shíkè	hangers on; retainers
	衣廩	yīlǐn	clothes and stipend

	倦色	juànsè	colour of fatigue; sign of fatigue
4	欺	qī	to deceive; to cheat; to mislead
	予	yú	me; I
	豈獨	qǐdú	How can there be only . . . ?
	不覺	bùjué	unconsciously; unknowingly
	斂容	liǎnróng	to wear a serious expression
5	翌日	yìrì	the following day
	敢造門下	gǎnzàoménxià	May I venture to come under your roof?; May I venture to visit you?
	求觀	qiúguān	to beg to see
	明旦	míngdàn	the following morning; at dawn the next day
6	寂然	jírán	all quiet
	升其堂	shēngqítáng	to enter his inner hall
	疑	yí	to doubt; to suspect
	意	yì	to think; to discern
	良久	liángjiǔ	for quite a while; for a good while
7	詰	jié	to question; to ask
	安在	ānzài	Where are . . . ?
	悵然	chàngrán	disappointedly; annoyedly
	暮	mù	late
	胡盧	húlú	to laugh with a hand on the mouth
	退	tuì	to retire; to go; to leave
9	大概	dàgài	probably; for the most part; generally speaking
	杜撰的	dùzhuànd	trumped up; fabricated
	作者	zuòzhě	author
	假托	jiǎtuō	to simulate
	附會	fùhuì	to gloss; to force an interpretation

10	後人	hòurén	successors; heirs; posterity
	諷刺	fěngcì	to ridicule; to satirise
	嫉妒	jídù	to envy; to be jealous of
11	養	yǎng	to feed and clothe
	胡亂	húluàn	at random; in great confusion; foolishly
	經不住	jīngbúzhù	unable to stand; unable to withstand
	實地觀察	shídìguānchá	field observation; field survey
	漏底	lòudǐ	to leak from the bottom hole; to reveal
12	目的	mùdì	purpose; aim
	教育	jiàoyù	to educate
	承認	chéngrèn	to admit
	善意	shànyì	good will
13	考證	kǎozhèng	to prove; to verify
	斤斤計較	jīnjīnjìjiào	to count one catty by one catty; to think about narrow personal gains and losses; minute squaring of accounts
14	類似	lèisì	similar; similarity
	例如	lìrú	for instance
	方士	fāngshì	a necromancer; a Taoist
	自稱	zìchēng	to assert; to allege; to call oneself
15	以致	yǐzhì	so as to
	沉醉	chénzuì	intoxicated; infatuated; very drunk
16	猶未	yóuwèi	still not yet
	甲子	jiǎzǐ	first of each group 天干 and 地支, which combine to form a cycle of sixty, used primarily for chronological purposes; time of the year
	恰好當時	qiàhǎodāngshí	just then
	墮馬	duòmǎ	to fall off a horse

	胁	xié	the ribs; the flank

page 65

1	血竭	xuèjié	dragon's blood, a red gum from a species of palm, used as an astringent, etc.
	敷之	fūzhī	to dress it; to apply to it
	乃瘥	nǎichài	would then be convalescent
	不啻	bùchì	not less than
2	执	zhí	to hold; to hold in custody
3	老姥	lǎolǎo	an old lady
	過度	guòdù	excessive
4	叱	chì	to scold; to abuse; to reprimand
	赦	shè	to remit; to pardon; to forgive
5	饒命	ráomìng	to spare life
	一派胡言	yīpàihúyán	all nonsense
	倒打一耙	dàodǎyībà	to hit back for once
6	誣	wū	to accuse falsely
	用心	yòngxīn	intention
	反映	fǎnyìng	to reflect
	情況	qíngkuàng	situation
7	秉性難移	bǐngxìngnányí	it is difficult to change one's natural disposition
	死不覺悟	sǐbùjuéwù	to refuse to be enlightened or sensible even at the cost of one's life
8	編造	biānzào	to trump up; to fabricate; to make up
	富有	fùyǒu	full of; rich in
	概括性	gàikuòxìng	generalisation
9	伎倆	jìliǎng	tricks
	集中	jízhōng	to concentrate; to centralise

	典型	diǎnxíng	typical
	情節	qíngjié	details
	引人注意	yǐnrénzhùyì	to call to people's attention
	提高警惕	tígāojǐngtì	to heighten vigilance
	因而	yīnér	thus; hence; therefore
10	教育	jiàoyù	education; to educate; educational
	意義	yìyì	significance; meaning

事事關心　Show Concern for All Things

page 66

	事事	shìshì	anything and everything
	關心	guānxīn	to be concerned with; to take an interest in
3	撰寫	zhuànxiě	to compose; to write; to edit
	副	fù	measure word for couplets, ear-rings, chess, cards, etc.
	對聯	duìlián	couplets
4	遺跡	yíjì	historical remains; traces; vestiges
5	認為	rènwéi	to think; to deem; to believe
6	認識	rènshí	knowledge; belief; understanding
	不合	bùhé	do not tally with; do not correspond to
	事實	shìshí	facts; reality
7	提起	tíqǐ	to mention; to speak of
	介紹	jièshào	introduction; recommendation
	必要	bìyào	need; necessity
8	上聯	shànglián	first line of a couplet
	意思	yìsī	meaning; idea
	環境	huánjìng	circumstances; surroundings
	便於	biànyú	good for; convenient for; suitable for
	專心	zhuānxīn	to employ all one's power and attention on; to devote to; to concentrate on
	生動地	shēngdòngd	vividly
	描寫	miáoxiě	to describe; to depict
	自然界	zìránjiè	the natural world; the world of nature
9	交織	jiāozhī	to be intermingled or interwoven with
	情景	qíngjǐng	state; setting; atmosphere
	令人	lìngrén	to cause; to make; to make one feel

	彷彿	fǎngfú	as if; seemingly; like
	置身	zhìshēn	to place oneself in
10	一片	yīpiàn	a wave of
	朗誦	lǎngsòng	recitation
	講學	jiǎngxué	lecturing; giving lectures; to lecture
	天籟	tiānlài	sound of nature
11	下聯	xiàlián	the second line of a couplet
	充分地	chōngfèn	fully; completely; sufficiently
	表明	biǎomíng	to express; to show
12	抱負	bàofù	aspiration; ambition
	主張	zhǔzhāng	to advocate; to uphold; to stand for

page 67

2	并提	bìngtí	to metion side by side
	可見	kějiàn	evidently; obviously; perceptibly
	指	zhǐ	to point at
	限於	xiànyú	to be confined to; to be limited to
3	貫串	guànchuàn	to thread through; to link up; to run through
	明顯	míngxiǎn	obvious; evident
	致力	zhìlì	to exert effort; to devote to; to endeavor
4	緊密	jǐnmì	closely
	結合	jiéhé	to connect; to combine
	理解	lǐjiě	to understand; to consider as
	雙關	shuāngguān	a pun; a phrase with a double meaning
	兼	jiān	simultaneously; at the same time; also
5	意義	yìyì	meaning; significance
	實在	shízài	indeed; actually; really

	相當	xiāngdāng	rather; considerably
	深長	shēncháng	profound; far-reaching
6	眼光	yǎnguāng	viewpoint; insight
	顯然	xiǎnrán	obviously; apparently
	盡管	jǐnguǎn	in spite of; despite; although 盡管 is also written as 儘管 (jǐnguǎn)
7	限制	xiànzhì	limitation; restriction
	封建	fēngjiàn	feudal
	階級	jiējí	class; social class
	立場	lìchǎng	stand; political stand
	維護	wéihù	to safeguard; to defend; to protect
	制度	zhìdù	system
8	鬥爭	dòuzhēng	to struggle; struggle
	班	bān	a group of; grade; class
	讀死書	dú sǐ shū	to read or to study without application
	追求	zhuīqiú	to seek for; to run after
	功名	gōngmíng	honour; rank; credit
	利祿	lìlù	wealth and position
	總算	zǒngsuàn	nevertheless; may be counted or taken as
	進步	jìnbù	progressive
9	代表	dàibiǎo	representative; to represent
	君子	jūnzǐ	a gentleman
	小人	xiǎorén	a mean man, the opposite of a gentleman
10	區別	qūbié	to distinguish
	正	zhèng	upright; good
	邪	xié	evil

	派	pài	factions
	忠心	zhōngxīn	faithful; loyal
	事主	shìzhǔ	to serve the master
	留心	liúxīn	to pay attention to
	民生	mínshēng	the life of people
11	隱居	yǐnjū	to live in seclusion
	講求	jiǎngqiú	particular about; to search for; to seek
	正義	zhèngyì	justice
	不配	búpèi	not good for; unworthy; unfit
	接着	jiēzhe	to follow; to succeed in
	主持	zhǔchí	to direct; to be in charge of
	講席	jiǎngxí	"chair" at a university; professorship
12	品評	pǐnpíng	to criticise; to judge
	議論	yìlùn	to discuss; to talk over; to criticise
	時政	shízhèng	popular politics
13	從根本上說	cónggēnběnshàngshuō	basically speaking
	超出	chāochū	to go beyond; to exceed; to break through
	理學	lǐxué	metaphysics
	學說	xuéshuō	theory
	範圍	fànwéi	sphere
14	創立	chuànglì	to establish; to found
15	門徒	méntú	disciples
	正宗嫡傳	zhèngzōngdíchuán	an orthodox accomplishment learned directly from a master
	弟子	dìzǐ	disciples
	重修	chóngxiū	to repair; to renovate; to restore

16	清楚地	qīngchǔd	clearly; mainfestly; beyond doubt
	宣佈	xuānbù	to declare; to proclaim
	繼承	jìchéng	to inherit; to take over
	衣鉢	yībō	the mantle; the cassock and bowl of a Buddhist priest

page 68

1	因素	yīnsù	element; factor
	恐怕	kǒngpà	perhaps
2	恢復	huīfù	to re-establish; to recover; to restore
	遺風	yífēng	customs which have been handed down
	歷史	lìshǐ	historical; history
	陳迹	chénjì	old traces; remains
3	道理	dàolǐ	principle; reason
4	片面地	piànmiànd	one-sidedly; unilaterally; arbitrarily
	強調	qiángdiào	to stress; to emphasise; to underline
5	極端	jíduān	absolutely; extremely; exceedingly
	空談	kōngtán	idle talk; to talk idly; to discuss aimlessly
	空頭的	kōngtóud	hollow-headed or arm-chair (politician)
6	不可思議	bùkěsīyì	unimaginable; inconceivable
	不問政治	búwènzhèngzhì	to be indifferent to or to take no interest in politics
7	書呆子	shūdāiz	book-worm
	有學問的	yǒuxuéwènd	learned; knowledgeable
	學者	xuézhě	scholar
8	就	jiù	merely; only
	所謂	suǒwèi	so-called
9	實際上	shíjìshàng	in reality; actually

	包含	bāohán	to contain; to imply
10	既……又	jì...yòu	both ... and ...
	愈來愈	yùláiyù	more and more
	尚且	shàngqiě	even; however
11	宣揚	xuānyáng	to advertise; to publicise
	難道	nándào	Can it be possible that..? Is it conceivable that..?
	無論如何	wúlùnrúhé	anyway
12	深刻	shēnkè	deeply; profoundly
	透徹	tòuchè	thoroughly

亂彈雜記　Report What Comes Handy

廖沫沙　Liao Mo-sha (1910?– 　　　) Essayist. Liao first became known in 1934 when he ridiculed Lu Hsun's essays as "decorative literature" in *Ta Wan Pao* (大晚報). During the Sino-Japanese War, he began writing essays as well as short stories.

In 1949, he was a member of the preparatory committee of the All-China Journalists' Association. In 1957, he became the chairman of the Department of Educational Work of the Peking Municipal Party Committee. He took office in the Department of United Front Work of the Peking Municipal Party Committee as director in 1961, and became a vice-chairman of the Peking branch of the CPPCC (Chinese People's Political Consultative Conference) in 1962.

He was one of the three authors of the much-disputed *Notes from a Three-Family Village* (三家村札記) which was published in 1962 in the *Frontline* (前綫) and branded as "anti-Party gusts of ill wind" during the Cultural Revolution. His historical work *Excursion in Hsienyang*, written in 1943, was also criticised for "slandering the liberated areas under the Chinese Communist Party".

page 69

1	破題	pòtí	presentation; lit. to open up a theme; to untangle a puzzling title
2	亂彈	luàntán	to play (an instrument) in a disorderly and capricious manner
	就是	jiùshì	namely; that is; merely
	東拉西扯	dōnglāxīchě	going about aimlessly; disconnected; to talk at random
	南腔北調	nánqiāngběidiào	tunes from the south and the north; a mixture of various dialects
	沒有譜	méiyǒupǔ	not according to the music book – disorderly
3	雜記	zájì	notes and comments on various matters
	不成文章	bùchéngwénzhāng	essay written in an unorganised manner
4	八股文	bāgǔwén	the eight-legged essay of the old examination system; Chinese classical style of writing

	入門	rùmén	an introduction; a shortcut; the ABC's; guidelines
6	茫茫然	mángmángrán	utterly ignorant of; uncertain; unsure
7	出生得晚	chūshēngdéwǎn	to be born too late
	時代	shídài	age; period; epoch
	這門專業	zhèménzhuānyè	this branch of specialised profession
	去古不遠	qùgǔbùyuǎn	not far away from the past
8	皮毛	pímáo	skin and hair – superficial
	承題	chéngtí	amplification
9	起講	qǐjiǎng	preliminary exposition
	提比	tíbǐ	initial argument
	虛比	xūbǐ	inceptive paragraphs
	中比	zhōngbǐ	middle paragraphs
	後比	hòubǐ	rear paragraphs
	大結	dàjié	concluding paragraphs
	內容	nèiróng	content
10	規定	guīdìng	regulations
	不可破格	bùkěpògé	not allowed to break the rule
	格式	géshì	style; pattern
	公式	gōngshì	general formula

page 70

1	按股入格	àngǔrùgé	to fit pattern to the rule
	套進公式	tàojìngōngshì	to fit the formula
	名登金榜	míngdēngjīnbǎng	to have one's name on the golden placard – to pass an examination
2	身入仕途	shēnrùshìtú	to be an official
	幹部	gànbù	cadre

– 70 –

3	填	tián	to fill in
4	登記表	dēngjìbiǎo	registration form
	統計表	tǒngjìbiǎo	statistical chart
	分明	fēnmíng	obviously
5	無理可講	wúlǐkějiǎng	having nothing to say
6	爲聖賢立言	wèishèngxiánlìyán	to propagate the teachings of sages
	四書五經	sìshūwǔjīng	the Four Books and Five Classics
	不知所云	bùshīsuǒyún	not knowing what one is talking about
	言之無物	yánzhīwúwù	talk without substance; empty talk
7	廢話	fèihuà	nonsense
8	科擧	kējǔ	the old examination system
	解釋	jiěshì	to explain
9	考選	kǎoxuǎn	to select through examinations
	升官發財	shēngguānfācái	official promotion and prosperity
	敲門磚	qiāoménzhuān	a brick that is used to knock at the door to fame and riches and is to be thrown away after the door is open; "the trump"
10	入迷	rùmí	fascinated; captivated
	儒林外史	rúlínwàishǐ	"Anecdotes of the Academic World"; a Ching novel by Wu Ching-tzu (1701–1754)
	湘劇	xiāngjù	Hunan opera
11	領會	lǐnghuì	to comprehend; to understand; to grasp the essence of
	流毒之深	liúdúzhīshēn	How great the bad influences are!
	爲禍之烈	wéihuòzhīliè	What impetuous calamities it brings!
12	廢除	fèichú	to abolish
	壽終正寢	shòuzhōngzhèngqǐn	to die of old age
	吸鴉片	xīyāpiàn	to smoke opium

	戒絕烟癮	jièjuéyānyǐn	to stop smoking
13	慢性病	mànxìngbìng	a chronic disease; creeping illness
	恢復健康	huīfùjiànkāng	to recover
14	習慣勢力	xíguànshìlì	a habitual force
15	滋生不絕	zīshēngbùjué	to grow endlessly

page 71

1	一首一尾	yīshǒuyīwěi	the beginning and the end
2	屈指一算	qūzhǐyīsuàn	to count on the finger
	優點	yōudiǎn	advantage; merits
	缺點	quēdiǎn	disadvantage; demerits
	原因	yuányīn	cause; reason
	經驗	jīngyàn	experience
	存在的	cúnzàid	existing; prevailing
3	解決	jiějué	to solve
	題旨	tízhǐ	theme; subject matter; essence
	分析	fēnxī	to analyse
4	基本情況	jīběnqíngkuàng	fundamental facts; basic conditions
	是否有當	shìfǒuyǒudàng	whether it is proper or not
	指示	zhǐshì	to instruct
	意見不成熟	yìjiànbùchéngshóu	opinions not well formed
5	指正	zhǐzhèng	to correct
6	略具形式	lüèjùxíngshì	to have a kind of form
	本義	běnyì	original meaning; the aims
7	掌握	zhǎngwò	to grasp
	論文	lùnwén	essay; thesis
	講稿	jiǎnggǎo	draft of a lecture

	報告	bàogào	report
	總結	zǒngjié	summary; conclusion
9	滔滔天下	tāotāotiānxià	throughout the world; in the whole wide world
	觸目可見	chùmùkějiàn	visible everywhere; seen everywhere
10	時文	shíwén	current literature; literature of the time
	雖不中也不遠	suībùzhòng-yěbùyuǎn	If it does not hit the target, it will not be far away from it — If it is not completely right, it will not be altogether wrong either.
12	養士	yǎngshì	to bring up the educated
13	取士	qǔshì	to select the educated
	謹防	jǐnfáng	to guard against
15	唸	niàn	to read aloud; to recite

page 72

1	翻尋	fānxún	to search into (documents); to investigate
2	翻來了	fānláile	to have introduced
	洋	yáng	foreign
3	抄筆記	chāobǐjì	to take notes
4	下堂	xiàtáng	after class
	對筆記	duìbǐjì	to compare notes
	背誦	bèisòng	to learn by heart; to recite from memory
	畢業	bìyè	to graduate; graduation
	摘引	zhāiyǐn	to quote
	傳爲「佳話」	chuánwéijiāhuà	being circulated as "fine tales"
	教學方法	jiāoxuéfāngfǎ	teaching methods; pedagogics
	道道地地	dàodàodìdì	typically
7	杞人之憂	qǐrénzhīyōu	the worries of the man of Chi, fearing that the sky would fall down

8	胆量	dǎnliàng	courage; guts
	文科	wénkē	department of literature; studies of Humanities
9	傳統	chuántǒng	tradition
11	難關	nánguān	dilemma; quandary
	災難	zāinàn	calamity; disaster
	士子	shìzǐ	scholar
	知識份子	zhīshífènz	intellectual; intelligentsia
	嚴重注意	yánzhòngzhùyì	to pay great attention
13	傳聲筒	chuánshēngtǒng	a sound transmitting tube
	社論	shèlùn	editorial
	往好處着想	wǎnghǎochùzháoxiǎng	to think optimistically; to look on the bright side of things

page 73

2	有朝一日	yǒuzhāoyīrì	some day
	碰釘子	pèngdīngz	to meet with a refusal
	偷偷地	tōutōud	stealthily; secretly
	改變	gǎibiàn	to change
4	讚揚	zànyáng	to praise
	深得我心	shēndéwǒxīn	impressed me deeply
5	借此	jiècǐ	to take the opportunity
	揭發	jiēfā	to uncover; to disclose; to expose
6	隱惡揚善	yǐnè-yángshàn	to conceal other people's weaknesses and make known their merits
	美德	měidé	virtues
	相關聯	xiāngguānlián	in connection with
8	無保留地	wúbǎoliúd	without reservation
	浙江省	zhèjiāngshěng	Chekiang Province

	稅務局	shuìwùjú	tax bureau
	草擬	cǎonǐ	to draft; to draw up a draft
9	秘書	mìshū	secretary
	科員	kēyuán	clerk
	水平	shuǐpíng	level; standard
11	擬稿人	nǐgǎorén	one who makes out a draft
12	無的放矢	wúdìfàngshǐ	to shoot an arrow without aiming at a target—not to the point
13	引經據典	yǐnjīngjùdiǎn	to quote from the classics
	抄摘	chāozhāi	to copy; to quote
	土教條	tǔjiàotiáo	a native dogma
14	文章結構	wénzhāngjiégòu	structure of an article
16	審查	shěnchá	to examine
	全文批准	quánwénpīzhǔn	to approve (or endorse) an official writing as it is

page 74

1	很全面	hěnquánmiàn	very comprehensive
	很正確	hěnzhèngquè	very accurate
2	總而言之	zǒngéryánzhī	in a word; to sum up
	泛濫	fànlàn	in flood; wide-spread
4	老子	lǎozǐ	Lao Tzu, a leading Taoist philosopher
	聖人不死大盜不止	shèngrénbùsǐ-dàdàobùzhǐ	Bandits will not cease to exist until all sages are dead
	發現	fāxiàn	to discover
	官僚	guānliáo	bureaucracy
5	官僚主義	guānliáozhǔyì	bureaucratism
	下限	xiàxiàn	limit; the lowest in scale

6	題目	tímù	topic; theme
	倒霉的	dǎoméid	unlucky; unfortunate
	土地爺	tǔdìyé	Chinese god of earth
7	立此存照	lìcǐcúnzhào	to write as evidence; to acknowledge in receipt
8	錯覺	cuòjué	illusion; false impression
9	團支書	tuánzhīshū	branch secretary of the Communist Youth League
	最沒威信	zuìméiwēixìn	having the lowest prestige
10	工會主席	gōnghuìzhǔxí	chairman of a labor union
11	科長	kēzhǎng	head of a department
12	漫畫	mànhuà	cartoon; caricature
	小品	xiǎopǐn	informal essays
	通訊	tōngxùn	correspondence; a bulletin
	描繪	miáohuì	to depict; to sketch
	扮演主角	bànyǎnzhǔjiǎo	to play the main role in a play
14	報紙刊物	bàozhǐkānwù	newspapers and publications
15	醜態可掬	chǒutàikějú	visible repulsive features

page 75

1	毛病	máobìng	weakness; shortcoming; disease
2	官卑職小	guānbēizhíxiǎo	unimportant positions
	領導同志	lǐngdǎotóngzhì	leading comrades
	保險櫃	bǎoxiǎnguì	safe
	沾染	zhānrǎn	to taint with; contaminate; to be affected by
3	塵土	chéntǔ	dust
4	觸犯	chùfàn	to offend; to affront
	平均主義	píngjūnzhǔyì	egalitarianism; equalitarianism
5	障眼的東西	zhàngyǎnd-dōngxī	something that blocks one's eyesight

	基層工會	jīcénggōnghuì	a basic-level trade union
7	隨風飄揚	suífēngpiāoyáng	to float in the air; to flutter in the air
	洗澡	xǐzǎo	to bathe
8	職權	zhíquán	authority; power
	空間愈廣	kōngjiānyùguǎng	the broader the space
9	一巴掌大	yībāzhǎngdà	of the size of a palm
	危害性	wēihàixìng	harm; damage
10	牽涉	qiānshè	to implicate; to involve
	無關大局	wúguāndàjú	having not much influence on the whole; insignificant
	片面	piànmiàn	partial; biased; one-sided
12	嚴重性	yánzhòngxìng	seriousness
	時下	shíxià	current; of the time; prevailing
	指責	zhǐzé	censure
13	逍遙	xiāoyáo	to wander about at leisure; to be at ease
14	古史家	gǔshǐjiā	historians in the field of ancient histories
	爭論	zhēnglùn	to contend; to dispute; to debate
	奴隸制社會	núlìzhìshèhuì	slave society
	朝代	cháodài	dynasty

page 76

1	遺傳	yíchuán	heredity
	變異	biànyì	evolution
2	生物學家	shēngwùxuéjiā	biologist
	遺傳因素	yíchuányīnsù	hereditary factor
	變異的規律	biànyìdeguīlù	law of evolution
3	生物	shēngwù	creature; a living thing

4	先代	xiāndài	former generations; ancestors
	差別	chàbié	difference
5	並存的	bìngcúnd	co-existing
8	理論	lǐlùn	theory
	思想	sīxiǎng	thought; ideology
	略抒管見	lüèshūguǎnjiàn	to express some of one's limited views
9	•理論家	lǐlùnjiā	theoretician
	思想家	sīxiǎngjiā	thinker
11	全面發展	quánmiànfāzhǎn	all-round; over-all; all embracing
	教育方針	jiàoyùfāngzhēn	educational policy
13	個性	gèxìng	individuality

page 77

1	後代	hòudài	posterity; descendants; future generations
2	馬克思	mǎkèsī	Karl Marx
4	原理	yuánlǐ	principles
	恩格斯	ēngésī	Friedrich Engels
5	遺著	yízhù	posthumous works; works left behind
	行世	xíngshì	to circulate in the world
	有書可考	yǒushūkěkǎo	demonstrable; able to stand the proof through books
	考證	kǎozhèng	to verify; to prove
6	痕迹	hénjì	a trace of
7	五味湯	wǔwèitāng	soup which has the five flavours — sweet, sour, bitter, pungent and salt
8	消滅	xiāomiè	to destroy
	腦力勞動	nǎolìláodòng	mental labour
	體力勞動	tǐlìláodòng	physical labour

	界限	jièxiàn	boundary
9	片面發展	piànmiànfāzhǎn	partial development
11	擴大	kuòdà	to enlarge
12	五育	wǔyù	five aims in education—love for motherland, love for the people, love for labour, love for science and love for public property

page 78

1	針對	zhēnduì	to aim at
3	冒昧	màomèi	to take the liberty of
4	持之有故	chízhīyǒugù	enough reason to stand by; there is precedent for it
	言之有理	yánzhīyǒulǐ	to speak with logic; logical
	交待明白	jiāodàimíngbái	to make oneself clear
5	標籤	biāoqiān	label
	貨眞價實	huòzhēnjiàshí	genuine goods and real prices
6	樓梯	lóutī	staircase; escalator
	晒衣竿	shàiyīgān	a pole used to hang clothes in the sun
7	文人	wénrén	intellectuals
	文壇	wéntán	the world of letters; literary circle
	詩人	shīrén	poet
	詩壇	shītán	the world of poetry
8	不甘庸俗	bùgānyōngsú	cannot stand being commonplace
	伸長脖子	shēnchángbózi	to stretch out the neck
	瞭望	liǎowàng	to be on the lookout
	藝術化	yìshùhuà	artistic
9	欣賞者	xīnshǎngzhě	admirer
10	大地回春	dàdìhuíchūn	return of the spring

	百花齊放	bǎihuāqífàng	all flowers bloom
12	杜甫	dùfǔ	Tu Fu, one of the best T'ang poets (A.D. 712-770)
	不薄今人愛古人	bùbójīnrénàigǔrén	kind to the new and love the old. 薄 means to slight, to belittle
13	一視同仁	yīshìtóngrén	to be equally kind to all
	今古一律	jīngǔyīlǜ	to treat the contemporary and the ancient in the same way
14	發生疑問	fāshēngyíwèn	to have doubt; to be sceptical

page 79

4	格式	géshì	a pattern of writing; form
5	橫排	héngpái	to arrange in a horizontal line
	豎排	shùpái	to set up vertically
7	廻廊九曲	huílángjiǔqū	a winding corridor with many ins and outs
9	齊齊整整	qíqízhěngzhěng	regular; in good order; tidy
	七長八短	qīchángbāduǎn	very uneven; varying in lengths
10	褲衩	kùchà	the open seam of trousers
	曝晒	pùshài	to dry in the sun
	形象	xíngxiàng	appearance; look; image
	不美觀	bùměiguān	not good-looking
11	形式主義	xíngshìzhǔyì	formalism
12	講	jiǎng	to be particular about; to be choosy; to stress
	意境	yìjìng	poetic state
	辭藻	cízǎo	diction; vocabulary; flowery language
	音節	yīnjié	syllable
	韻律	yùnlǜ	laws for rhyming
	如所周知	rúsuǒzhōuzhī	as is known by all
13	不相連貫	bùxiāngliánguàn	incoherent; unconnected

	唸不上口	niànbushàngkǒu	unreadable
	韵脚	yùnjiǎo	rhyme
14	聽便	tīngbiàn	at will; as (one) pleases
	散文	sǎnwén	prose
15	氣味	qìwèi	characteristics

page 80

2	澆冷水	jiāolěngshuǐ	to pour cold water on–to discourage
3	雜誌	zázhì	magazine; periodical
	競相	jìngxiāng	to compete with each other for
	登載	dēngzài	to publish; to print
	古詩古詞	gǔshī, gǔcí	ancient poems
	古曲	gǔqǔ	classical opera
4	棄新從舊	qìxīncóngjiù	to reject the new for the old
5	冷落之感	lěngluòzhīgǎn	feeling of being neglected
6	剩下	shèngxià	to leave behind; to remain
7	自強不息	zìqiángbùxī	to push forward through endless efforts
	擺字遊戲	bǎiziyóuxì	play of words; to bandy with words
8	學學前人	xuéxuéqiánrén	to learn from one's predecessors
9	用點苦心	yòngdiǎnkǔxīn	to work harder
	太方便	tàifāngbiàn	too convenient
	信口開河	xìnkǒukāihé	to talk nonsense; to jabber; to babble
	提筆亂寫	tíbǐluànxiě	to pick up the pen and dash off a piece of writing without thinking carefully
12	百家爭鳴	bǎijiāzhēngmíng	hundred schools of thought contend
	音樂週	yīnyuèzhōu	musical week
	音樂家	yīnyuèjiā	musician

	口頭	kǒutóu	orally
	筆下	bǐxià	in writing
13	洋腔	yángqiāng	foreign tunes
	土腔	tǔqiāng	native tunes; broad accent
	一竅不通	yīqiàobùtōng	utterly ignorant

page 81

1	共同性	gòngtóngxìng	something in common; of a joint nature
2	科學	kēxué	science
	高論	gāolùn	high-flown talk; harangue
3	西醫	xīyī	Western medicine
	中醫	zhōngyī	Chinese medicine
	先進	xiānjìn	advanced; progressive
	落後	luòhòu	backward
4	啞口無言	yǎkǒuwúyán	to be dumb-stricken; to be silent
	宣言投降	xuānyántóuxiáng	to declare surrender
5	名堂	míngtáng	reason; definition
	黃帝內經	huángdìnèijīng	title of the oldest Chinese medicine book
	本草綱目	běncǎogāngmù	title of an illustrated materia medica compiled by Li Shih-chen
6	玩意	wányì	game; toy
8	證據	zhèngjù	evidence; proof
	作曲法	zuòqǔfǎ	theory of musical composition
9	發聲法	fāshēngfǎ	vocalism; vocalisation
	音域	yīnyù	vocal reach; sound volume
	樂器	yuèqì	musical instrument
	沒有準	méiyǒuzhǔn	having no standard; without established rules

10	嗓門	sǎngmén	larynx; voice
12	判斷能力	pànduànnénglì	the ability to judge
	揣測	chuǎicè	to estimate; to judge
13	國樂家	guóyuèjiā	traditional Chinese musician
	瞠目結舌	chēngmùjiéshé	with a staring look and tongue-tied; speechless
14	遜色	xùnsè	inferior; less colourful
	拉胡琴	lāhúqín	to play Chinese violin
	敲鑼鼓	qiāoluógǔ	to beat the gong and drum
15	聖手	shèngshǒu	expert; the best performer
16	抵抗	dǐkàng	to resist; to hold out against; to stand up to

page 82

2	聲明在案	shēngmíngzàiàn	it has been stated on record
	主觀主義	zhǔguānzhǔyì	subjectivism
	承認	chéngrèn	to recognise; to acknowledge
5	倒嗓子	dǎosǎngz	to lose voice; to miss a scale
	免俗	miǎnsú	to be free from what is common
7	客觀事物	kèguānshìwù	objective things
	發展規律	fāzhǎnguīlù	law of development
	否定	fǒudìng	to deny; to negate
10	行行出狀元	hánghángchūzhuàngyuán	狀元: **highest** graduate of the Hanlin Academy (or the Imperial Academy). The best found in every profession.
12	向科學進軍	xiàngkēxuéjìnjūn	to march forward to science
	號召	hàozhào	to call on; to call for; to appeal
13	響應	xiǎngyìng	to answer; to respond
	理所當然	lǐsuǒdāngrán	naturally; of course; both natural and right
15	自然科學	zìránkēxué	natural sciences

	數理化生	shùlǐhuàshēng	abbreviations for mathematics, physics, chemistry and biology

page 83

1	自然現象	zìránxiànxiàng	natural phenomena
2	大類	dàlèi	big category; general category
	社會科學	shèhuìkēxué	social sciences
3	啃書本	kěnshūběn	bookwork; to read as a bookworm
	背教條	bèijiàotiáo	to repeat dogmas
	記公式	jìgōngshì	to memorise formulas
	科學遺產	kēxuéyíchǎn	scientific heritage
4	記載	jìzài	to record
5	成果	chéngguǒ	results
	脫離實際	tuōlíshíjì	divorced from reality; not in accordance with practice
	教條主義	jiàotiáozhǔyì	dogmatism
6	研究機構	yánjiūjīgòu	research organisation
	副博士	fùbóshì	doctoral candidate
8	狹窄	xiázhǎi	narrow
9	誤解	wùjiě	wrong interpretation; misunderstanding
11	荒乎其唐	huānghūqítáng	absurd; ridiculous. Same as 荒唐
	怪想法	guàixiǎngfǎ	strange idea
12	各行各業	gèhánggèyè	each and every trade
14	借鑒	jièjiàn	a warning example; to serve as an example
	授以學位	shòuyǐxuéwèi	to confer an academic degree
15	農業合作社	nóngyèhézuòshè	Agricultural Producer's Cooperative
	工廠管理	gōngchǎngguǎnlǐ	factory management
16	售貨員	shòuhuòyuán	salesman or saleswoman in a store

page 84

1	行家	hángjiā	expert
	考問	kǎowèn	to question: to examine
	對答如流	duìdárúliú	to give quick answers
2	勞動模範	láodòngmófàn	labour model
	先進工作者	xiānjìngōngzuòzhě	advanced worker
3	降低	jiàngdī	to lower; to humble; to bring down
4	尊嚴	zūnyán	dignity
5	蠢想法	chǔnxiǎngfǎ	stupid idea
	學術	xuéshù	academic learning
	實際問題	shíjìwèntí	practical problem
	理論科學	lǐlùnkēxué	theoretical sciences
6	應用科學	yìngyòngkēxué	applied sciences
	寧缺而無濫	níngquēérwúlàn	better to have too little than too much
	擺設品	bǎishèpǐn	an ornament; a decorative object
8	總結報告	zǒngjiébàogào	summary; report
10	勞力	láolì	manual labour
	勞心	láoxīn	mental labour
	尊卑之分	zūnbēizhīfēn	distinction between superiority and inferiority
11	駁	bó	to argue; to refute; to repudiate
	業務工作	yèwùgōngzuò	profession; business operations
	在職	zàizhí	working; on the job
15	一句俗話	yījùsúhuà	(to use) a common saying

page 85

2	教育家	jiàoyùjiā	educator
3	幼兒園	yòuéryuán	kindergarten

	兒童心理學	értóngxīnlǐxué	child psychology
4	私塾	sīshú	private school in old China
6	壽命	shòumìng	the span of life
7	害	hài	to suffer from
	肺結核	fèijiéhé	tuberculosis; pulmonary tuberculosis
	疾病	jíbìng	disease
9	端端正正	duānduānzhèngzhèng	properly
	描畫	miáohuà	to sketch; to trace writing
11	腦筋	nǎojīn	the brain; nerves of the brains
14	發育過程	fāyùguòchéng	the process of development
	估量	gūliàng	estimation; deliberation
15	老老實實	lǎolǎoshíshí	honestly

page 86

3	成人	chéngrén	adult; grown-ups
	老頭	lǎotóu	old man
	成長發育	chéngzhǎngfāyù	to grow up
	襁褓嬰兒	qiǎngbǎoyīngér	an infant wrapped in a piece of cloth
4	發蒙書	fāméngshū	a book used to enlighten the young
5	人性哲學	rénxìngzhéxué	philosophy of human nature
6	教育學	jiàoyùxué	pedagogy
9	保險	bǎoxiǎn	to guarantee; to make sure
11	下死勁	xiàsǐjìn	to make great efforts
14	少年先鋒隊	shàoniánxiānfēngduì	Young Pioneers
15	檢討	jiǎntǎo	self-criticism
16	聯繫	liánxì	to link with; having bearing on
	變魔術	biànmóshù	to conjure (tricks); magic

| | 拉扯 | lāchě | to stretch; to chat |

page 87

1	壓縮	yāsuō	to squeeze; to compress; to condense
	餵飯	wèifàn	to feed
2	咀嚼	jǔjiáo	to chew
6	公開	gōngkāi	publicly
	發表宣言	fābiǎoxuānyán	to make a public statement; to declare oneself
7	服務態度	fúwùtàidù	service
8	千眞萬確	qiānzhēnwànquè	true and real
10	視而不見	shìérbújiàn	look but do not see – to be absent-minded
	聽若罔聞	tīngruòwǎngwén	to hear but pay no attention
	緣故	yuángù	cause; reason
11	吉人天相	jíréntiānxiàng	Heaven protects the good, used to comfort the sick or those in trouble
12	走了眼	zǒuleyǎn	to have read the wrong words; to misread
13	威風	wēifēng	dignity; majesty; pomposity
14	電車	diànchē	tram; street car
	公共汽車	gōnggòngqìchē	bus
	司機	sījī	driver; chauffeur
	售票員	shòupiàoyuán	bus conductor
	罵	mà	to scold
15	挑肥擇瘦	tiāoféizéshòu	fussy; critical; fastidious
	百問一煩	bǎiwènyīfán	saying "please" only once while making a hundred requests

page 88

1	笑臉歡送	xiàoliǎnhuānsòng	to see (someone) out with a smiling face
	質問	zhíwèn	to question; to interpellate

	揍	zòu	to beat
2	挨打	āidǎ	to be beaten
	醫院	yīyuàn	hospital
3	精神不振	jīngshénbúzhèn	tired; listless; sapless
	有氣無力	yǒuqìwúlì	weak; feeble; unnerved
	醫生	yīshēng	doctor
	護士	hùshì	nurse
4	急躁	jízào	impatient and irritated
	歇息	xiēxī	to take a rest
	眼睛一翻	yǎnjīngyìfān	to turn up the whites of the eyes — expressing anger
	怒目相待	nùmùxiāngdài	to eye (people) angrily
	老子	lǎoz	I, me — a term implying self-importance and arrogance; lit. your father
5	伺候	cìhòu	to wait upon
6	理由充足	lǐyóuchōngzú	having sufficient reasons
8	大夫	dàifū	medical doctor
	熱衷	rèzhōng	to be enthusiastic about; to be highly interested in
9	處之泰然	chǔzhītàirán	to take things calmly
	證明人	zhèngmíngrén	witness
	猜想	cāixiǎng	to guess
10	出席	chūxí	to be present
12	好	hǎo	what; how (interj.)
	厲害	lìhài	severe; terrible
	一言以斃之	yīyányìbìzhī	to kill the whole with one sentence, derived from the phrase 一言蔽之 (to sum up). 斃 meaning to shoot to death and 蔽 to cover, are pronounced in the same way
13	天津	tiānjīn	Tientsin

14	辛辛苦苦	xīnxīnkǔkǔ	laboriously; toilsomely
	制訂	zhìdìng	to enact; to draw up
	文明行為	wénmíngxíngwéi	civilised behaviour

page 89

1	野蠻	yěmán	uncivilised; barbarous
2	好走極端	hàozǒujíduān	fond of going to the extreme
	撒野	sāyě	to be unmannerly
3	綑仙索	kǔnxiānsuǒ	a magic rope used to tie up supernatural beings
4	束縛	shùfú	bonds; fetters; restraints
	亂蹦亂跳	luànbèngluàntiào	jumping around recklessly
5	規矩	guījù	rules; manners
	側目而視	cèmùérshì	with a side glance—indicating disapproval or distrust
6	絕無僅有	juéwújǐnyǒu	unique; uncommon
	正在開端	zhèngzàikāiduān	just the beginning
7	冬烘	dōnghōng	a village schoolmaster—sitting over the stove in winter
	引以為奇	yǐnyǐwéiqí	to find it strange
	妨碍	fáng'ài	to hinder; to prevent from
10	搞典型	gǎodiǎnxíng	to set up models and examples
	標準的	biāozhǔnd	standard
12	區區	qūqū	small; insignificant
	無組織	wúzǔzhí	unorganised
	無紀律	wújìlǜ	undisciplined
13	頭兒	tóur	head (of an organisation)
15	檢查	jiǎnchá	to examine; to investigate
16	農業合作化	nóngyèhézuòhuà	agricultural co-operation
	右傾偏向	yòuqīngpiānxiàng	rightist tendencies

	鄉社幹部	xiāngshègànbù	village – and commune-level cadres

page 90

1	時髦話	shímáohuà	in fashionable terms
	不公平	bùgōngpíng	injustice; unfairness
3	課堂上	kètángshàng	in class
	飯廳	fàntīng	dining hall; canteen
	圖書館	túshūguǎn	library
4	分貼	fēntiē	to post (proclamations, notices, etc.) in different places
5	公共場所	gōnggòngchǎngsuǒ	a public place
	遵守	zūnshǒu	to observe; to obey; to follow
6	限制	xiànzhì	restriction
9	辮子	biànz	a braid; a queue
	披頭散髮	pītóusànfà	dishevelled hair
10	無例外的	wúlìwàid	without exception
	鼓掌	gǔzhǎng	to clap hands
13	籠統	lóngtǒng	general; over-simplification
14	憲法	xiànfǎ	constitution
16	不分皂白	bùfēnzàobái	not to distinguish black from white – indiscriminate

page 91

1	隨風倒	suífēngdǎo	to bend with the wind
	虛無論	xūwúlùn	nihilism
3	守則	shǒuzé	rules; regulations
7	頑皮處	wánpíchù	mischievousness
8	想盡法子	xiǎngjìnfǎz (fàz)	to try every means
	欺負	qīfù	to take advantage of; to bully

9	靈機一動	língjīyīdòng	to come upon a clever contrivance
	掐住	tāozhù	to clutch; to hook
12	惱恨	nǎohèn	to hate
13	偏愛	piān'ài	to love one more than the other
14	討厭	tǎoyàn	to dislike
	嫉妒	jídù	to be jealous of

page 92

4	不理睬	bùlǐcǎi	to pay no attention to; to take no notice of
	瞪眼	dèngyǎn	to stare in anger
	恍然大悟	huǎngrándàwù	to begin to apprehend after moments of confusion
5	關心	guānxīn	to show concern for; to care for
7	出乎意外	chūhūyìwài	beyond expectation
8	順手	shùnshǒu	in passing; while convenient
	抽	chōu	to draw out; to take out
	人民幣	rénmínbì	Chinese currency
12	補充	bǔchōng	to add; to supplement

爭鳴的風度 Manner of Contention

章白 Chang Pai. It is not certain whether Chang Pai is the pen name for Wu Han or Liao Mo-sha. However, Chang Pai's style seems most to resemble that of Liao.

page 93

	爭鳴	zhēngmíng	contention
	風度	fēngdù	deportment; refined manners
2	贊成	zànchéng	to agree
	貫徹	guànchè	to carry out completely; to implement
3	何以見得	héyǐjiàndé	Whence do we see this?
	例子	lìzǐ	examples; instances
	證	zhèng	proof; evidence
4	許	xǔ	to allow; to promise
	討論	tǎolùn	to discuss; discussion
	著文	zhùwén	to write an article or articles
	立說	lìshuō	to set up a theory or theories; to theorise
5	道理	dàolǐ	reason; principle
	不見得	bújiàndé	unlikely; not necessarily
	細心	xìxīn	careful; carefully
	分析	fēnxī	to analyse; analysis
	吸取	xīqǔ	to absorb; to take
	綜合	zōnghé	to gather together; to sum up
6	合理	hélǐ	reasonable
	部份	bùfèn	part
	解決	jiějué	to solve; to settle
	即使	jíshǐ	even if
	暫時	zhànshí	temporarily

	擱一下	gēyīxià	to put it down or to drop it for a while
	留待	liúdài	to wait until
	材料	cáiliào	material
7	發見	fājiàn	to discover; to find out
	再加	zàijiā	to have it again (brought out and discussed)
	採取	cǎiqǔ	to adopt; to select (one out of many)
	堅持	jiānchí	to insist on
	己見	jǐjiàn	one's own opinion
8	宣稱	xuānchēng	to proclaim; to declare
	擺出	bǎichū	to put on; to display
	權威	quánwēi	authority
	專家	zhuānjiā	expert
9	却步	quèbù	to step back; to withdraw
	其實	qíshí	actually; in fact
10	否定	fǒudìng	to negate
	論點	lùndiǎn	viewpoint
	實在	shízài	indeed; actually; really
	高明	gāomíng	intelligent; competent
	降低	jiàngdī	to lower
	削弱	xuēruò	to weaken
11	加強	jiāqiáng	to strengthen
12	根據	gēnjù	source; ground; evidence
	就	jiù	only; then
	列舉	lièjǔ	to enumerate; to illustrate one by one
13	越……越	yuè…yuè	the more … the better
	持有	chíyǒu	to have; to hold; in possession of

page 94

1. 看法　　　　kànfǎ　　　opinion; viewpoint
   一方　　　　yīfāng　　　one party
   提出　　　　tíchū　　　 to put forward; to make a remark; to state
2. 以求　　　　yǐqiú　　　 so as to
   符合　　　　fúhé　　　 to correspond to; to fit; to agree with
   指出　　　　zhǐchū　　　to point out
   也罷…也罷　yěbà...yěbà　whether...or...; be it...or...
3. 主觀　　　　zhǔguān　　 subjective
   能動性　　　néngdòngxìng　initiative; activity
   發生　　　　fāshēng　　 to take place; to play; to work
   作用　　　　zuòyòng　　 function; role
   版本　　　　bǎnběn　　　edition; 版本上的 written, printed
   證據　　　　zhēngjù　　 evidence; proof
   這樣　　　　zhèyàng　　 thus; in this way
4. 深入　　　　shēnrù　　　to deepen; to investigate closely
   科學　　　　kēxué　　　 science; scientific
   阻礙　　　　zǔài　　　　to hinder; to obstruct; to prevent...from
   展開　　　　zhǎnkāi　　 to launch (a movement); to unfold; to expand
5. 張三李四　　zhāngsānlǐsì　third son of Chang and fourth son of Lee -- this one and that one; anybody
6. 國有制　　　guóyǒuzhì　 nationalisation; the system of nationalisation
   分歧　　　　fēnqí　　　 difference in opinion; disagreement over
   到底　　　　dàodǐ　　　 actually; after all
   指　　　　　zhǐ　　　　 to point to; to pinpoint; to mean exactly
   統治集團　　tǒngzhìjítuán　ruling clique

7	其次	qícì	next
	應用範圍	yìngyòngfànwéi	sphere of application
	整個	zhěnggè	the whole
8	賬	zhàng	accounts; an account book
	湊	còu	to add up to; to put together
	七嘴八舌	qīzuǐbāshé	many people talking confusedly together
	總	zǒng	by any means; on all accounts; always
	對不上	duìbúshàng	does not correspond to (something); **does not fit**; does not agree
	口徑	kǒujìng	calibre
	總之	zǒngzhī	in a word
	經典著作	jīngdiǎnzhùzuò	classical works
9	理解	lǐjiě	to understand; understanding
	結合	jiéhé	to combine; to go with
	實際	shíjì	actuality; actual; actually
	各取所需	gèqǔsuǒxū	to each according to his needs
10	糊塗	hútú	confused; bewildered
	弄	nòng	to make; to do; to end in
	服氣	fúqì	to accept defeat; to submit
	究	jiū	to examine; to investigate; to get down to
	根源	gēnyuán	root; origin; cause
	唸通	niàntōng	to understand thoroughly
11	試問	shìwèn	let me ask; allow me to put it to you
	要是	yàoshì	if
12	態度	tàidù	attitude; manner; behaviour
	絕大多數	juédàduōshù	overwhelming majority

	不免	bùmiǎn	unavoidably
13	個把	gèbǎ	one or two; a few
	漏洞	lòudòng	loop-holes
	要求	yāoqiú	to demand; to ask for
	學術論文	xuéshùlùnwén	dissertation or thesis of learning
	顛撲不破	diānpūbùpò	irrefutable
	一絲一毫	yīsīyīháo	in the least
	缺點	quēdiǎn	weakness; shortcoming; fault; defect
14	經過	jīngguò	to go through; to undergo
	不斷	búduàn	repeated; continual
	辯駁	biànbó	to refute; refutation
	修改	xiūgǎi	to alter; to revise; revision
	逐步	zhúbù	step by step; gradually
	完善	wánshàn	to attain perfection; perfection
	提高	tígāo	to raise; to heighten
	認識	rènshí	to know; to realise; to acquaint
15	必經過程	bìjīngguòchéng	inevitable process
	理論	lǐlùn	theory
	水平	shuǐpíng	level
	發展	fāzhǎn	to develop
16	抓住	zhuāzhù	to seize; to get hold of; to grasp firmly
	大作文章	dàzuòwénzhāng	to make a great fuss
	冷嘲熱諷	lěngcháorèfěng	scorching satire and freezing irony; to ridicule in various ways
	與人爲善	yǔrénwéishàn	to be friendly; to do good for others

1	不久前	bùjiǔqián	not long ago
	留	liú	to keep
	便	biàn	exactly; precisely; no more and no less
2	眞眞	zhēnzhēn	really; sincerely
	推動	tuīdòng	to motivate; to move forward; to give impetus to; to push ahead
3	心情舒暢	xīnqíngshūchàng	ease of mind; in a happy frame of mind
	還得	háidé	must in addition
	講究	jiǎngjiū	to carefully study; particular about; choosy
	一下	yīxià	about; a little
	那就是	nàjiùshì	namely; that is
	平等	píngděng	equal; equality
4	有權	yǒuquán	having the right to; be entitled to
	講道理	jiǎngdàolǐ	to talk sensibly; to argue reasonably
	說服	shuōfú	to convince; to persuade
	共同的	gòngtóngd	common; known to all
	一致的	yīzhìd	unanimous
5	透	tòu	thoroughly

態度，使人讀了很不愉快，不久前一篇討論古人留不留鬍子的文章便是一個例子。

由此看來，要使學術爭論健康地展開，真真做到百家爭鳴，推動學術水平的提高，而又心情舒暢，知無不言，言無不盡，還得講究一下爭鳴的風度，那就是第一大家都平等，有權講道理；第二道理要科學，能夠說服人；第三共同的語言，一致的口徑；第四道理要講透，態度要正確。

1. 同看法，爭來爭去，爭不清楚。這時候，爭論的一方忽然提出，這條材料應該加一個字，或者減一個字，甚至改一個字，以求符合自己的論點。
2. 改也罷，都是主觀能動性在發生作用，並沒有版本上或其他的證據。這樣，問題也就不好說了，不能深入了。這種不科學的風度，確也阻礙了爭鳴的展開。
3. 第三種情況，是你說的張三，我說的李四。題目雖同，內容卻異。例如歷史上土地國有制問題，首先是國的分歧，這個國到底指的是什麼，是皇帝個人？還是他的統治集團？其次是應用範圍，是指的整個東方國家，還是專指某些國家？第三是有，如何有法？討論的各方，各有各的一本賬，湊到一起，七嘴八舌，總對不上口徑。總之，就經典著作的學術名詞說，各人理解不同，對結合自己的歷史實際說，卻又各取所需，越爭越糊塗，弄個沒完沒了，卻又誰都不服氣。究其根源，還是經典著作沒有唸通，自己的歷史也沒唸通，試問要是通了，口徑怎麼會不對？
4. 第四種呢？道理有些對，態度卻不好。絕大多數人在提出自己論點的時候，總不免有個把漏洞，要求每一個新論點，每一篇學術論文顚撲不破，一絲一毫缺點也沒有，是不可能的。總要經過不斷討論，辯駁，修改，逐步完善，逐步提高，這是一個認識新事物的必經過程，也是學術理論水平不斷提高發展的必需過程。於此，有的人卻不能理解，抓住一個漏洞，大做其文章，道理是對的，態度卻不好，冷嘲熱諷，不是與人爲善的

爭鳴的風度

章白

百家爭鳴，這四個字，好得很！字只有四個，誰都認得，誰都懂得，誰都贊成，但貫徹這四個字，卻並不是容易的事。何以見得？有以下一些例子為證。

一種情況，是只許我有理，不許你有理。在討論的時候，各家著文立說，各說各的道理，其中有些道理不見得全對，也不一定全不對。要是能夠細心分析，吸取，綜合各家所鳴的合理部分，是可以解決問題，即使不能完全解決，暫時擱一下，留待以後有材料發見時再加討論，也是可以的。但是，有些人卻不願採取這種方法，堅持己見，並且宣稱，只有他的道理對，別人的全不對，擺出權威，專家的臉孔，使人望而卻步。這樣，就使人不敢爭，也不敢鳴了。其實，這不是一個好辦法，堅持己見，當然可以，但完全否定別人的論點，卻實在有點不大高明。這種風度，只能是降低、削弱權威、專家的地位而不是加強。

第二種情況，是我的根據對，你的就不對。在爭論時各家列舉自己論點的根據，擺**出事實，越多越好**，這是必需的。但也有這種情況，兩家擺的是同一件根據，卻持有不這真是奇怪。我又問：那麼你為什麼不問問他，他愛不愛他的媽媽？他媽媽可是個女的呀。

那位老師笑了：「怎麼沒有問過？他說：我把媽媽恨死了。問他為什麼恨？他回答我：媽媽十天半月都見不到面，見了面也不理睬他，說不定還瞪着眼看他。」我恍然大悟：原來如此。大概他對爸爸也不會好感，估計他的爸爸是不會比媽媽更關心他的。可是不，據那位老師說：他很愛他的爸爸，滿口說他的爸爸比誰的爸爸都好。

「是怎麼好法呢？」這又出乎我的意外了。

老師告訴我：她也問過那孩子，他爸爸怎麼好法。他順手從衣口袋抽出兩張一元的人民幣一揚，說：「你看，這就是我爸爸給的。他不光是給一塊錢，還給兩塊錢。如果我再要，他也會給我。他多麼好！」

故事并沒有講完，但是我記到這裏為止，不想再記下去了。這是一對怎樣的父母，請讀者來作評判吧。補充一句：這男孩子的爸爸媽媽都是幹部。

一個孩子和他的父母

皂白；二、隨風倒，一講「個性」，就什麼全不要了；三、學校教育的「虛無論」，對學生不許有任何限制，連學習紀律都不許有，可以來去自由。

按照這種批評的標準，中學生守則十八條，也是「好厲害的十八條」！

一位小學老師向我說出這樣一段故事：她所教的班上所有的孩子都好教，只有一個孩子她沒有辦法教好。

那是個男孩子，十二三歲了，卻不講任何道理，他要怎麼着就怎麼着。別的頑皮處都不必說，頂奇怪的是，他見到女同學就要想盡法子欺負她。下了課追打女生不算，連上着課他忽然靈機一動，伸出雙手一把掐住坐在他前面的一個女生的脖子，再也不肯放手。你看看，這有什麼辦法？

我聽完這個故事，也同樣覺得奇怪：小男孩不愛同小女孩在一塊玩，倒是常事，可是對女孩子惱恨得這麼厲害的，真是不多見；我甚至沒有見過。

是什麼原因呢？是他的爸爸媽媽偏愛他的姐姐或妹妹，所以他惱恨女孩子麼？我問那位老師：你為什麼不仔細調查研究，是不是他很討厭或者嫉妒他的姐姐妹妹？她說：

「他沒有姐姐，也沒有妹妹。」

1. 放火，不許百姓點燈」的批評方法，用一句時髦話來說，叫「嚴重的」不公平。

2. 天津十六中學的七十二條是怎樣「好厲害」的呢？我特意尋出報紙細讀過兩遍，無

3. 非是教學生在課堂上如何作，在飯廳裏如何作，在圖書館又如何等等。條文雖多達七十

4. 二，如果分貼在學校的各個地方或學生在校外的各種地方，也並不算太多了；而且大多

5. 數是在公共場所應該遵守的一些對集體有利的規則。「發展個性」，如果發展到不管公

6. 共和集體的利益，發展到不管任何限制的極端「自由」，那麼對這種「個性」和這種「

7. 自由」，我以為妨礙妨礙，束縛束縛，是有益而無害的。這並不叫「好厲害」。七十二

8. 條中免不了若干條是不必要的廢話，例如女生留長頭髮必須編成小辮，紮上彩帶之類。

9. 我看完全是廢話。哪有一個留長髮的女生不結辮子、披頭散髮上學的？當然也還有若干

10. 做不到或不必要做的，例如：「無例外的鼓掌」之類。但是我就看不出有半數以上的條

11. 文都是這樣的廢話，而且都妨礙「個性發展」。即使它真有半數以上的條文都要不得，

12. 至少也有十條八條是規定得對的，並不妨礙「個性發展」吧？怎麼能得出「好厲害的七

13. 十二條」的籠統的「一言以蔽之」呢？

14. 如果只是因為它是七十二條，多了，就「好厲害」。那麼看看我們國家的憲法，何

15. 止七十二條？一百以上。

16. 這個「一言以蔽之」的批評，據我的看法，犯了三條（只有三條）毛病：一、不分

1. 學校裏的「文明行為」既然「一言以斃之」，自然「野蠻行為」接着登場。青年們

2. 一個可愛的特點，是好走極端，不許他們「文明」，他們就會撒野。小學生還不懂得什

3. 麼文明和野蠻，只知道照常上學；大中學校的學生卻不然，身上的綑仙索一解開，就免

4. 不得手脚齊動。如果你告訴他們：解開一切束縛，并不是叫你亂蹦亂跳，學校有學校的

5. 規矩。他會側目而視：怎麼着，你還敢來束縛我的「個性發展」麼？

6. 這并不是講笑話，的確有這種情況，而且不算絕無僅有，正在開端。

7. 我不是冬烘老先生，也并不怕青年們「發展個性」。不過我引以為奇是妨碍學生個

8. 性發展的，難道只是一個天津第十六中學所訂的七十二條「文明行為」的規則麼？別的

9. 中學如何？大學又如何？

10. 有人說：這是搞典型。要批評就批評這種典型。七十二條，是一個標準的「典型

」。

11. 那我又要問：天津第十六中學不過是區區一個中學，即使他們無組織無紀律，上面

12. 也該有個管他們的頭兒吧？請問頭兒們是怎樣領導和指示他們的？

13. 我并不是要請出天津十六中學上面的頭兒來「一言以斃之」，因為頭兒之上還有頭

14. 兒，天外還有一層天。明擺着的一件事實是，學校教育的方針，是應該有人管理和檢查

的。農業合作化的右傾偏向，難道都是鄉社幹部們搞出來的嗎？恐怕未必。「只許州官

笑臉歡送。倘使笑得不夠勁，他就會質問：你的服務態度怎麼是這樣的？該揍你一頓。——果然有揍的售貨員。因爲「服務」也包括揍打在內。他生病進醫院了，總該是精神不振，有氣無力了吧？可是不，他見了醫生打醫生，看到護士罵護士。要是有人勸他：您身體不好，別那麼急躁，快歇息歇息吧。他會眼睛一翻，怒目相待：「老子花了錢，他就得伺候我」。——「伺候」，就是「服務」的別稱。他花了錢，難道不該爲他服務？他的理由充足極了。

你不相信有這樣的人和這樣的事麼？挨打過的電車、汽車司機或售票員，受過罵的商店店員，既挨過打又受過罵的大夫和護士，都大有人在。儘管他們熱衷於爲人民服務，還不至於挨了打不覺得痛，受了罵能處之泰然。如果要請他們來作證明人，據我猜想，他們是沒有理由不肯出席的。

抱有這種「被人民服務」的思想的人，我看不在少數。

好厲害的「一言以斃之」

報紙上登出過這樣一篇批評：「好厲害的七十二條」。一言以斃之，天津第十六中學的教師們辛辛苦苦制訂出來的七十二條「文明行爲」，看來是一條不剩，都拉出來「斃」了。

被人民服務的人

1. 「為人民服務」這問題似乎已經解決了，又似乎還沒有解決。說它已經解決了吧，可是誰也沒有公開發表過宣言，說他「反對為人民服務」。說它已經解決了吧，可是報紙上的批評，刊物上的「小品」，經常在揭發那些不安心工作和服務態度很不好的人。
2. 而且這些都是千真萬確的事實，十目所視，十手所指。
3. 服務態度不好，不肯老老實實為人民服務，當然應該受批評。可是另外有一種人，卻為眾人視而不見，聽若罔聞。批評這件物事，不知為了什麼緣故，很少落到這種人的頭頂。好像是「吉人天相」。
4. 這種人並不反對「為人民服務」。但是他們大概是這幾個字走了眼，把「為人民服務」看成了「被人民服務」或者看成了「人民為我服務」。所以他們威風不小：出門上電車或公共汽車，只要那些司機或者售票員稍不如他的意，開口就罵，舉手就打。到商店買東西，挑肥擇瘦，百問一煩，到頭來卻什麼東西亦不買，扭身便走；而售貨員還得

1. 個問題爭鳴起。

2. 我爲什麼要提這個問題？因爲我們的教育從古至今都沒有解決這個問題，不是把兒童當作成人甚至老頭來教育，就是把他們看作永久不成長發育的襁褓嬰兒來教育。古時候（其實并不止古時候），五、六歲兒童一入學就讀四書五經，詩云子曰，起碼的發蒙書也是「人之初，性本善」，是一套連大人都說不清所以然的人性「哲學」。這是把小孩看作老頭。後來有人從外國學了洋教育學回來，說這樣教法不行，得由淺入深，把發蒙書改了：「人、手足、刀尺」，似乎合理一些。可是兒童的語文程度愈來愈下降，到了現在，中學生連水滸傳都得請老師一字一句的講解，大學畢業生能不能把一封普通信寫得一字不錯，每一句都通順，就很難保險。

3. 學生的語文程度如此，其他學科是不是很高了呢？誰都知道，蘇聯的中、小學一共才十年，而我們是十二年，程度還趕不上人家，要趕上就非下死勁不可。請問這是什麼道理？是我們的孩子比別人低能些麼？恐怕未必。分明是我們把中、小學生的孩子看得太年小了，教的東西很不夠，怕傷了他們的腦筋。

4. 另一方面，又時常把孩子看成大人，連少年先鋒隊員也得像黨團員一樣，開起會來滿口的批評、檢討。我就親身參加過少年先鋒隊的隊會，親耳聽到他們背述故事，要「聯繫自己的思想」。──我們的教育眞像是在變魔術，能夠把受教育的兒童一會兒拉扯

老少難分

1. 教育家「百家爭鳴」的問題很不少，問題之一，是幼兒園該不該教識字。
2. 幼兒園該不該教幼兒識字呢？對這點我提不出「科學」的意見。因為我既不懂兒童心理學，也不懂幼兒教育。我只知道，我自己是整五歲時上私塾唸書，一開始就讀「子
3. 曰，學而時習之，不亦悅乎！」和我的年齡不相上下的同學，是唸（其實是喊叫）「關
4. 關雎鳩，在河之洲」。比我所讀的更難懂。我的同學的壽命如何，我不知道，至於我自
5. 己，一直活到現在，除開害過肺結核以外，腦子卻似乎并無疾病。此外還有我的孩子。
6. 現在雖已上小學，可是他遠在入幼兒園之前——三歲左右，在家看見哥哥姐姐上學識字
7. ，他也要求識字，而且教他幾個簡單的生字，他不但識熟了，并且能端端正正地描畫出
8. 來。至今也看不出他的腦子因此受了傷害，影響健康。
9. 這就可見，七歲以下的兒童不能教識字，教了就會傷害他的小腦筋，是道理不充足
10. ，缺乏證據的，說不出理由，找不出證據，我看這就不能算科學。
11. 我并不是要參加這個爭論，堅持幼兒園應該教識字，而是要問一問：我們對兒童和
12. 青少年的心理發育過程，到底有沒有個比較正確——也就是比較合乎實際的估量或看法
13. 。我要求一切心理學家和教育家老老實實地研究研究這個問題。假如要爭鳴，就先從這

1 ——當然，他們必須是行家，工作的確作得極好，考問起來對答如流。有人說：各行各業不是都有勞動的模範和先進工作者的稱號麼？博士這種學位是授與科學或學術研究有成就的人，你這種主張，豈不是把學術研究和一般的工作混為一談，降低了科學或學術的尊嚴和地位了麼？

2 我有一個蠢想法：：科學也好，學術也好，不都是解決實際問題的麼？無論是理論科學或應用科學，倘使它最後是與實際無關，那就寧缺而無濫。科學並不是擺設品，只能看看的。如果這也算是一個道理，那我就要問：科學和實際工作既然都是解決實際問題的，為什麼要分出高下？某一科學的一篇論文和某一革命工作的一篇總結報告，如果都不是教條主義和八股文，請問它們的價值和作用有多麼大的分別呢？這裏應該解決一個問題，勞力和勞心的尊卑問題。我以為它們是不應該有尊卑之分的。

3 也許還有人要駁我：：按照你這樣說，科學研究和一般的業務工作意義相同，在職的青年就不用向科學進軍了。

4 這樣一駁幾乎要把我駁倒。但是我還有一說，國家需要我們幹什麼就幹什麼。它需要誰向科學進軍，就該向科學進軍；它需要誰作一般工作，就該作一般工作。而一般工作也同樣可以向科學進軍，同樣有科學，同樣需要科學研究。一句俗話：「行行出狀元」，當然也就「門門有博士」。

1. 們所研究的是自然現象的發展規律；但是科學並不止是研究自然規律，它也研究社會發
2. 展的規律。還有一個大類，叫社會科學。不應該忘了。
3. 有人以為，研究科學就是啃書本、背教條、記公式。研究科學要接受前人的科學遺產，啃書本也是必需的。但是科學研究的對象是客觀事物，前人的著作也都是記載他們研究客觀事物的成果。脫離實際的研究並不叫科學研究，只能叫「教條主義」。
5. 還有人以為，向科學進軍就是進大學，進研究機關，考副博士和博士，把「向科學進軍」看作「向博士進軍」。這種看法並不完全正確。
8. 第一種「以為」，是把科學看得太狹窄；第二種「以為」，是脫離實際；而第三種「以為」，我說什麼好呢？是把科學看成很簡單的公式：科學＝博士。這是一種誤解。
11. 怎樣使那些響應國家號召的可愛青年不發生誤會呢？我倒有一個荒乎其唐的怪想法：我主張各行各業都應該出博士。只要他能夠從各種客觀事物和一切實際工作中發現它的發展規律，而且能總結出適應這種規律的辦法和解決問題的經驗，有助於同類性質的工作的借鑒，就應該授以學位，從副博士到博士。
15. 如果這樣，辦農業合作社的，可以當農業合作社博士，管理工廠的，可以當工廠管理博士，做機關工作、當小學教師、商店的售貨員等等，也都可以當各種各樣的博士。

可是究竟什麼叫「科學」呢？

聲明在案：我並不懂科學。不過憑我的一點「主觀主義」看法，科學總得承認事實，講出道理。已經存在的東西，而不承認它的存在自有道理，恐怕不能算是科學。存在並不等於合理，中樂可能有不合理的地方，正像西樂不可能絕對合理一樣。比如發音法，中國的舞台上有倒嗓子的，西洋音樂家也不能免俗，同樣有倒嗓子的。當然兩家也都各有不倒嗓子的名家。可見洋唱法有洋科學，土唱法也有土科學，各有各的律規和辦法。科學家應該是研究客觀事物的發展規律，而不是否定客觀存在的事物，說它根本沒有規律，說它的存在是不科學的。西樂家否定中國樂的規律性，說它不科學，也正像否定一個人，說他生長得不科學一樣。我看這樣的「科學論」自己就很不科學。

行行出狀元

我們中國的確是太需要科學了。不僅現有的科學水平太低，而且有好多門科學根本還沒有。需要科學，就需要研究科學的人。所以國家提出「向科學進軍」的號召。

青年們響應這個號召，理所當然，是件極好的事。不過在向科學進軍之前，先把科學是個什麼東西，如何研究科學，為什麼研究科學，這幾件事認識清楚，倒很有必要。

有人以為，科學只是自然科學，數、理、化、生……，這些當然是科學，因為它

1. 我忽然發現這些爭鳴有一個共同性：凡是一牽涉到中西（中國和西洋）兩方，就有

2. 人抬出兩個大字「科學」。人們大概還記得，在中西醫之爭的時候，曾經有過這樣的高

3. 論：西醫為什麼是先進的呢？因為它科學；中醫為什麼是落後的呢？因為它不科學。

4. 於是乎中醫的一方啞口無言，只好宣言「投降」。因為講到「科學」，中醫們的確

5. 說不出個名堂。「黃帝內經」和「本草綱目」中，哪有什麼「科學」這種東西呢？

6. 據我看，現在的中樂與西樂之爭，「科學」這玩意似乎又被人抬出來當武器了。調

7. 子相同：西樂的先進，是因為它科學；中樂的落後，是因為它不科學。

8. 中國音樂什麼地方不科學呢？證據是很多的：它的作曲法講不出個道理，不科學；

9. 它的發聲法，不但音域少，而且不科學；樂器製作沒有準，當然更不科學。似乎生為中

10. 國人，連耳朵和嗓門都不如西洋人長得「科學」似的，發出的聲音竟比人家少，而且有

11. 些音，叫聽衆根本聽不出來。

12. 這種理論的是非如何，我毫無判斷能力。因為我既不懂音樂，也不懂科學。據我揣

13. 測（也許揣測錯了），國樂家遇到這種「科學論」，恐怕也會像中醫們一樣瞠目而結舌

14. ，說不出話來。而且他們比中醫們更加遜色，無論是唱戲唱曲的名家，拉胡琴、敲鑼鼓

15. 的聖手，能寫會說，善於講出一篇科學大道理的人，根本就數不出幾位，叫他們用什麼

16. 來抵抗西樂家的「科學」，這眞叫：有口開不得，科學嚇倒人！

1. 我並不是要給今人的「新詩」澆冷水,其實澆冷水的何嘗是我們這些並不寫詩只是
2. 讀詩的人?試看時下的報紙雜誌,不是在競相登載今人寫的古詩、古詞、古典麼?其中
3. 就有棄「新」而從「舊」的詩作家。
4. 百花齊放,連古詩、古詞、古典都開放了,而新詩卻漸有冷落之感。可見「不薄今
5. 人愛古人」這句詩,現在快剩下下半句了。
6. 「新詩」如何才能自強不息呢?我看第一條是拉下「樓梯」,不作擺字的遊戲;第
7. 二條是,也如杜甫老先生所說的:「竊攀屈宋方宜駕,頗學陰何苦用心」,學學前人,
8. 用點苦心。藝術是「苦心」得來的,太方便太容易,信口開河,提筆亂寫,哪裏能寫得
9. 出一首好詩?連一句好詩都不可得。

根本不科學

果然是「百家爭鳴」。剛舉行過全國音樂周的音樂家們,口頭和筆下都「爭鳴」開
了:中樂、西樂、洋腔、土腔,十分熱鬧。對於音樂,我是一竅不通,插不上嘴去的。
不過凡是「百家爭鳴」,我都想聽聽和看看,不管他是那一家。所以凡是我能看到的「
爭鳴」的文章,我都看。

1. 而是它們薄我。

2. 我並不是說今人的「新詩」沒有一首好的。不過無論如何，自有「新詩」以來，我沒有讀過一千首，也讀過八九百首，而我至今連半首詩都背誦不出來，沒有留下一點深的印象。假如說我對「新詩」有印象的話，那就是說詩中有那麼一種格式：兩三個字一行，不論橫排或豎排，都像樓梯似的，一行行低下去，低下去；然後又忽然提高，成為另一張樓梯。

3. 大約那就是步上詩壇的樓梯吧？可是那些樓梯往往長得很，廻廊九曲，眞叫走（也就是讀）它的人走個不完。

4. 還有一種不是樓梯的格式：上面齊齊整整，下面卻七長八短，像一竿長竹竿穿上長短不齊的衣服褲衩，橫在太陽下曝晒。形象也並不美觀。

5. 這都是說的形式，人們要說這是形式主義論。

6. 是的，詩應該講內容，講意境，講辭藻，講音節，講韵律。可是如所周知，我們「新詩」不是呼天喚地，就是哎喲喧天，句子前後不相連貫，音節唸不上口，韵脚也沒有，長短聽便。即使是寫得極好的一首詩，也不過是一段散文，分開來一句寫成一行罷了，那有點詩的意境和氣味？

7. 當然，思想內容很正確的「新詩」，那是不少的。可惜思想正確並不能說它是「詩」是針對什麼問題來說的；第二、他們究竟是怎麼說的；第三、請你找出一段原文來證明他們所說過的「全面發展」是五育並進，缺一不可。

當然，我是在給新觀察寫「亂彈」，而不是冒昧參加「百家爭鳴」。力爭全面發展和五育不可缺的學說，仍然是「持之有故」而「言之成理」的。不過得交待明白：這並不是馬克思學說的原物，應該取下標籤，才能「貨真價實」。

樓梯和晒衣竿

文人作文的地方叫「文壇」，詩人寫詩的地方叫「詩壇」。我是站在離這些「壇」遠遠的人，但也不甘庸俗，常常伸長脖子，向這些壇上遠遠的瞭望。——用一個「藝術化」的名稱，叫「文藝的欣賞者」。

我常常瞭望我們的「詩壇」，想看看是不是大地回春，百花齊放。然而至今沒有望到。

杜甫有一句詩：「不薄今人愛古人」。這是講他自己對詩的看法，他對今人的詩和古人的詩一視同仁。我也正是這個看法：今古一律，我都喜好。

但是看來看去，我對杜甫這句詩的前半句發生疑問：「不薄今人」，是不是即使今人不如古人，也不可「薄」呢？就今人寫作的新詩來說：我實在感覺得不是我薄它們，

1. 第一代的學說，是怎麼說的呢？從後代的「遺傳」中，也就是從現在所有的爭論中

2. ，雖然誰都在說他是根據馬克思的學說原理在作爭辯，卻很少見到人們再提到它的原來

3. 面目。似乎他們所說的就是馬克思所說過的。只有「遺傳」而沒有「變異」。

4. 「儒墨皆稱堯舜，而堯舜不復生」，相信誰說的是對的呢？馬克思和恩格斯雖然不

5. 可復生，卻並不像堯舜沒有遺著行世，馬、恩學說是有書可考的。那就考證考證他們的

6. 原作吧。考證馬克思和恩格斯的原作，果然發現出一條「變異」的痕迹。原來馬克思和

7. 恩格斯口中或筆下所提到的「全面發展」，並不是現在人們所爭論的「五味湯」。他們

8. 所說過的道理很容易懂（當然並不簡單）：消滅腦力勞動與體力勞動的界限，人類就可

9. 以全面發展；不消滅這條界限，人類就只能片面發展。所謂「全面」，不過只包括腦力

10. 勞動和體力勞動。止此而已。

11. 而後代的「全面發展」學說，卻真的是「發展」了，也就是擴大和「變異」了：從

12. 腦力勞動、體力勞動擴大為五育「全面發展」。全面發展是更加全面了，可惜已經不是

13. 馬克思、恩格斯在講「全面發展」時所親口講過或親筆寫過的本來面目了。這不是直接

14. 「遺傳」，而是「變異」以後的新種。屬於「遺傳」因素的，只是「全面發展」這幾個

15. 字面而已。

16. 有人不肯相信麼？那就請看馬克思和恩格斯的原著，第一、請看他們講「全面發展

遺傳與變異

1. 生物學家正在對遺傳學中的遺傳因素和變異的規律作「百家爭鳴」。
2. 雖然我自己也是個生物，但是我所知道的僅止於此；我之所以成為人這種生物，而不
3. 成為別的生物，據我推想，是由我先代「遺傳」而來；可是我和我先代畢竟有若干差別
4. ，生物學家可能稱這種差別為「變異」。我相信這兩者是並存的，否則猴子變人這個學
5. 說就不能成立了。但是為什麼既遺傳，又為什麼變異？這個道理我卻說不明白。反正我
6. 不是生物學家，想錯了或者講錯了，也不害怕人們笑話。
7. 錯就讓它錯下去吧，我現在要對理論或思想中的「遺傳」與「變異」略抒管見。當
8. 然，這不是說我是個理論家或思想家。因此我也同樣說不清這種「遺傳」和「變異」的
9. 道理。我只知道這種現象在一些理論或思想工作中確實存在。現在從大學教育到中、小
10. 學教育，都在爭論的一個問題是「全面發展的教育方針」。這爭論就很有「遺傳」和「
11. 變異」的規律在起作用。
12. 「個性全面發展」或「全面發展的教育」這個名稱，是從哪兒來的呢？人們說，這
13. 是馬克思和恩格斯的學說傳下來的。因此說馬、恩學說是「全面發展」的第一代，大概
14. 是沒有什麼錯誤的。

1. 沒有告訴過我們還有別的人是官僚主義者。似乎天下最愛犯官僚主義毛病的,只有這些官卑職小的「下面」的幹部;科長以上的領導同志,就都是裝在保險櫃中,不沾染任何官僚主義塵土的。

2. 批評官僚主義,如果觸犯到科長以上的領導同志,是不是犯了「平均主義」的錯誤呢?我看未必。但是不知道有一種什麼障眼的東西,使人們的眼睛不敢往科長、基層工會的主席和團支書以上的領導同志身上碰一碰,是不是比科長高一級的同志就眞的不沾染官僚主義的塵土呢?我看也未必。官僚主義的塵土是隨風飄揚的,如果不經常洗臉洗澡,任何人都可能沾染上。而且事實上官愈高,職權愈大,面臨的空間也愈廣,沾染的塵土也就可能更厚更多;官卑職小,所管的空間不過一巴掌大,即使犯點官僚主義,危害性倒牽涉很小,無關大局。這是我的一種「不成熟」的「片面」的看法。

3. 凡是官僚主義,不論大小,都不是好東西,都應該批評、反對。但是據我的看法,從嚴重性來說,小官僚主義不如大官僚主義;從時下的批評指責來說,又似乎大官僚主義不如小官僚主義。因為大官僚主義是逍遙於批評之外的。

4. 古史家正在爭論中國奴隸制社會的「下限」期在哪一朝代。我心裏在設想:我們對官僚主義的批評,是不是也應當有個「下限」?這種「下限」不是哪一朝代,而是「下限」到哪一級的幹部,例如科長以上。

這樣的「八股文」才會得到領導人的讚許：因為它寫得「很全面」，「很正確」。

結果如何，大家都已知道。總而言之，在這些領導人之下，「八股文」就是這樣泛濫天下的。

老子說：「聖人不死，大盜不止」。我現在發現：官僚不死，八股文不止！

官僚主義的「下限」

「文藝學習」有段「忽然想到」，題目是「倒霉的土地爺」。我覺得寫得很好。摘出幾句來，「立此存照」：

「但願這是一種錯覺：

在『中國青年報』上，團支書是最沒威信的人；

在『工人日報』上，工會主席是最沒威信的人；

在『新觀察』上，科長是最沒威信的人⋯⋯

不是麼？在漫畫、小品、通訊裏所描繪的官僚主義劇，常常是由這些同志扮演主角的。」

完全不是「錯覺」：我們從報紙刊物（不止是這幾家）上所看到的正是這樣，並沒有看錯；報紙刊物告訴我們，犯官僚主義錯誤而醜態可掬，就是這些同志；很少、甚至過的只佔少數。至於那些沒有讀過，或者沒有想到去讀一讀的領導人，我也同樣往好處着想，有朝一日，他會碰個小小的釘子（又稱爲批評），自己就偷偷地改變辦法，不一定都要到報紙上和大家見面。

而我所想說的，倒不是讚揚這封「黨員來信」和這篇「社論」如何深得我心，更不是想借此再揭發一些我所目見的同一類事實，唯恐人們不知道這樣的領導人咱們這裏也有。隱惡而揚善，這是我們中國人的「美德」。我所想到的，還是與「八股文」相關聯。

我幾乎可以無保留地相信：浙江省稅務局的那幾位代替領導同志草擬一切報告或講稿的秘書、科員，不管他們的水平多麼高，他們所寫出來的東西，少不得是道地的「八股文」。

理由何在呢？我的理由是：這些報告或講稿既然不是擬稿人自己要講的話，當然是「無的放矢」，滿篇空話；沒有話要說出話來，沒有文章要寫文章，講什麼或寫什麼好呢？當然可靠的辦法是引經據典，抄抄摘摘，土教條或洋教條能搬出多少搬多少，寫的方法和文章結構怎麼樣呢？基本情況、優點、缺點、原因、經驗……第一、第二、第三、甲、乙、丙、丁……

稿子寫出來，交呈領導同志審查指正——其實不審查、不指正、全文批准。也只有

八股文領導

人民日報發表過一封黨員來信：「是領導人呢？是傳聲筒呢？」一篇社論：「從一封黨員來信說起」。

凡事總該往好處着想，我希望天下的領導人讀過這篇來信和社論的佔多數，沒有讀

是些什麽？但是如果有人去翻尋翻尋，恐怕難免他們抱着經書，寫了或講了不少的「詩云」，還從外國翻來了洋「詩云、子曰」。因爲現在不僅有我們中國自己的「詩云、子曰」，洋「子曰」。至於大學的學生們，是上課抄筆記（也就是記老師所唸的講稿），下堂對筆記，考試以前背誦筆記，畢業寫論文摘引筆記，這已經在報紙上傳爲「佳話」，當是事實。不管這些講稿和筆記原來是不是「八股文」，這樣一個口誦、手抄、心記的教學方法，就算本來不是「八股文」也道道地地成了「八股文」的讀書法——養士法。怎麼能不使人有杞人之憂呢？

當然，我沒有這個胆量，敢說現在的大學文科是「八股文」養士。但是「八股文」在我們中國是有「傳統」的，現在也還是「千百萬人的習慣勢力」，這幾年又從外國翻譯過不少的洋「八股文」，所以「八股文」養士的危險，是從多方面來的。要逃脫這個難關，或避免這場災難，須請士子們——也就是知識份子們——嚴重注意！

那麼，新「八股文」有哪幾股？一首一尾有相似的地方，可稱為「破題」和「大結」；至於中間，我屈指一算，也恰巧算出六股，名稱是：優點、缺點、原因、經驗、存在的問題、解決問題的辦法。首股「破題」，倒不像老「八股文」只解釋題旨，而是分析「情況」或稱為「基本情況」；末段「大結」就只是：「是否有當，請指示」「意見不成熟，請同志們批評、指正」之類。至於「請指示」「請批評」是不是真心誠意，或有無必要這麼寫，那就又當別論。略具形式，就是「八股文」的本義。

只要掌握這個「八股」，就可以寫出論文、講稿、報告、總結或其他所需要的一切新「八股文」。

也許有人要問，你所指的新「八股文」是那一篇？我說：滔滔天下，觸目可見。只要你按照我所總結出來的公式，去套一套眼前的「時文」，就可以發現，雖不中，也不遠。

八股文養士

明清兩代以「八股文」取士，我們新中國當然不以「八股文」取士。但是要謹防以「八股文」養士。

有沒有這個危險呢？我看有。大學的教授們寫講稿，唸講稿，寫的和唸的雖不知道

1. 有思想內容，或者內容有多少，你得按股入格，套進這個公式。套得好的就名登金榜，

2. 身入仕途，成為皇帝的「幹部」。

3. 這種文章，看來并不難作，因為有格式可以填，有公式可以套，就像我們現在常常

4. 填寫登記表或統計表一樣，照着格子填寫；但是也不容易作好，因為分明是無話可說，

5. 卻要說出話來，分明無理可講，也要講出一篇大道理；而且不許說你自己想說的話，講

6. 你自己所懂得的理，只許為聖賢立言，講四書五經所講過的道理。結果是不知所云，言

7. 之無物，通篇是廢話，寫了等於沒有寫。

8. 明清時代的考試，就是寫「八股文」，稱為「科學」。——用現代的話來解釋，就

9. 是用「八股文」來考選幹部。「八股文」既是跟皇帝當「幹部」和升官發財的「敲門磚

10. 」，當然使人入迷。讀過「儒林外史」這部名著小說，看過「祭頭巾」這齣湘劇的人，

11. 就可以領會「八股文」對人類社會流毒之深，為禍之烈。

12. 現在科舉制度是早廢除了，老「八股文」總算壽終正寢，但是吸過鴉片的人，要戒

13. 絕烟瘾是很不容易的；患過某些慢性病的人，要完全恢復健康也是件難事。寫「八股文

14. 」似乎也有瘾，寫過的人固然愛寫，沒有寫過的人也愛學愛寫，成了一種「習慣勢力」

15. 。老「八股文」死了，新「八股文」滋生不絕，我們現在不僅有「八股文」，而且寫「

16. 八股文」的人還不在少數。真所謂「八股文」精神不死。

亂彈雜記

廖沫沙

破題

亂彈，就是東拉西扯，南腔北調，沒有譜；雜記，就是想到哪裏，寫到哪裏，不成文章。

1

寫上了「破題」兩字，就聯想到「八股文」。「八股文」的名稱雖在，而「八股文」是個什麼，你我似乎都茫茫然。

2

八股文入門

我出生得晚，沒有趕上作「八股文」的時代，沒有學過這門專業。但是去古不遠，畢竟還可以知道一些「皮毛」。所謂「八股」，是一篇文章分爲八個部份：破題、承題、起講、提比、虛比、中比、後比、大結。每一部分講什麼內容，佔多少字數，全文共多少字，都有個規定，不可破格。這是一種寫文章的「格式」或「公式」。不管你有沒

3

4

5

6

7

8

9

10

如果要想從他的身上，找到反封建的革命因素，那恐怕是不可能的。我們決不需要恢復所謂東林遺風，就讓它永遠成為古老的歷史陳迹去吧。我們只要懂得努力讀書和關心政治，這兩方面緊密結合的道理就夠了。片面地只強調讀書，而不關心政治；或者片面地只強調政治，而不努力讀書，都是極端錯誤的。不讀書而空談政治的人，只是空頭的政治家，決不是真正的政治家。真正的政治家沒有不努力讀書的。完全不讀書的政治家是不可思議的。同樣，不問政治而死讀書本的人，那是無用的書呆子，決不是真正有學問的學者。**真正有學問的學者決不能不關心政治。完全不懂政治的學者，無論如何他的學問是不完全的**。就這一點說來，所謂「事事關心」實際上也包含着對一切知識都要努力學習的意思在內。既要努力讀書，又要關心政治，這是愈來愈明白的道理。古人尚且知道這種道理，宣揚這種道理，難道我們還不如古人，還不懂得這種道理嗎？無論如何，我們應該比古人懂得更充分，更深刻，更透徹！

1. 世界的事情。那個時候的人已經知道天下不只是一個中國，還有許多別的國家。所以，

2. 他們把天下事與國事並提，可見這是指的世界大事，而不限於本國的事情了。

3. 把上下聯貫串起來看，它的意思更加明顯，就是說一面要致力讀書，一面要關心政

4. 治，兩方面要緊密結合。而且，上聯的風聲、雨聲也可以理解為語帶雙關，即兼指自然

5. 界的風雨和政治上的風雨而言。因此，這副對聯的意義實在是相當深長的。

6. 從我們現在的眼光看上去，東林黨人讀書和講學，顯然有他們的政治目的。盡管由

7. 於歷史條件的限制，他們當時還是站在封建階級的立場上，為維護封建制度而進行政治

8. 鬥爭。但是，他們比起那一班讀死書的和追求功名利祿的人，總算進步得多了。

9. 當然，以顧憲成和高攀龍等人為代表的東林黨人，當時只知道用「君子」和「小人

10. 」去區分政治上的正邪兩派。顧憲成說：「當京官不忠心事主，當地方官不留心民生，

11. 隱居鄉裏不講求正義，不配稱君子。」在顧憲成死後，高攀龍接着主持東林講座，也是

12. 繼續以「君子」與「小人」去品評當時的人物，議論萬曆、天啓年間的時政。他們的思

13. 想，從根本上說，並沒有超出宋儒理學，特別是程、朱學說的範圍，這也是可以理解的

14. 。因為顧憲成講學的東林書院，本來是宋儒楊龜山創立的書院。楊龜山是程灝、程頤兩

15. 兄弟的門徒，是「二程之學」的正宗嫡傳。朱熹等人則是楊龜山的弟子。顧憲成重修東

16. 林書院的時候，很清楚地宣佈，他是講程朱學說的，也就是繼承楊龜山的衣鉢的。人們

事事關心

鄧拓

風聲、雨聲、讀書聲，聲聲入耳；
家事、國事、天下事，事事關心。

這是明代東林黨首領顧憲成撰寫的一副對聯。時間已經過去了三百六十多年，到現在，當人們走進江蘇無錫「東林書院」舊址的時候，還可以尋見這副對聯的遺迹。

為什麼忽然想起這副對聯呢？因為有幾位朋友在談話中，認為古人讀書似乎都沒有什麼政治目的，都是為讀書而讀書，都是讀死書的。為了證明這種認識不合事實，才提起了這副對聯。而且，這副對聯知道的人很少，頗有介紹的必要。

上聯的意思是講書院的環境便於人們專心讀書。這十一個字很生動地描寫了自然界的風雨聲和人們的讀書聲交織在一起的情景，令人彷彿置身於當年的東林書院中，耳朵裏好像真的聽見了一片朗誦和講學的聲音，與天籟齊鳴。

下聯的意思是講在書院中讀書的人都要關心政治。這十一個字充分地表明了當時的東林黨人在政治上的抱負。他們主張不能只關心自己的家事，還要關心國家的大事和全血竭敷之乃瘥。下令求血竭不可得。艾子言於王曰：此有方士，不啻數千歲，殺取其血，其效當愈速矣。王大喜，密使人執方士，將殺之。」這才嚇得方士不得不「拜且泣曰：昨日吾父母皆年五十，東隣老姥，攜酒爲壽，臣飲至醉，不覺言詞過度，實不曾活千歲。艾先生最善說謊，王其勿聽。趙王乃叱而赦之。」

這個方士最後要求饒命的時候說的這一段話，當然還是一派胡言，並且倒打艾子一耙，誣他說謊，可見方士的用心頗爲不善。這又反映了一種情況，就是說大話的人也有秉性難移，死不覺悟的。

歷史上說大話的眞人眞事，雖然有許多，但是這些編造的故事卻更富有概括性，它們把說大話的各種伎倆集中在典型的故事情節裏，這樣更能引人注意，提高警惕，因而也就更有教育意義了。

一九六一年六月十一日「北京晚報」

事，我看很有意思。一個故事寫道：「艾子在齊，居孟嘗君門下者三年，孟嘗君禮為上客。既而自齊返乎魯。季孫氏遇。季孫曰：先生久於齊，齊之賢者為誰？艾子曰：無如孟嘗君。季孫曰：何德而謂賢？艾子曰：食客三千，衣廩無倦色，不賢而能之乎？季孫曰：嘻，先生欺予哉！三千客予家亦有之，豈獨田文？艾子不覺斂容而起，謝曰：公亦魯之賢者也；翌日敢造門下，求觀三千客。季孫曰：諾。明旦，艾子衣冠齊潔而往。入其門，寂然也；升其堂，則無人焉。艾子疑之，意其必在別館也。良久，季孫出見。詰之曰：客安在？季孫悵然曰：先生來何暮？三千客各自歸家吃飯去矣！艾子胡盧而退。」

這個故事大概是杜撰的。不但艾子是作者的假託，而且季孫氏也是由附會得來的。凡是春秋戰國時代魯國桓公的兒子季友的後人，都稱為季孫氏。陸灼諷刺季孫氏嫉妒孟嘗君能養三千食客，就胡亂吹牛說自己也有三千食客，可是經不住實地觀察，一看就漏底了。陸灼寫出這個杜撰的故事，其目的是要教育世人不可吹牛。我們應該承認他是善意的，似乎不必用考證的方法，對它斤斤計較。

在同書中，還有類似的一些故事。例如說趙國有一個方士好講大話，自稱見過伏羲、女媧、神農、蚩尤、蒼頡、堯、舜、禹、湯、穆天子、瑤池聖母等等，以致「沉醉至今，猶未全醒，不知今日世上是何甲子也」。恰好當時「趙王墮馬傷脇，醫云：須千年

說大話的故事

鄧拓

看過「三國演義」的人都記得，諸葛亮揮淚斬馬謖的時候，曾經提到劉備生前說過，馬謖言過其實，不可大用。演義上的這一段話是有根據的。陳壽在「三國誌」的「蜀誌」中確曾寫道：「先主謂諸葛亮曰：馬謖言過其實，不可大用。」看來，劉備對於馬謖的了解，實在是很深刻的。馬謖在劉備的眼裏就是一個好說大話的人。說大話的害處古人早已深知，所以，管子說過：「言不得過其實，實不得過其名。」這就是告誡人們千萬不要說大話，不要吹牛，遇事要採取慎重的態度，話要說得少些，事情要做得多些，名聲更要小一些。

歷來有許多名流學者，常常引用管子的這些話，作為自己的座右銘。然而，也有的人並不理會這個道理。據漢代的學者王充的意見，似乎歷來忽視這個道理的以書生或文人為最多。王充在「論衡」中指出：「儒者之言，溢美過實。」他的意思顯然是認為，文人之流往往愛說大話。其實，愛說大話的還有其他各色人等，決不只是文人之流而已。

古人的筆記小說中寫了許多說大話的故事。明代陸灼在「艾子後語」中寫的幾個故民的利益，他堅決向反動黑暗勢力鬥爭，百折不撓。他值得我們學習的地方，第一是明辨是非，第二是和黑暗勢力鬥爭到底的精神。當然，海瑞是三四百年前封建社會的人物，他的是非觀點同我們現在的是非觀點並不完全一樣，但是他的立場的鮮明與戰鬥精神的旺盛卻是值得我們效法的。

海瑞罵皇帝

海瑞大罵皇帝,同情他和支持他的人到處都是,他的名聲越來越大了,萬曆十四年(公元一五八六年),海瑞被人向皇帝誣告,青年進士顧允成、彭遵古、諸壽賢替他辯誣申救,寫的文章中說:「我們從十幾歲時,就聽說海瑞的名聲,認為是當代的偉人,永遠被人瞻仰,這是任何人都不能趕得上的。」這是當時青年人對他的評價。

❖

海瑞在當時,是得到人民愛戴,為人民所歌頌的。

他反對貪污,反對奢侈浪費,主張節儉,打擊豪強,幫助窮人,主持清丈田畝,貫徹一條鞭法,裁革常例,興修水利,這些作為對農民是有利的,農民愛戴他,歌頌他。

他對城市人民,主要是商戶,裁減派差捐,禁止無償供應物品等等,這些措施對減輕城市工商業者的負担,是有好處的。城市人民也愛戴他,歌頌他。此外,他還注意刑獄,特別是人命案件,著重調查研究,在知縣和巡撫任上,都親自審案,處理了許多積案,判清了許多冤獄。海知縣,海都堂是當時被壓抑、被欺侮、被冤屈人們的救星。他得到廣大人民的稱譽,贊揚,被畫像禮拜,被謳歌傳頌。死後,南京人民罷市,喪船過江,兩岸站滿了穿白衣來送葬的人羣,奠祭拜哭的百里不絕。他的事迹,主要是審案方面的故事,一直到今天,還流傳在廣大人民中。

在封建時代,海瑞是個清廉正直的官吏。他反對壞人壞事,支持好人好事。為了人

「目前的問題是君道不正，臣職不明，這是天下第一件大事。這事不說，別的還說什麼！」

嘉靖看了，大怒，把奏本丟在地下，叫左右立刻逮捕海瑞，不要讓他跑了。宦官黃錦在旁邊說：「聽說這人自知活不了，已向妻子作臨死告別，托人準備後事，家裏的傭人都嚇得跑光了，他不會逃。這個人素性剛直，名聲很大，居官清廉，不取官家一絲一粟，是個好官呢？」嘉靖一聽海瑞不怕死，倒楞住了，又把奏本拾起來，一面讀，一面嘆氣，下不了決心。過了好些日子。想起來就發脾氣，拍桌子罵人。有一天發怒打宮婢，宮婢私下哭著說：「皇帝挨了海瑞的罵，卻拿我們來出氣。」嘉靖又派人私下查訪，有誰和海瑞商量出主意的。同官的人都怕連累，看到海瑞就躲在一邊，海瑞也不以為意，在家等候坐牢。

嘉靖有時自言自語說：「這人真比得上比干，不過我還不是紂王。」他叫海瑞是畜物，口頭上和批處海瑞案件的文件上都不叫海瑞的名字。病久了，又有氣，和宰相徐階商量，要傳位給太子，說：「海瑞的話都對，只是我病久，怎麼能上朝辦事呢？」又說：「都是自己不好，不自愛惜，鬧了這場病。要是能上朝辦事，怎麼會挨這個人的罵」下令逮捕海瑞下獄，追查主使的人。刑部論處海瑞死刑，嘉靖也不批復。過了兩個月，嘉靖死了，新皇帝即位，才放海瑞出來，仍回原職，作戶部主事。

當時的問題，向皇帝提出的質問，要求改革。他在疏中說：

1. 「你比漢文帝怎麼樣？你前些年倒還做些好事。這些年呢，只講修道，大興土木。以猜疑誹謗殺謬臣下，濫派官職給人。跟兩個兒子也不見面，人家以為你薄于父子。弄得天下吏貪將弱，到處有農民暴動。這種情況，你即位初年也有，但沒有這樣嚴重。現在嚴嵩雖然罷相了，但是沒什麼改革，還不是清明世界。我看你遠不如漢文帝。」

嘉靖自比為堯，號堯齋。海瑞說他連漢文帝也不如，他怎麼能不冒火。海瑞接着又說：

2. 「天下的人不滿意你已經很久了，內外大小官員誰都知道。
3. 「你一意修道，只想長生不老，你的心迷惑了。過于苛斷，你的性情偏了。你自以為是，拒絕批評，你的錯誤太多了。你一心想成仙得道，長生不老。你看堯、舜、禹、湯、文王、武王那個活到現在？你的老師陶仲文教你長生之法，他已經死了。他不能長生，你怎麼能求長生呢？你說上天賜你仙桃、藥丸，那就更怪了，桃、藥是怎麼來的呢？是上天用手拿着給你的嗎？
4. 「你要知道，修道沒有什麼好處，應該立即醒悟過來，每天上朝，研究國計民生，痛改幾十年的錯誤，為人民謀些福利。

海瑞罵皇帝

吳晗

在封建時代，皇帝是不可侵犯的，連皇帝的名字都要避諱，一個字不幸成為「御諱」，就得缺筆鬧殘廢，不是缺胳膊，就是缺腿，成為不全的字。人們不小心把該避「御諱」的字寫了正字，就算犯法，要吃官司，判徒刑。至于罵皇帝，那是很少聽說過的事。

真正罵過皇帝，而又罵得非常痛快的是海瑞。海瑞罵嘉靖皇帝最厲害的幾句話說：「現在人民的賦役要比平常多許多，到處都是這樣。你化了許多錢，用在宗教迷信上，而且一天比一天多。弄得老百姓都窮的光光的，這十幾年來鬧到極點。天下人民就用你改元的年號嘉靖，取這兩個字音說，『嘉靖』皆淨，家家窮得乾乾淨淨，沒有錢用。」這樣大胆直接罵皇帝的話，不僅嘉靖當了幾十年皇帝沒有聽見過，就是從各朝各代的古書上也很難找到。但御句句刺痛了他的要害，嘉靖又氣又惱，十分冒火。

原來嘉靖做皇帝時間長了，懶得管事，不上朝，住在西苑，成天拜神作齋醮【宗教儀式】，上青詞。青詞是給天神寫的信，要寫得很講究，宰相嚴嵩、徐階都因為會寫青詞得寵。政治腐敗到極點，朝臣中有人提意見的，不是殺頭，便是革職，監禁，充軍，嚇得沒人敢說話。海瑞在嘉靖四十五年（公元一五六六年）二月上的治安疏，便是針對

1 2 3 4 5 6 7 8 9 10 11 12 13

還有一個大眼鬼。南皮許南金膽很大，在和尚廟裏讀書。夜半忽然牆上出來兩個燈，一看是一個大臉孔，兩個燈是一雙大眼睛。他說：正說好，要讀書，蠟燭完了。拿一册書背着牆，坐下就朗誦，念不了幾頁，燈光沒有了。又一個晚上上厠所，一個小孩給拿蠟燭，不料這個大眼鬼又出來了，扣壁叫喚，也不出來。他撿起蠟燭，就放在大眼鬼頭上，說沒有燈台，你來得正好。大眼鬼仰着頭看，一動也不動。他又說：你哪裏不好去，偏要到這裏來！聽說海上專有人趕臭地方走的，大概就是你了。萬不可以對不起你，隨手拿一張用過的手紙抹鬼的嘴巴，大眼鬼大嘔大吐，狂吼幾聲，就不見了。從此再也不來了。

這幾個故事很不錯，蔑視，鄙視，仇視種種形色的鬼，完全合理。人氣盛了，鬼氣就衰了；人不怕鬼，鬼就怕人了。

不但對死鬼該這樣，對活鬼也該這樣。

人不可以迷信，要相信科學，尊重科學，但也不妨研究研究鬼話，鬼故事，從中得到益處。講人話的書要多讀，講鬼話的書，我以為也不妨讀讀。

一九五九年五月十八日「人民日報」

鬼和人

1. 第一個是蒲松齡寫的青鳳。說有一個狂生叫耿去病，聽說有一個荒廢的大宅子鬧鬼。堂門自己會開關，有時還會笑語歌吹聲。晚上正在用功時，一個披髮鬼進來了，臉黑得像漆一樣，張着眼對他笑。耿去病也對着笑，順手把倪台的墨汁塗上一臉，面對面瞪着眼睛看。鬼看着不對頭，滿臉羞慚溜走了。

2. 第二個是紀曉嵐寫的吊死鬼。說是有一個姓曹的，住在一個人家。半夜裏有一個東西從門縫進來，像一張紙，變成人形，是個女人。他一點也不怕。鬼又披髮吐舌，作吊死鬼模樣，他笑說，頭髮還是頭髮，只是亂一些，舌頭還是舌頭，只是長一些，有頭都不怕，何況沒頭？鬼沒有辦法，可怕。鬼又把頭摘下來，放在桌上，他笑說：有頭都不怕，半夜門縫又響了，剛一露頭，他就嚷，又是這個討厭東西，下不見了。後來又住這房子，

! 鬼一聽只好不進來了。

· 另一個是大鬼。說戴東原的族祖某人膽大不怕鬼。住進一座空宅子，到晚上，陰風慘慘，出來一個大鬼，說，你真不怕？答：不怕。大鬼做了許多惡樣子，又問，還不怕？答：當然。大鬼只好客氣地說：我也不一定趕你走，只要你說一聲怕，我就走了。他說：真是豈有此理，我實在不怕，怎能說假話。你要怎樣就怎樣吧。鬼再三央告，還是不理。鬼只好嘆一口氣說，我在這兒三十多年了，從來沒見過你這號頑固的人，這樣蠢才，怎能住在一起。只好走了。

鬼和人

1. 怕的原因是，據說鬼又要投生變人，屈死鬼投生之前，總得要找一個替身，將人變
2. 鬼。以此人們談鬼就怕，更不用說見鬼了。倒過來，據說人死了就成鬼，人和鬼到底有
3. 關係。自己沒有作鬼的經驗，聽聽別人的也好，以此又喜歡聽鬼故事，大概也是借鑒的
4. 意思吧。
5. 自從有了科學知識，自從有了唯物主義，懂得科學和唯物主義的人們不再相信有鬼
6. 了。但是，研究一下過去的若干鬼故事，從中了解這一時代的社會相，也畢竟有些好
7. 處。
8. 何況，死鬼雖然不存在，活鬼卻確實有之呢！他們成天張牙舞爪要吃人，青面獠牙
9. 嚇唬人，鬼頭鬼腦擺弄人，鬼心思，鬼主意，鬼行當，鬼伙伴，總之，有那末一小撮活
10. 鬼在興風作浪，造謠生事，播弄是非，造成緊張局勢，擺出鬼架子，鬼威風。你愈怕，
11. 他就愈狠，非把你吃掉不可。
12. 對付活鬼的辦法是大喝一聲，你是鬼！揭穿他，讓人人都知道這是鬼。把鬼揪到陽
13. 光底下，戳穿鬼把戲，鬼伎倆，讓人們認識鬼樣子，鬼姓名，鬼親眷，鬼朋友。鬼在人
14. 們中間孤立了，也就搞不成鬼玩意了，或者變人，或者真的變鬼，這倒不妨隨他的便。
15. 要對付活鬼，首先要不怕鬼。道理是你不怕，他就怕。這裏有幾個鬼故事是很有意
16. 思的。

人和鬼

吳晗

鬼和人

在過去的時代裏，人們講迷信，相信有鬼。

據說鬼也和人一樣，有好鬼，有惡鬼。有大鬼，小鬼，男鬼，女鬼，好看的鬼，難看的鬼，文鬼，武鬼，以至大頭鬼，吊死鬼等等。總之，人世間有的事，鬼世界裏也都有。

有了鬼的故事，自然也有說鬼話的書。從「太平廣記」所引的「靈鬼誌」，到「太平御覽」，「太平廣記」都專門有幾卷講鬼的。清朝有幾個人特別喜歡講鬼故事，一個是蒲松齡，他寫了「聊齋誌異」，一個是紀曉嵐，他寫了「閱微草堂筆記」，還有一個是袁子才，也喜歡講鬼。

蒲松齡和紀曉嵐筆下的鬼，形形色色，甚麼樣子脾氣的都有，其中有些鬼寫得實在好，很使人喜歡。他們通過鬼的故事來諷刺，教育活着的人，說的是鬼話，其實是人話。也寫有一些活人，看着是活人，說的卻是鬼話，做的是鬼事。

大體上說來，雖然鬼是從人變的，人死後是鬼，但是人卻又怕鬼。另一面，人雖然怕鬼，卻又喜歡聽鬼故事。

毒物和藥

1. 對某些人是險阻道路的事情，對某些人卻可以是陽關大道。
2. 這，怎能不使人想起良醫化毒物為妙藥的事蹟呢？由於醫生水平的高低，醫療對象及其病況的不同，用藥劑量的輕重，決定了毒物能否轉化的妙藥。
3. 這樣說，自然不是講藝術工作沒有什麼根本規律。否認這些根本的東西，等於瘋子以為揪住自己的頭向上提，自己就能飛了起來。但是，「大體則有，定體則無。」一個作家，越是能夠具備那些根本條件，他的直接的生活經驗豐富，知識越淵博，他在藝術園地裏就越是能夠縱橫馳騁，越不會去「劃地為牢」。
4. 我想，這樣說，該不致於被人誤認是宣傳把毒物當飯吃，或者宣傳培植毒草，或者宣傳踢倒一切規律吧？這個譬喻，僅僅是說明：致人於死的東西適當運用尚且可以轉化為妙藥，那麼藝術工作中，不屬根本規律的某些「條條」和「框框」，又有什麼不可打破的呢！

毒物和藥

1. ；但是除了這些根本要求之外，其他許許多多的「小道理」，卻往往只是「相對眞理」，參考是可以的，但是把它們絕對化起來，卻必定成了所謂「條條」和「框框」。

2. 舉例來說，「眼見爲實，耳聽爲虛」，自己親眼看過的東西，描繪起來總是比較生動的。但這也只是一般而論罷了。對於一個直接的生活經驗很豐富的人，聽來的東西也可以把它描繪得栩栩如生。施耐庵大概自己是沒有打過虎，甚至也不曾看見人家打過虎的吧，然而他描寫武松打虎，卻是多麼的生動精彩！古今文學作品中，有什麼人刻劃這種場面超越過他呢！

3. 根據一點點兒的歷史傳說材料，出之於百分之九十以上的想像，這樣「架空」的作品大概是沒有什麼眞實感吧？但是，許多名家筆下的耶穌、伊索、蘇格拉底之類的故事，馬克•吐溫的「夏娃日記」、魯迅的那些「故事新編」，卻使人讀了極爲親切和感動。

4. 一個人沒有到過某個時期的某個外國，卻去描繪外國生活，這該是荒誕不經的吧？但是，「牛虻」、「尤利烏斯•伏契克」、「羅森堡夫婦」那一類的小說、劇本，卻爲我們留下了良好的範例，那些作者生動表現了外國志士的鬥爭生活。……

類似這樣的例子少嗎？不少！

毒物和藥

傳說舊時代有這樣的軼事：有一個人參加詩酒之會，和朋友聯句吟詩。這人根底很差，一下筆竟寫出了一句不成話的詩「柳絮飛來片片紅」。柳絮怎麼會是紅的呢？此語一出，四座嘩然。另一個人忍受不了，就提筆在這句子上面加了一句「夕陽方照桃花塢」，這一來，「柳絮飛來片片紅」那不成話的一句詩，竟忽然間一變而成為動人的詩句了。

同類的一個故事，說有個詩人給一個富貴人家的老太婆題詩賀壽。他寫了這一句「這個婆娘不是人」，舉座失色；但是他接着寫第二句「九天仙女下凡塵」，那人家的兒孫們看見，就轉怒為喜了。詩人又寫了第三句「兒孫個個都成賊」，大家看了不禁又勃然震怒；但是詩人把筆鋒輕輕一轉，寫出了結句「偷個蟠桃奉至親」，大家又只好改顏贊許了。

舊時代，這一類的文談詩話是不少的。假如說這一類的笑談有什麼思想性的話，我覺得在於它給了我們一點重要的啟示：事物因時因地因條件而變異，決非一成不變；在藝術表現方法上，「絕對不行」的事是極少的。

在文學史上，常常有許多「文章法則」被人粉碎的故事，那道理，和這一類的軼談如出一轍。這和良醫可以使毒物成為妙藥的道理，也有共通的地方。

健康的思想、豐富的生活經驗、熟練的藝術技巧，這些自然是藝術工作的根本要求

毒物和藥

秦牧

有一些被人公認是毒物的東西，一到了良醫的手裏，卻往往變成了妙藥。

砒霜，這東西夠毒了，但是醫生有時治皮膚病，卻用得着它。

蛇毒，它的乾粉一克就可以殺死整百的牛羊。現在，卻有一些人專門養蛇採毒入藥。越毒的蛇就越好，人們專找些眼鏡蛇、響尾蛇之類來飼養。

蝎子，這也是夠毒的東西了。東北地區的人民公社就有專門建築蝎房來養蝎的。

蜂毒，這也是夠厲害的東西了，但是用它製成針劑，卻又可以醫療關節炎。

「箭毒」（一種樹的毒汁，用以塗抹箭鏃殺獸）、蟾酥（癩蛤蟆皮膚的分泌物，有劇毒）、鴉片、嗎啡……這些東西，在對症施用，並且份量適當的時候，也都變成了妙藥。

知道某種東西是毒物，這是重要的；但是知道了之後，又能在某種場合適當加以運用，使它一變而為妙藥，這卻要比僅僅知道它是毒物的那種認識，更跨前一步了。在藝術工作中有沒有這種類似情形呢？我想也是有的。

1. 是要知道那位親密的同窗原來是個姑娘,但是我們不能認定除了師母說穿,梁山伯就始終不會明白。假如在我們觀念上「情節總是這樣固定的」,川劇、淮劇、潮劇就會狠狠地給我們當頭一棒了。

2. 對於社會生活中許多細節的了解,假如有一種簡單化、劃一化的觀念,也總是要碰壁的。

3. 有時看到一些批評文章,指責那些文學作品細節「不真實」,所持的理由不是別的,總是根據一些社會科學上的結論,去套每一個生活的細節,不相符合的就以為不對。在這一類批評者心目中,好像全世界發生的每一個故事細節都要由他來批准似的。這真是奇怪的事情!社會、歷史有一個總的流向,這是完全肯定的。而生活的細節則像是浪花飛濺似的,可以有無窮無盡的樣式。如果不能容忍許多曲折獨特的細節出現在文學作品中,勢必影响某些作者不能創造性地處理豐富多采的題材,而總是滿足於「一般的情節」。結果就會使這部分人的作品減少了光輝。

4. 如果我們沒有理由反對川劇、淮劇、潮劇那樣演他們的戲,我們也沒有理由為文學作品隨意規定細節。生活的海洋是多采多姿的,我們可以知道海洋的一般性質,但是那裏面我們不知道而等待人們告訴我們的魚蝦、海獸、貝類、水藻,卻是太多太多了。

錯綜汊河 49

1. ，像樹葉的支脈那樣，歸根到底總是滙集到主脈上面，而主脈，又總是有一定的流向的。
2. 這種水網地帶的景象，和社會生活的事象道理上頗有一脈相通的地方。反映生活的文學作品，千差萬殊的情節，和這種道理也是有相通之處的。
3. 那就是：不管形式上怎樣錯綜複雜，變化詭奇，實際上總有一個基本的道理貫串其間。
4. 但是基本道理只體現在它的總的方面。至於細節，卻盡有許許多多的表現形式。
5. 一條大河，總有一定的流向。譬如長江、黃河，都是從西向東的。但這只是就整體而言，這樣地作出結論，並不等於說長江、黃河的任何一小節，流向都是自西向東。在某一小節上，長江、黃河可以由北向南，由南向北，甚至有由東向西的反常曲折，這都是可能的，任何人只要翻看一下地圖就明白。我們不能因爲只看到總的流向，就以爲每一小節的流向都是這樣；也不能因爲看到一小節江河流向的殊異，就忘記了那個總的流向。
12. 在「白蛇傳」中，白娘娘有個隨身女侍，但是我們決不可認定小青一定是雌蛇變的，雄蛇就變它不成。在「秦香蓮」中，秦香蓮的寃抑總是要設法伸雪的，但是我們不能認定除了包公出現，決不會有報仇的結局。在「梁山伯與祝英台」中，梁山伯到最後總

河汊錯綜

1. 初初看到這個情節的時候，也是覺得特別的。但仔細吟味，它又何嘗不是言之成理呢？情節的河流曲折地經過這麼一個河床，也是未嘗不可的。

2. 「梁山伯與祝英台」的故事，在十八相送那一折之後，全國許多劇種，都是描述由於師母做媒，梁山伯才恍然大悟，知道那位在路程上說了許多迷離惝怳的話的同學原來是個少女。但是在廣東的潮州戲中，這情節卻又是另外一個面貌了：它表現梁山伯送走祝英台後，歸程時疲倦已極，在樹下入睡，夢境中卻見到祝英台已經裝上女裝，把在十八相送路程上和他說過的話重說一遍。於是，梁山伯驚覺過來了，仔細推敲，不待別人提醒，自己就斷定祝英台是女扮男裝的了。

3. 我十分喜歡這個細節。它是有充份的心理科學的根據的。一個人在睡夢中，由於擺脫了習慣觀念的羈絆，隱約感到的事情突然清晰起來，是完全可能的。而且在舞台上這樣來表現，也充滿了抒情的優美氣氛。

4. 這些神話、傳說、民間故事在各地舞台上的差異，充分地告訴我們：生活的細節是千變萬化的，決不是一成不變的。

5. 你登高看過水網地帶河汊錯綜的景象嗎？從高山上俯瞰下去，河汊溪流像是葉脈似的，錯綜複雜。它們熠熠發亮，四面放射。乍看起來，好像互相糾纏，沒有什麼條理；但是仔細辨認，就會覺察氣勢萬千的溪流

河汊錯綜

秦 牧

同樣一個劇本，因為演出地區不同，經過長期衍變的結果，常常在同樣故事骨幹的基礎上，出現許多十分懸殊的小節，比較這種差別，是一種發人深思的事。

「白蛇傳」故事，在全國各個劇種中，白娘娘的女侍小青，都是雌蛇變成的，唯獨在川劇中，卻是雄蛇變的。川劇的「白蛇傳」故事，講白蛇下山的時候，遭到一條青色的雄蛇的追逐，青蛇被擊敗後，就俯首貼耳，心悅誠服，化成小青，服侍著白娘娘，永無異心。

初看川劇「白蛇傳」的時候，覺得十分奇特。但細想一下，這又有什麼不好呢？這不也同樣表現了青蛇的義氣嗎？它又何損於整個神話故事的發展呢？

「秦香蓮」的故事，國內許許多多的劇種，描述的都是：秦香蓮被陳世美拋棄和逼害之後，死裏逃生，向包公投訴，包公鍘了陳世美，給她伸了冤。唯獨淮劇卻有另一番情節：秦香蓮被陳世美的刺客義釋以後，死裏逃生，遇到道行深厚的人物的搭救練得一身好武藝，終於女扮男裝，改姓換名在邊關立了戰功，逐漸升為統帥，後來自己回京的時候，親自違旨殺了陳世美，反出京師……這就是淮劇「女審」中的故事。

1 2 3 4 5 6 7 8 9 10 11 12 13

［邯鄲學步］

1. 發揮了創造性而形成的。「諸家」仍然是它的源流）。但是光會模仿的人，卻只知有「一家」，而不知道有和這「一家」密切關係的「諸家」。這就使得學習的範圍大大的狹隘了。四來，「取法於上，僅得其中；取法於中，僅得其下。」模仿總是不能達到十全十美的，所以顧炎武才說「效『楚辭』者必不如『楚辭』」。就是學到維妙維肖，也並不怎樣可貴（優秀的臨摹之作不就是這樣的作品麼）；何況，這一個境界也難以達到呢？……僅僅上面談的這些，就足見何以模仿之作一般在藝術水平上是這樣的低下，「邯鄲學步」一語，何以引起歷代優秀的藝術家們那樣多的警惕了。

2. 差不多藝術任何部門的大師，在他們的經驗談中都講到廣泛師承與獨特創造的可貴。齊白石有兩句話說得很有風趣：「學我者生，似我者死。」實際上表現的也正是這個道理。

3. 「取法於上，僅得其中。」那麼怎樣才能超越這個「上」呢？我想應該是「取法眾上」，取法上的結果，就可能超越某一個別的「上」。這正是何以一代代的學生，在整體來說，到頭來終於能夠超過一代代的老師的關鍵所在。怪不得那種釀取百花成蜜、「蜜成花不見」的蜜蜂，多少世代以來，受到思想家、藝術家們那麼多寓意深長的讚美了。

者必不如『楚辭』，效『七發』者必不如『七發』，蓋其意中先有一人在前，既恐失之，而其筆力復不能自逡。此壽陵？餘子學步邯鄲之說也。」（「日知錄」）可知，這個典故所包含的令人警惕的意義，歷代許多大師都是深爲讚許的。

我常常這樣想：拋棄自己的風格來模仿別人，既然在理論上和事實上都可以完全證明是一條「死胡同」，爲什麼歷代還是有許多人醉心於模仿呢？這大概是由於，初學者往往從「模仿」開始，少年的模仿，成人是不便加以責難的。但是一個人學習達到一定水平，或者說，到了應該長成的階段之後，如果不能推陳出新，不能發揚自己的風格，也就談不上什麼創造了。「模仿」比起「創造」來不知道要容易多少萬倍，唯其容易，所以貪圖方便的人就往往鑽進這條死胡同去了。

模仿之所以必然糟糕，我想有許許多多方面的原因存在。一來，藝術是反映生活的，生活變動不居，藝術表現形式也就應該不斷地隨着發展，一個僵硬了的殼（不管它昨天還是怎樣美好），是總不能和新鮮的內容完全適應的。二來，藝術應當給人強烈的新鮮感，離開了「個性」、「獨特風格」一類東西，這種新鮮味兒就要大大地打個折扣。三來，藝術學習應該注意廣泛的繼承，藝術家得像海洋那樣地善於容納「百川」，即使是着重學習「一家」吧，也應該涉獵「諸家」（因爲任何精彩的「一家」，都是在批判地繼承諸家的基礎上

「邯鄲學步」

秦　牧

每次乘坐京漢列車，經過河北古城邯鄲的時候，在月台上散步，想起這個兩千多年前趙國京都的往事陳迹，那些名將、策士、俠客、美人，尤其是「燕趙慷慨悲歌之士」的故事，就彷彿出現在眼前。同時，由於是在邯鄲的地面上走路的緣故，也禁不住常常想起「邯鄲學步」這個可笑的典故來。

傳說，古代的邯鄲人是很會走路的，大概是京都大邑之所在，人們很講究姿勢和風度，決不能容許任何鵝步和八字脚之類出現吧。總之，古代邯鄲人走路得美妙大有名氣。於是，有些人就特地到邯鄲來學樣了。一個燕國壽陵地方的少年人也趕來學習，他全力去模仿邯鄲人走路的樣子，沒有學會，自己原來走路的樣子卻又拋掉了，最後，簡直狠狠到只好爬回去。

這段掌故，因為對那些完全拋棄自己風格一味模仿的人諷刺得很有力量，頗為歷代文人所重視。自從莊子的著作中叙述了它以後，「邯鄲學步」或者「壽陵失步」這句成語，常常被許多人所引用。李白的一首「古風」中，就有這樣的句子：「醜女來效顰，還家驚四鄰。壽陵失初步，笑殺邯鄲人……。」顧炎武也說過這樣的話：「效『楚辭』

1
2
3
4
5
6
7
8
9
10
11
12
13

在廣大羣衆喜愛的菊花和金魚身上,也許就藏着這麼一些藝術的道理。

全包括一部分成年人，看來就不會感到那麼夠味了。一切藝術的道理也是這樣，單一必然導致枯燥。而豐富多采、目不暇接則是絕大多數人所歡迎的。一個人可以有自己藝術上的偏愛，但切忌「以宮笑角，以白詆青」（袁枚語）。你只愛「十丈珠簾」這麼一種菊花；你只愛「珍珠鱗」這麼一種金魚，自然悉聽尊便。但決不應該因為自己有這樣的偏愛，就把其他所有的菊花，所有的金魚都說得一文不值！正像一個人不能因為自己喜愛長篇小說，就去貶低其他的文學樣式；或者自己喜愛樸素的風格，就認為華麗的、纖巧的東西都沒有美的價值一樣。在政治方向上，永遠都需要一致性，在藝術風格上，任何時候都應該提倡多樣化，那種在藝術風格上，揚此抑彼甚至主張定於一尊的論調，是最妨碍「百花齊放」的。即使從觀賞菊花、觀賞金魚時所領略的情趣中，我們稍加思索也可以體會到這樣一點道理。

第三、從菊花和金魚的多姿多采，也使我想到「風格」是大胆發揚特點之後才能夠形成的。我們不妨說，菊花中「朱砂牡丹」、「芙蓉托桂」等等品種都各有自己獨特的風格，如果不是瓣內瓣外都那麼紅，「朱砂牡丹」就失掉它的風格了；如果不是有一個巨大的花心，「芙蓉托桂」也失掉它的特色了。「水泡眼金魚」如果失掉那兩個水泡，也就沒有獨特風格可言了。不敢大胆發揚特點，就談不上風格。不僅菊花和金魚這樣，一切藝術創造的道理，恐怕也都是這樣的吧。

，投以激賞的眼光的時候，我彷彿聽到了一個讚美的聲音：「多行呀！人類又給大自然增添新的花樣。」

我們不妨把菊花和金魚看做一種活的藝術品。在花盆、魚缸間徜徉，我不禁有這樣的感觸：

第一、「人工」是多麼可貴啊！人類的勞動眞是「功參造化」、「巧奪天工」，如果不是人為的選擇作用，菊花還不是一種野外平平常常、貌不驚人的小花？金魚還不是一種平平常常、只配被人作爲普通看饌的鯽魚？但是一經人們長期把勞動貫注到它們身上，奇迹就出現了。在藝術創造上，也讓我們讚美人爲的加工的作用，放棄那種原始的、自然崇拜的觀點吧！

第二、從菊花、金魚的品種繁多，人們仍然沒有感到滿足，還在不斷地創造新的品種這樣的事情上面，讓我們更深地體會多樣性的重要吧。那種飄逸灑脫、雅致大方的「嫦娥牡丹」、「十丈珠簾」之類的名菊固然是異常珍貴和令人喜愛的。但是「滿天星」、「萬壽菊」之類的普通菊花，也仍然不失爲菊花中的一些值得重視的品種。如果沒有各式各樣的菊花，而僅有幾盆名菊的話，「菊花之海」就不可能出現了，菊花展覽也不能吸引這樣廣大的羣衆了。金魚也是一樣，如果僅僅有「珍珠鱗」、「鶴頂紅」之類品種，而沒有「朝天眼」、「水泡眼」之類充滿了丑角情趣的金魚，也許小孩子們，甚

菊花與金魚

1. 那場面真可以說多姿多采，儀態萬千了！
2. 古代荒郊寒傖的野菊，一經過人類的加意選種培育，歷時數千年，終於大放異采。
3. 光說一樣花瓣，菊花就有平瓣、管瓣、匙瓣、管舌瓣等等，還有些瓣端有鉤或者捲成球形的。
4. 談到顏色，它們又有紅、紫、黃、白、以至於綠（綠荷）和墨（墨菊）等等之別；至於花型，樣式更是多到難以數說。有一種「標本菊」，一株只有一兩朵，而花型大如牡丹；有一種「大立菊」，一株可以開花千朵以上。它們有的端雅大方；有的龍飛鳳舞；有的瑰麗如彩虹；有的潔白賽霜雪；有的像火焰那麼熱烈；有的像羽毛那樣輕柔……。這難道只是一類花麼，它簡直令人想起羣芳競妍的江南的「花朝」！
5. 金魚也是這樣，它們像是活在水裏的能夠游動的花朵。什麼珍珠鱗、獅頭、鶴頂紅、扯蜓、水泡眼、朝天眼……品種多得令人吃驚。每一種都各有它的妙處，你說「珍珠鱗」才好看麼，但是有些人一看到水泡眼，才高興呢，那些眼睛上面長着兩個大水泡的金魚，簡直像是魚類中的丑角，有時竟使人們笑得直不起腰，甚至流出眼淚來。
6. 菊花和金魚的品種現在已經夠紛繁了，試想光是菊花，叫得出名字的就有兩千多個品種，這還不夠瞧麼？但是人們欣賞的興趣是無窮無盡的，羣眾仍在歡迎新的品種。而那些栽培菊花和養殖金魚的老行尊，不但要滿足羣眾的這樣心願，自己也充滿了勞動創造的豪情勝慨；結果，幾乎年年都有新的品種被創造出來。每當人們圍觀新出現的品種

菊花與金魚

秦牧

菊花與金魚，是中國人培育出來的兩種絕妙的東西。我想，把它們稱做藝術品也無不可，它們一種是植物性藝術品，一種是動物性藝術品，都是經過歷代巧匠的苦心培育才繁衍出現在這樣豐富的品種的。

世界各國的人民，都各有各的藝術天才。世界文明是各大洲的勞動人民共同創造的，你提供這樣，我提供那樣，才使得這個本來相當乏味的地球變成了個光華璀璨的大千世界。在培植奇花異卉和人工選擇有趣的小生物方面，世界各國的人民，有的馴養了金絲雀，有的培植了品種紛繁的蘭花，有的養了鴿子，有的養了長尾雞……而歷史悠久的中國，則特別端出了菊花和金魚。中國人種植菊花已經有三千年的歷史了；把鯽魚變成金魚，也已經有千年以上的歷史了。我國郵局曾經發行過一套菊花郵票和一套金魚郵票，這兩套小彩畫都是令人看了愛不釋手的。它使我們想起歷代許多藝菊和養魚的能手，無數「功參造化」的能工巧匠；以至於祖國悠久的歷史和深厚的文化。

每年秋天，許多城市的公園都在舉辦菊花展覽，至於金魚，更是不分季節，任何時候都可以看到。每次觀賞菊花和金魚展覽的時候，我都深深地體會到「豐富」的含義。

1 2 3 4 5 6 7 8 9 10 11 12 13

張獻忠不殺人辨

是普通人民（自然在刀兵之中，普通人民也難免有誤傷誤殺之事）。革命就是階級鬥爭的最高形式，絕不是吃素念佛的人所幹的事，而被革命者所希望的，也正是只有他們來屠殺革命者，反過來卻不許革命者動刀槍進行革命。當然，我講這些，並無提倡殺人，主張多殺人之意。我只是希望，對張獻忠其人其事，還以一個歷史本來面目。因此，就不必斤斤沾着在一個「殺」字上去理解，倒是趙太爺准不准阿Q革命的問題了。

1. 正是給張獻忠殺人的誑言增加了添油加醬的材料，也正中了地主，資產階級的「上懷」，樂於廣爲傳播的。

2. 關於張獻忠不殺人的說法，當然不如說張獻忠「殺人成性」的多，但也不是沒有的。

3. 劉獻廷「廣陽雜記」卷二載：「余聞張獻忠來衡州，不戮一人，以問婁聖功，則果然也。」這一記載究竟詳情如何，現在當然很難考查，也許出之於劉獻廷同情農民起義，

4. 故而出此；也許張獻忠大軍到達衡州之日，地主官吏早已望風逃盡，農民以及被壓迫被剝削者又歸附獻軍，因此無可殺之對象。

5. 但有些歷史學家根據這一記載，而在大做翻案文章，由此而證明張獻忠並不殺人，這也是違反歷史眞實的，我就很難同意這一結論。

6. 自然我也知道說張獻忠不殺人，是出於有些歷史學家的好心，是由於同情農民革命而發，特別是以「不殺一人」與地主，資產階級誣蔑張獻忠「屠殺」卅人盈野，恰恰的翻了一個個兒。

7. 看來像是十分鮮明強烈的對比；可是歷史不離乎現實，不離乎事理。當一個階級對另一個階級，進行民衆性的武裝革命之時，既已訴之於刀兵，就很難想像不會殺人；而況作爲革命對象的階級，又那裏會自動的滾下統治的寶座，而不去加以凶殘的鎮壓與撲滅革命力量呢？我看農民革命不發生則已，如果一發而不可遏止之時，即使革命者主觀上不欲多所誅殺，但爲了革命，爲了對付統治者的鎭壓，也勢難由己，所以問題不在於農民起義殺人不殺人，而在於殺的是什麽人？是敵對的統治者、壓迫者，還

張獻忠不殺人辨

孟　超

說張獻忠是殺星下界，所到之處，殺人如麻，這種說法顯然是出自封建地主階級對於農民革命領袖的詆誣毀謗，只是反動宣傳，毫無歷史真實價值；但另一方面，爲了同情張獻忠，爲了同情農民革命，一反其道而行之，偏說張獻忠不殺一人，或者根據一點一滴的筆記記載，就得出了張獻忠不曾殺人的結論，我看不但同樣是不合歷史實際，也是有害的論斷。

誇張的去描繪張獻忠殺人的「事實」，過去「官書」「半官書」以及所謂「私家史乘」眞也成篇累牘，難於勝計；他們也許因爲製造詆言，尙不足以解對農民起義的心頭之恨，又從而歸之於因果報應，甚至假以神話，迷惑世人。如所謂獻忠立「七殺碑」，碑上鐫「天生萬物以養人，人何以對天，……」然後接連着刻上七個大「殺」字。這一「碑文」，從文字上看，已難索解，也許是出於憤世嫉俗者流，指獻忠爲「代天行刑」，乃担當起殺人的使命；也許由於獻忠幼時，隨父販棗，誤將驢糞玷污地主石坊，不但其父被打，且迫其用手擦淨驢糞，而給他埋下深刻的階級仇恨的種子。從這一事實出發，從石坊引伸到石碑，因而製造出這一「傳說」。不管動因如何，但「七殺碑」之說，客觀的弊病，因而也就符合了客觀事物的規律，而不爲片面的主觀揣測、表面的一般現象所迷惑，因此他的估計才對了頭。別看調查、研究、觀察、判斷一個小小的白蟻的秘密，這中間卻存在了極深的學問，如果推而廣之，用之於對待其他事物，我看，也是同具此理的！

在這裏，並不是對那三位青年研究員有所苛求，更不是對一個專門研究白蟻問題的專家僅僅從這一點上加以讚許；但得失之間，正確與否，關鍵所系就不能不使我如獲智珠了！

1. 梯旁邊，又靠近廚房，常有音響和烟熏，因而蟻王、蟻后，早已離「宮」他去。
2. 這一段情節，真像一個有趣的故事。我們如果仔細地追究一番，同是對一個「蟻宮」秘密的探索，李始美和那三位青年研究員，竟而得出不同的判斷，作出不同的結論，等到證實之後，誰得誰失，得在哪裏，失在哪裏，這就很耐人尋味了。
3. 那三位青年研究員，你說他沒有進行觀察，我看也不能那樣說，他們也是對「蟻宮」作了調查研究，但都是不符合實際。問題在哪裏呢？我看就在於他們僅僅局限在從這個蟻巢的表面形狀去測斷內在的實質，孤立地從這一蟻巢的一般現象去判斷內在情況；或者更可以說離開周圍環境、具體條件去認識物象，因而不能不帶有某種的片面性。
4. 同時他們也正由於研究蟻巢已經有了一定的認識經驗，於是也就忘掉其他的客觀條件，根據已往的認識，跳脫不出固有的看法，因此也無法放開眼光，看得準確。當然對於白蟻——特別蟻王、蟻后的習性的認識，也還研究得不夠到家，因此就無法知道樓梯之下，人類腳步的驚擾，足以使它們難以安然靜處；廚房之內，烟熏火炙，對它們生活要求也是不適合的。天下的事物，絕不會簡單得都是從一個樣子裏鑄造出來的，它是會隨着不同的條件而產生不同的內在的變化的，你能簡單化地認識一切問題，解決一切問題嗎？
5. 李始美則剛剛相反，他不但研究有素，更重要的是他的調查方法、研究方法、觀察方法、判斷方法，這一整套的認識方法和思想方法，是以客觀為依據，絕沒有以主觀代替

白蟻宮的秘密

孟超

最近許多報紙都登載了「李始美帶領青年研究人員，深入探索白蟻世界的秘密」的消息，很能引起人的興趣。別看這段消息雖微雖小，亦足供我們見微而知著，因小而喻大，作為一把開動思想方法的鎖匙，啓示出認識複雜事理，解決縈繁問題的某些規律。

我看小事小節，也有絕大的意義的。

在這裏，我不想去描述白蟻之為害，因為只要知道白蟻的人，誰都知道它是能蠹蝕木材，甚至大樹、屋宇、船舶、橋樑都能從內部蛀嚙侵害，以至於朽枯，點點微物，害人極大。我也不想再重複地去讚許李始美作為一個農民科學家的種種事迹，因為過去報紙上都已作了詳細介紹了。在這裏只想以李始美探索白蟻宮的奧秘，而着重談談他所給我的思想啓示。

且說李始美帶領三個青年研究人員，到湛江市防治白蟻，在一座房屋內發現一個蟻巢，青年人根據蟻巢外形特徵，判斷是白蟻的主巢，而李始美卻搖了搖頭，認為可能是副巢。經過解剖，果然發現裏邊有一個白蟻的「皇宮」，卻找不到指揮一切的蟻王，和專司繁殖的蟻后，只有一些工蟻和兵蟻。原來這個蟻巢過去確是主巢，但由於它築在樓

從點戲說起

1. 又可愛了，她敢於在皇帝的寵妃面前「執意不作」「非本角之戲」，而「定要」演自己
2. 對工的戲，這種有主見而又敢於堅持的風格，是難能可貴的。
3. 賈元春點戲只是「紅樓夢」中的一個小小的插曲，但是我覺得這插曲很值得我們深思。

熙。元春認為齡官的戲演得好，加點兩齣，不拘那兩齣就是了」。賈薔看來並不內行，而且也還有點主觀主義，所以就「命」齡官作「遊園」、「驚夢」，而齡官卻頗有一點藝術家脾氣（當然，也可以解釋作是對賈薔的拿腔作勢），堅持不演「非本角之戲」，賈薔「扭她不過」，也許還有別的原因，但是他並不一朝權在手，便把令來行，總比韓復榘的副官通情達理得多了，齡官很有主見地演了自己的對工戲，而賈妃則不僅「甚喜」，而且還給了「不可難為了這女孩子，好生教習」的鼓勵。

點戲者，戲提調和演戲者之間的矛盾，看來是很難避免的，問題只在於如何妥善地處理。處理得好，看戲的滿意，演戲的高興，戲提調也可以順利完成任務，上下兩不得罪，處理得不好，那麼正如韓復榘的老太爺點「秦瓊打關公」一樣，不僅演戲者受罪，戲提調為難，而點戲者呢，也適足以暴露他的狹窄，專橫無知而已。曹雪芹筆下的元春的性格是可愛的。她欣賞齡官的藝術，加點了兩齣戲，但是她並不下死命令，只是說「不拘那兩齣就是了」，這中間就不僅有鼓勵，而且還有了愛護和尊重的意思，從這裏可以看出，這個點戲的人是有氣度而又有教養的。賈薔為了賣好，也許為了表現自己的戲提調有功，也許是為了要讓齡官露一手，可是這一下就表現了他的主觀和不了解演員的特長和性格，至於齡官，那就刻劃得

1 2 3 4 5 6 7 8 9 10 11 12 13 14 15 16

從點戲說起

夏衍

從廣播裏聽了相聲「秦瓊打關公」的故事，忽然想起另一件事來。這件事出在「紅樓夢」第十八回，同樣是點戲，卻表現出點戲者與被點者之間的不同的態度，也許可以說是不同的風格。

……賈薔急將錦冊呈上，並十二個花名單子。少時太監出來。只點了四齣戲。[1]

剛演完了，太監執一金盤糕點之屬進來，問誰是齡官？賈薔便知是賜齡官之物，喜得忙接了，命齡官叩頭。太監又道，貴妃有諭，齡官極好，再作兩齣戲，不拘那兩齣就是了。賈薔忙答應了，因命齡官作「遊園」、「驚夢」二齣，齡官自為此二齣原於非本角之戲，執意不作，定要作「相約」、「相罵」二齣，賈薔扭她不過，只好依她作了。賈妃甚喜，命不可難為了這女孩子，好生教習，額外賞了……金銀錁子食品之類。[2]

在這裏，點戲者賈元春，是皇帝的寵妃，地位當然要比韓復榘的老太爺高得多了，賈薔是戲提調之類，但他也算是賈門子弟，而齡官，卻只不過是從蘇州「採買」了來的小女伶，論身份，是連人身自由也沒有的奴隸，可是，這三個人在這裏都表現得很有特

「耐」與「愛」之志同論

1. 是同志與同志間的「耐」——說服，教育，理解——只有這才是一條最可寶貴的韌帶！

2. 我就是缺乏這樣東西的，但我一定要獲得它。

3. 也是前面那本書後面有一段，安娜喝了酒和司令陳柱吵着要回上海，陳柱不允許，安娜就撒了嬌，「沒有端緒的她响着門扇走了。」這時陳柱也沒擺出「上級」的架子來，要「處分」她，「陳柱他了解為甚麼，安娜今夜會這樣完全失卻理性的狂言！他看着這個初次被愛情所咬傷的孩子，自己感到一種輕微的悲傷！他準備着該怎樣使她更切實的接近『鬥爭』。」——這是一種「耐」罷。「愛」和「耐」是分不開的，只有真正的愛，才有真正的耐，反過來說也應該如此。——且不管你愛的是甚麼。——題外寫幾句：

4. 以堅定的心，堅決的言語和革命結了契約的——應該尊敬。

5. 為革命，從血和鐵裏滾爬出來，賺得遍體瘡疤，仍然不倦地戰鬥着——這是最應該尊重的。此外也還有這樣的，在血和鐵底試煉中，偶爾軟弱了，做下了一點使革命的尊嚴受到損失的人，而後仍然回到革命隊伍來戰鬥，不管別人對這樣的人如何看法，我是尊敬他們，比對那從來就沒見過血和鐵，在「保險箱」裏逞英雄的英雄們，似乎更尊敬些——他們終究是「試煉」過了。

6. 「浪子回家」不是很可貴的麼，何況他們也還並不是浪子。

1. 」正存在着很多（而且是現代化了的），你稍一馬虎，他們就要以細菌和「閃擊戰」的方式向你反攻過來。——危乎哉！

2. 我願意在這裏向一些被冤枉或被誤解的青年同志問一聲：你們之中，可有受過七十二難或者「撒旦」試煉的麼？革命是艱苦的，更是作爲一個履行組織決定的革命黨員，如果不懷抱着「登淨土的希望」，入地獄的精神」，這一生也要不安和痛苦下去的，一個革命者的任務，就是要隨時隨地和醜惡與不義來戰鬥，爲後來者開路。只要有一分退敗的想頭，「撒旦」就要攢進你的心了。

3. 另一面我也願意向那些，從自己的瞳孔裏引伸出兩條綫來，交會在自己鼻子前面，就在那交會點上永久蹲着「地位」和「權威」，自己就一直看着這類東西的人說一聲：「地位」和「權威」，全不是壞東西，人也應該獲得它，但那要由正路，不要像個沒品行的賽跑員，穿上釘鞋子，從你底後來者或者同伴們的鼻子踏過去呀！何況這樣也並不能保證就弄個第一？人不是也常常講說着尊敬敵人麼？只要算爲一個同志的，無論他怎樣不如人，難道比你的敵人還可惡，還不值得一尊敬麼？

這裏我提到的「耐」字，是有兩方面解釋的。一面是說我們既然要幹一番事情——不必說改造人類——第一個字需要的那就是能「耐」，而後才能說到其他。另一面那就

「耐」

年來，和一些革命的同志接觸得更多一些，我卻感到這「同志之愛」的酒也越來越稀薄了！雖然我明白這原因，但這卻阻止不了我心情的悲愴。

近來竟常常接到一些不相識的同志們底信，信裏面大致是述說自己的痛苦和牢騷，不滿意環境，不滿意人，不滿意工作⋯⋯甚至對革命也感到倦怠了⋯⋯。沒有條件，我對這些向我申訴的人——大部是比我小幾歲的青年男女——我是寄以眞情的同情和尊重的。因爲他們敢於信賴了我，我也不願在這裏擺出指導者的架子——還沒有這條件和資格——賣狗皮膏藥，說一些連自己也不能辦到的理論，這是可恥的。但卻樂意說一些自己的意見，算作一點鹽，給與一些對於我這人敢於信賴過「西遊記」的，那師徒四衆不是經過七十二難，出生入死，終於把「經」取回來了麼？還有法國小說家福樓拜爾也寫過一本小說「聖安東的誘惑」，那是說一個聖者怎樣和各種「撒旦」來戰鬥。我們革命當然不是取「經」，更不是尋上帝，但這種「宗教的情操」無論幹什麼事都一定要具備，否則就不行。

宗教裏「撒旦」在試煉人。「聖經」裏有「九妖十八洞」在搗亂。

革命的過程中——隊伍內，隊伍外，自己的心裏——那大大小小各式各樣的「撒旦

「耐」與「愛」之志同論

另外一段：那是蕭明和安娜戀愛了，引起隊員們不滿，司令陳柱為了顧慮整個影响，就決定讓安娜和蕭明暫時分開。這時候蕭明是被大家看不起的了，每個人全要向他「冷嘲」一下，只有「鐵鷹」隊長還是照常。當安娜隨着本隊出發，蕭明目送着每個人走出去的時候，曾有如下一段這樣的描寫：

鐵鷹隊長，手槍又開始在他的腰間出現了。他懇切的捉住蕭明的手沉重的說：

「蕭同志！一切要當心！鬥爭的時候，把鬥爭以外的事情，全忘掉了吧！這裏不久會有敵人來的。」

他戀戀地撒開蕭明的手，站着，似乎等待蕭明的說話。但蕭明只是說了一句：

「鐵同志！我敬重你，一直到我死的時候！」

因為我不願看，也不願讓讀者們看，同志的子彈打進同志的胸膛；但也不願革命的紀律因此而墮落了。所以就借日本兵的子彈結束了這個給革命隊伍招來損害和誤解，老疙瘩──前一段我是那樣地寫了的。後一段，這是說明了當一個人正被圍攻和誤解，能有一個人──而且是鐵鷹隊長那樣出身的人──給與你一種真誠的溫暖，你將怎樣呢？「鐵同志！我敬重你，一直到我死的時候！」這又是怎樣和着一種悲痛的血而迸出來的人底聲音啊！……

1
2
3
4
5
6
7
8
9
10
11
12
13
14
15

論同志之「愛」與「耐」

蕭 軍

「愛」

1　還記得當我寫「八月的鄉村」其中一段：一個革命隊員——唐老疙瘩——因為自己

2　的情婦被日本兵污辱了，他在樹林裏遇到她，要帶她一同走。她被傷害得很厲害，又不

3　能走。日本兵馬上就要追來，同志們為了避免整個隊伍底損害，勸他走，他的情人——

4　李七嫂——也勸他走，可是他卻耍起脾氣來，把槍也扔在地上，不幹「革命」了，要與

5　他的情人共存亡，若不，就讓他的隊長槍斃他，連他的情人一道。這個隊長外號「鐵鷹

6　」，「紅鬍子」出身，是以殺人不眨眼著名的。這時候為了敵人馬上就到，為了革命的

7　紀律，他雖然躊躇了一番，可是終於提起了手槍……。——寫到這裏那時是寫不下去了

8　，我不知道應該怎樣處理這場面。我看着海——那時在青島——看着山……從家裏走到

9　街上，又從街上走回來，而不是自己的同志。我記得自己那時的心情是很難受的。這已經是七八年

10　彈打死了他，足足思索了近乎兩夜兩天，直到後來，我才決定讓日本的流

11　前的事了，如今記憶起來還是有些不愉快。

12

的特性的虛偽，被襲人運用得極其徹底了。這徹底虛偽的結果，不但使得史太君主夫人極端信任她。而且使得賈寶玉，雖然痛惡她，卻又不能不歡喜她。（歡喜不等愛）而且不能不無可奈何地依從她。結果，是奴才服了主子，而又制服了主子。襲人的虛偽之徹底，又表現在平時雖然對主子十分眞誠，但一旦「樹倒猢猻散」的時候到來，她的行為，卻使人發生「堪嘆優伶有福，可憐公子無緣！」的感嘆。所以，眞正奴才氣的奴才，他的一點點愛人民固然是虛偽的，他對主子百般順從，同樣也是虛偽的。他的眞誠只是對他自己和自己的利益。

一九五七年北京

領導者，為什麼呢？據說也還是由於地位。

第三是「根據」。我看作為一個領導者，其言論的實際資料，那是沒有用的。對於這些文件，他也有他的處理法，反右時一定要左得徹底，反左時一定要右到極端。他再次「隨」的文件中的一面，但是，據說這就是黨性強，是對上級領導意圖的貫徹。還有次一個秘密，高級幹部常有「秘本」和「秘聞」的。這種領導者，在羣眾的威信確實是很高的。因為他常常能夠根據「秘本」和「秘聞」，說出一些羣眾在報紙上看不到的話，使羣眾相信他的葫蘆裏真有靈丹妙藥。

第四再談「根據」。我聽說有一位領導者，千方百計，捕風捉影，發動羣眾統一認識，嚴迫另一個人承認極大的罪名，這種事在每次肅反運動中常見的。當那人問這個罪名的定義的時候。他說：說到定義，可是經典著作裏也沒有根據呀！經典著作裏面沒有根據，那末，可以不成立了罷？但是，偏偏一定要成立，這是創造性。貓吃老鼠是不類相殘了，似乎得講一點理由，例如：「你反對我的領導，假若一隻貓要吃另一隻貓，這是同講任何理由，羣眾要我吃你」之類，說來說去，一定要吃！但到底卻只有一個根據，就是「一定要吃」。

第五是論「襲人的本質」。我這才知道，花襲人原來是個奴才，作為奴才的最本質

蟬噪居漫筆

蕭軍

由于到處的氣候關係，我已有好幾年不作聲了。眞是「噤若寒蟬」。今年到了北京，卻寫了一些雜文，在百家爭鳴的空間，散播了擾人午夢的噪音，明知擾人午夢是不識趣的。但爲氣候所感，欲罷而不能。而且螳螂沒有來追捕我，所以還是要叫下去。

第一關於「學習」。我常常聽說：許多高級幹部，甚至於自己辦學校，領導別人學習，日在叫忙。有些高級幹部，畢竟是馬克斯主義者，所以他「才略」是非凡的。我又看到有些不讀書的人，卻極善於領導別人讀書，而且極善於批評讀書的人從讀書得來的言論，他還作結論，據說，他的依據就是地位也。

第二是「思和隨」。我覺得現在有這樣一種人，自然也是馬克斯主義者，而且是領導者，他們行爲特點，可以這樣假定來形容：在文藝創作問題上，有一年他是主張「無衝突論」的。過了一年多，蘇聯反對「無衝突論」了，他也大張旗鼓的反對「無衝突」來反對暴露陰面了。但最近，他是毒草也可以大放的堅決主張者，他自己「隨」者，把「無衝突論」者，批評得體無完膚，又過了一個時期，他又來反對暴露陰面了。但最近，他是毒草也可以大放的堅決主張者，他自己「隨」之是無關緊要的。但他是領導者，於是被領導者，可眞是慢慢的毀了，他雖然「隨」，他永遠不會毀，永遠是英明的獨立的精神，藝術才能對社會改革的事業起推進的作用。尊重作家先要了解他的作品。作家在他作為作家的時候，不希望在他作品以外的什麼尊重。適如其份地去批評他，不恰當的讚美等於諷刺，對他稍有損抑的評價則更是一種侮辱。

讓我們從最高的情操上學習古代人愛作家的精神吧——

「**生不用封萬戶候，但願一識韓荊州。**」

一九四二年三月十一日延安「解放日報」

家作重尊，家作解了

1. 可以支持一個民族的自尊心理，從而換到了不止一個的印度。
2. 我常常聽人說：「某些人看了某篇作品不高興了。」我的心就非常高興。因為，由此我們可以知道那些作品的確起了作用了。
3. 作家並不是百靈鳥，也不是專門唱歌娛樂人的歌妓。他們竭盡心血的作品，是通過他的心的搏動而完成的。他不能欺騙他的情感去寫一篇東西，他只知道根據自己的世界觀去看事物，去描寫事物，去批評事物。在他創作的時候，就只求忠實於他的情感，因為不這樣，他的作品就成了虛偽的，沒有了生命的。
4. 希望作家能把癬疥寫成花朵，把膿包寫成蓓蕾的人，是最沒有出息的人——因為他連看自己醜陋的勇氣都沒有，更何況要他改呢？
5. 愈是身上髒的人，愈喜歡人家給他搔癢。而作家卻並不是喜歡給人搔癢的人。
6. 等人搔癢還是洗一個澡吧。有盲腸炎的就用刀割吧。有瘊眼的就用硫酸銅刮吧。鼻子被梅毒菌吃生了要開刀的病而怕開刀是不行的，患傷寒症而又貪吃是不行的。
7. 假如醫生的工作是保衛人類精神的健康——而後者的作用則更普遍，持久，深刻。
8. 作家除了自由寫作之外，不要求其他的特權。他們用生命去擁護民主政治的理由之一，就因為民主政治能保障他們的藝術創作的獨立的精神。因為只有給藝術創作以自由

家作重尊，家作解了

但是人類還會思索，還有感覺，還知道恥辱和光榮，還能嫉妒和同情，還懂得愛和恨，還常常心裏感到空漠因而悲哀，還要在最孤獨的時候很深沉地發問：「活着究竟爲什麼？」

這些事，都並不是凳子、牀、燈、臉盆、飯、衣服、藥、六〇六這些東西完全可以解決的。因爲這些事，同樣會發生在沒有物質憂慮的人們之間。就連最原始的人類，也有他們的心理活動；就連最不開化的民族，也有他們自己的詩歌。

當法國資產階級大詩人伐萊里的「水仙辭」出版的時候，一個同階級的批評家曾以這樣的話頌揚他的作品：「近年來我國發生了一件比歐戰更重大的事件，即伐萊里出版了他的『水仙辭』。」

這原因就在於「水仙辭」爲爛熟了的法國資產階級——也可以說全世界的資產階級——提出了許多使內心顫慄不安的問題，他的詩，通過他自己深沉的審視，從哲學上引起了對生命具體懷疑的問題。

好像有一個英國人曾說：「寧可失去一個印度，卻不願失去一個莎士比亞。」

這原因就在於莎士比亞是英國商業資本主義抬頭時代的代言人，是英帝國主義向世界擴展其勢力的鼓吹者，是大英帝國直到現在還用以驕傲於世界的偉大詩人。他的作品

16　15　14　13　12　11　10　9　8　7　6　5　4　3　2　1

了解作家，尊重作家

艾青

1. 作家是一個民族或一個階級的感覺器官，思想神經，或是智慧的瞳孔。作家是從精神上——即情感，感覺，思想，心理活動上——守衞他所屬的民族或階級的忠實的兵士。

2. 作家的工作就是把自己的或他所選擇的人物的感覺，情感，思想，凝結成形象的語言，通過這語言，去團結和組織他的民族或階級的全體。

3. 一首詩，一篇小說，或一個劇本，它們的目的，或是使自己的民族或階級給自己的省察，或是提高民族或階級的自尊，或是從心理上增加戰勝敵人的力量。

4. 有人問：「文藝有什麼用處呢？」

5. 文藝的確是沒有什麼看得見的用處的。它不能當板凳坐，當牀睡，當燈點，當臉盆洗臉……它也不能當飯吃，當衣服穿，當藥醫病，當六〇六治梅毒。

6. 所以反功利主義的唯美論者戈諦耶會滿懷憤慨地說：「……我們不能從物喻得到一只帽子，或者像穿拖鞋般穿比喻；我們不能把對偶法當雨傘用，我們不能，不幸，把音韻當背心穿。」

三八節有感

在大會中說來,或許有人認為痛快。然而卻寫在一個女人的筆底下,是很可以取消的,但既然寫了就仍舊給那些有同感的人看看吧。

一九四二年三月九日

延安「解放日報」

三八節有感

1. 能擔受一切磨難，才有前途，才有享受。這種愉快不是生活的滿足，而是生活的戰鬥和進取。所以必須每天都作點有意義的工作，都能有東西給別人，游惰只使人感到生命的空白，疲軟，枯萎。

2. **第三、用腦子** 最好養成一種習慣。改正不作思索、隨波逐流的毛病。每說一句話，每作一件事，最好想想這話是否正確，這事是否處理的得當，不違背自己作人的原則，是否自己可以負責。只有這樣才不會有後悔。這就是叫通過理性，這，才不會上當，被一切甜蜜所蒙蔽，被小利所誘，才不會浪費熱情，浪費生命，而免除煩惱。

3. **第四、下吃苦的決心堅持到底** 生為現代的有覺悟的女人，就要有認定犧牲一切薔薇色的溫柔的夢幻。幸福是暴風雨的搏鬥，而不是在月下彈琴，花前吟詩。假如沒有最大的決心，一定會在中途停歇下來。不悲苦，即墮落。而這種支持下去的力量卻必須在「有恆」中來養成。沒有大的抱負的人是難於有這種不貪便宜，不圖舒服的堅忍的。而這種抱負只有真正為人類，而非為己的人才會有。

三八節清晨

附及：文章已經寫完了，自己再重看一次，覺得關於企望的地方，還有很多意見，但為發稿時間所限，也不能整理了。不過又有這樣的感覺，覺得有些話假如是一個首長幣的壓迫，她們每人都有一部血淚史，都有過崇高的感情（不管是升起的或沉落的，不管有幸與不幸，不管仍在孤苦奮鬥或捲入庸俗），這在對於來到延安的女同志說來更不冤枉，所以我是拿着很大的寬容來看一切被淪為女犯的人的。而且我更希望男子們尤其是有地位的男子，和女人本身都把這些女人的過錯看得與社會有聯繫些。少發空議論，多談實際的問題，使理論與實際不脫節，在每個共產黨員的修身上都對自己負責些就好了。

然而我們也不能不對女同志們，尤其是在延安的女同志有些小小的企望。而且勉勵着自己，勉勵着友好。

世界上從沒有無能的人，有資格去獲取一切的。所以女人要取得平等，得首先強己。我不必說大家都懂的。而且，一定在今天會有人演說的：「首先取得我們的政權」的大話，我只說作為一個陣線中的一員（無產階級也好，抗戰也好，婦女也好），每天所必須注意的事項。

第一、**不要讓自己生病** 無節制的生活，有時會覺得浪漫，有詩意，可愛，然而對今天環境不適宜。沒有一個人能比你自己還會愛你的生命些。沒有什麼東西比今天失去健康更不幸些。只有它同你最親近，好好注意它，愛護它。

第二、**使自己愉快** 只有愉快裏面才有青春，才有活力，才覺得生命飽滿，才覺得們在沒有結婚前都抱着有凌雲的志向，和克苦的鬥爭生活，她們在生理的要求和「彼此幫助」的蜜語之下結婚了。於是她們被迫着做了操勞的回到家庭的娜拉，「落後」的危險，他們四方奔走，厚顏的要求托兒所收留她們的孩子，要求刮子宮，寧肯受一切處分而不得不冒着生命的危險悄悄的去吃着墜胎的藥。而她們聽着這樣的回答：「帶孩子不是工作嗎？你們只貪圖舒服，好高鶩遠，你們到底作過一些什麼了不起的政治工作？既然這樣怕生孩子，生了又不肯負責，誰叫你們結婚呢？」於是她們不能免除「落後」的命運。一個有了能力工作的女人，而還能犧牲自己的事業去作為一個賢妻良母的時候，未始不被人所歌頌，但在十多年之後，她必然也逃不出「落後」的悲劇。即使在今天以我一個女人去看，這些「落後」份子，也實在不是一個可愛的女人。她們的皮膚在開始有摺皺，頭髮在稀少，生活的疲憊奪取她們最後的一點愛嬌。她們處於這樣的悲運，似乎是很自然的，但在舊的社會裏，她們或許會被稱為可憐、薄命，然而在今天，卻是自作孽、活該。不是聽說法律上還在爭論着離婚只須一方提出，或者必須雙方同意的問題麼？離婚大約多半都是男子提出的，假如是女人，那一定更有不道德的事，那完全該女人受詛咒。

我自己是女人，我會比別人更懂得女人的缺點，但我卻更懂得女人的痛苦。她們不會是超時代的，不會是理想的，她們不是鐵打的。她們抵抗不了社會一切的誘惑，和無

"要不是我們土包子,你想來延安吃小米!"但女人總是要結婚的。(不結婚更有罪惡,她將更多的被作為製造謠言的對象,永遠被污衊。)不是騎馬的就是穿草鞋的,不是藝術家就是總務科長。她們都得生小孩。小孩也有各自的命運:有的被細羊毛線和花絨布包着,抱在保姆的懷裏,有的被沒有洗淨的布片包着,扔在坑頭啼哭,而媽媽和爸爸都在大嚼着孩子的津貼(每月二十五元,價值二斤半豬肉),要是沒有這筆津貼,也許他們根本就嘗不到肉味。然而女同志究竟應該嫁誰呢?事實是這樣,被迫着帶孩子的一定可以得到公開的譏諷:「回到家庭裏的娜拉」。而有着保姆的女同志,每一個星期可以有一天最衛生的交際舞。雖說在背地裏也會有難聽的誹語悄聲的傳播着,然而只要她走到那裏,那裏就會熱鬧,不管騎馬的,穿草鞋的,總務科長,藝術家們的眼睛都會望着她。這同一切的理論都無關,同一切主義思想也無關,同一切開會演說也無關。然而這都是人人知道,人人不說,而且在做着的現實。

離婚的問題也是一樣。大抵在結婚的時候,有三個條件是必須注意到的。一、政治上純潔不純潔,二、年齡相貌差不多,三、彼此有無幫助。而所謂幫助也可以說到鞋襪的縫補,甚至女性的安慰其備(公開的漢奸這裏是沒有的。),但卻一定堂皇的考慮到。而離婚的口實,一定是女同志的落後。我是最以為一個女人自己不進步而還要拖着他的丈夫為可恥的,可是讓我們一看她們是如何落後的。她

三八節有感

丁玲

「婦女」這兩個字，將在什麼時代才不被重視，不需要特別的被提出呢？年年都有這一天。每年在這一天的時候，幾乎是全世界的地方都開着會，檢閱着她們的隊伍。延安雖說今年不如前兩年熱鬧，但似乎總有幾個人在那裏忙着。而且一定有大會，有演說的，有通電，有文章發表。

延安的婦女是比中國其他地方的婦女幸福的。甚至有很多人都在嫉羨的說：「為什麼小米把女同志吃得那麼紅胖？」女同志在醫院，在休養所，在門診部都佔着很大的比例，卻似乎並沒有使人驚奇，然而延安的女同志卻仍不能免除那種幸運；不管在什麼場合都最能作為有興趣的問題被談起。而且各種各樣的女同志都可以得到她應得的誹議。這些責難似乎都是嚴重而確當的。

女同志的結婚永遠使人注意，而不會使人滿意的。她們不能同一個男同志比較接近，更不能同幾個都接近。她們被畫家們諷刺：「一個科長也嫁了麼？」詩人們也說：「延安只有騎馬的首長，沒有藝術家的首長，藝術家在延安是找不到漂亮的情人的。」然而她們也在某種場合聆聽着這樣的訓詞：「他媽的，瞧不起我們老幹部，說是土包子，似乎都還談不到「取值」和「享受」；相反，負責任更大的人，倒更應該表現與下層同甘苦（這倒是真正應該發揚的民族美德）的精神，使下層對他有衷心的愛，這才能產生真正的鐵一般的團結。當然，對于那些健康上需要特殊優待的重要負責者，予以特殊的優待是合理而且是必要的。一般負較重要責任者，也可略予優待。關于二，三三制政府的薪給制，也不應有太大的等差；對非黨人員可稍優待，黨員還是應該保持艱苦奮鬥的優良傳統，以感動更多的黨外人士來與我們合作。關于三，恕我冒昧，我請這種「言必稱希臘」的「大師」閉嘴。

我並非平均主義者，但衣分三色，食分五等，卻實在不見得必要與合理——尤其是在衣服問題上（筆者自己是所謂「幹部小廚房」階層，葡萄並不酸）一切應該依合理與必要的原則來解決。如果一方面害病的同志喝不到一口麵湯，青年學生一天只得到兩餐稀粥（在問到是否吃得飽的時候，黨員還得起模範作用回答：吃得飽！），另一方面有些頗為健康的「大人物」，作非常不必要不合理的「享受」，以致下對上感覺他們是異類，對他們不惟沒有愛，而且——這是叫人想來不能不有些「不安」的。

老是講「愛」，講「溫暖」，也許是「小資產階級感情作用」吧？聽候批判。

一九四二年三月十七日、二十三日延安「解放日報」

「首長」批評打擊，致陷于半狂狀態。我希望這是傳聞失實。但連稚弱的小鬼都確鑿什有瘋狂的，則大人之瘋狂，恐怕也不是不會有的事。雖然我也自覺神經不象有些人那麼「健康」，但自信還有足夠的生命，在任何情形下都不至陷于瘋狂，所以，敢繼某同志之後，也來談平均主義與等級制度。

共產主義不是平均主義（而且我們今天也不是在進行共產主義革命），這不需要我來做八股，因為，我敢保證，沒有半個伙伕（我不敢寫「炊事員」，因為我覺得這有些諷刺意味；但與他們談話時，我底理性和良心卻叫我永遠以最溫和的語調稱呼他們「炊事員同志」——多麼可憐的一點溫暖呵！）會妄想與「首長」過同樣的生活。談到等級制度，問題就稍微麻煩一點。

一種人說：我們延安並沒有等級制度；這不合事實，因為它實際存在着。另一種人說：是的，我們有等級制度，但它是合理的。這就需要大家用腦子想一想。

說等級制度是合理的人，大約有以下幾種道理：（一）根據「各盡所能，各取所值」的原則，負責任更大的人應該多享受一點；（二）三三制政府不久就要實行薪給制，待遇自然有等差；（三）蘇聯也有等級制。

這些理由，我認為有商量餘地。關於一，我們今天還在艱難困苦的革命過程中，大家都是拖着困憊的軀體支撐着煎熬，許許多多人都失去了最可寶貴的健康，因此無論誰，其實，不僅睡覺而已。在「必然性」底口號之下，「大師」們對自己也就很寬容了。他們在睡夢中對自己溫情地說：同志，你也是從舊社會裏出來的呀，你靈魂中有一點小小黑暗，那是必然的事，別臉紅吧。

于是，我們在那兒間接助長黑暗，甚至直接製造黑暗。

在「必然性」底「理論」之後，有一種民族形式的「理論」叫做「天塌不下來」。是的，天是不會塌下來的。可是，我們底工作和事業，是否因為「天塌不下來」就不受損失呢？這一層，「大師」們的腦子絕少想到甚至從未想到。如果讓這「必然性」「必然」地發展下去，則天——革命事業的天——是「必然」要塌下來的。別那麼安心吧。

與此相關的還有一種叫做「小事情」的「理論」。你批評他，他說你不應該注意「小事情」。有的「大師」甚至說，「媽的個×，女同志好注意小事情，現在男同志也好注意小事情！」是呀，在延安，大概不會出甚麼叛黨叛國的大事情的，但每個人做人行事的小事情，卻有的在那兒幫助光明，有的在那兒幫助黑暗。而「大人物」生活中的「小事情」，更足以在人們心裏或是喚起溫暖，或是引起寂寞。

四、平均主義與等級制度

聽說，曾有某同志用與這同樣的題目，在他本機關底牆報上寫文章，結果被該機關養。或許因爲沒有糖果吃就發起「牢騷」來。至於「醜惡和冷淡」對於他們也並不是「陌生」；正因爲認識了「醜惡和冷淡」，他們才到延安來追求「美麗和溫暖」，他們才看到延安的「醜惡和冷淡」而「忍不住」要發「牢騷」，以期引起大家注意，把這「醜惡和冷淡」減至最小限度。

一九三八年冬天，我們黨曾大規模的檢查工作，當時黨中央號召同志們要「議論紛紛」，「意見不管正確不正確都盡管提」，我希望這樣的大檢查再來一次，聽聽一般下層青年底「牢騷」。這對我們底工作一定有很大的好處。

三、「必然性」、「天塌不下來」與「小事情」

「我們底陣營存在于黑暗的舊社會，因此其中也有黑暗，這是必然性。」對呀，這是「馬克思主義」。然而，這只是半截馬克思主義，還有更重要的後半截，卻被「主觀主義宗派主義的大師」們忘記了。這後半截應該是：在認識這必然性以後，我們就必要以戰鬥的布爾塞維克能動性，去防止黑暗底產生，削減黑暗底滋長，最大限度地發揮意識對存在的反作用。要想在今天，把我們陣營裏一切黑暗消滅淨盡，這是不可能的；但把黑暗削減至最小限度，卻不但可能，而且必要。可是「大師」們不惟不曾強調這一點，而且很少提到這一點。他們只指出「必然性」就睡覺去了。

到的骯髒，他們先看到；別人不願說不敢說的話，他們大胆地說。因此，他們意見多一些，但不見得就是「牢騷」；他們的話或許說得不夠四平八穩，但也不見得就是「叫嚷」。我們應該從這些所謂「牢騷」「叫嚷」和「不安」的現象裏，去探求那產生這些現象的問題底本質，合理地（注意：合理地！青年不見得總是「盲目的叫嚷」。）消除這些現象的根源。說延安比「外面」好得多，教導青年不發「牢騷」，說延安的黑暗方面只是「些微拂意的事」，「算不得甚麼」，這絲毫不能解決問題。是的，延安比「外面」好得多，但延安可能而且必須更好一點。

當然，青年常表現不冷靜，不沉着。這似乎是「碰壁」作者底主題。但青年如果眞個個都是「少年老成」起來，那世界該有多麼寂寞呀！其實，延安青年已經夠老成了，前文所引那兩位女同志底「牢騷」，便是在昏黑中用低沉的聲音發出的。我們不但不應該討厭這種「牢騷」，而且應該把它當作鏡子照一照自己。

說延安「學生出身」的青年是「家庭和學校哺乳他們成人，愛和熱向他們細語着人生……」我認為這多少有些主觀主義。延安青年雖然絕大多數是「學生出身」，「入世未深」沒有「嘗夠人生冷暖」，但他們也絕大多數是從各種不同的痛苦鬥爭道路走到延安來的，過去的生活不見得有那樣多的「愛和熱」；相反他們倒是懂得了「恨和冷」，才到革命陣營來追求「愛和熱」的。依「碰壁」作者底看法，彷彿延安青年都是嬌生慣

二、碰「碰壁」

在本報「青年之頁」第十二期上，讀到一位同志底標題為「碰壁」的文章，不禁有感。

先抄兩段原文：

「新從大後方來的一位中年朋友，看到延安青年忍不住些微拂意的事，牢騷滿腹，到處發洩的情形，深以為不然地說：『這算得什麼！我們在外面不知碰了多少壁，受人多少氣！……』」

「他的話是對的。延安雖也有着令人生氣的『臉色』，和一些不能盡如人意的事物；可是在一個碰壁多少次，嘗夠人生冷暖的人看來，卻是微乎其微，算不得甚麼的。至於在入世未深的青年，尤其是學生出身的，那就迥乎不同了。家庭和學校哺乳他們成人，愛和熱向他們細語着人生，教他們描摹單純和美麗的憧憬；現實的醜惡和冷淡于他們是陌生的，無怪乎他們一遇到小小的風浪就要叫嚷，感到從來未有過的不安。」

我不知道作者這位「中年朋友」是怎樣的一個人，但我認為他底這種知足者長樂的人生哲學，不但不是「對的」，而是有害的。青年是可貴，在於他們純潔、敏感、熱情、勇敢，他們充滿着生命底新銳的力。別人沒有感覺的黑暗，他們先感覺；別人沒有看

「大頭子是這樣，小頭子也是這樣。我們底科長，×××，對上是畢恭畢敬的，對我們，卻是神氣活現，好幾次同志病了，他連看都不伸頭看一下。可是，一次老鷹抓了他一隻小鷄，你看他多麼關心這件大事呀！以後每次看見老鷹飛來，他都嚎嚎的叫，扔土塊去打它——自私自利的傢伙！」

沉默了一回。我一方面佩服這位女同志口齒尖利，一方面惘然若有所失。

「害病的同志太多了，想起來叫人難過。其實，害病，倒並不希望那類人來看你。他只能給你添難受。他底聲音、表情、態度，都不使你感覺他對你有甚麼關懷、愛護。」

「我兩年來換了三四個工作機關，那些首長以及科長、主任之類，真正關心幹部愛護幹部的，實在太少了。」

「是呀，一點也不錯！他對別人沒有一點愛，別人自然也一點不愛他。要是做羣衆工作，非垮台不可……。」

她們還繼續低聲興奮地談着。因為要分路，我就只聽到這裏爲止，這段談話也許有偏頗，有誇張，其中的「形象」也許沒有太大的普遍性；但我們決不能否認它有鏡子底作用。

我們生活裏到底缺少甚麼呢？鏡子裏看吧。

野百合花

1　命，所以……。另有人回答說：延安男女的比例是「十八比一」，許多青年找不到愛

2　人，所以……。還有人會回答說：延安生活太單調，太枯燥，缺少娛樂，所以……。

3　這些回答都不是沒有道理的。要吃得好一點，要有異性配偶，要生活得有趣，這些

4　都是天經地義。但誰也不能不承認：延安的青年，都是抱定犧牲精神來從事革命，並不

5　是來追求食色的滿足和生活的快樂。說他們不起勁，甚至肚子裏裝着不舒服，就是為了

6　這些問題不能圓滿解決，我不敢輕於同意。

7　那麼，我們生活裏到底缺些什麼呢？下面一段談話可能透露一些消息。

8　新年假期中，一天晚上從友人處歸來，昏黑裏，前面有兩個青年女同志在低聲而興

9　奮地談着話。我相距丈多遠，我放輕腳步凝神諦聽着：

10　「……動不動，就說人家小資產階級平均主義；其實他們倒真有點特殊主義。事

11　事都只顧自己特殊化，對下面同志，身體好也罷壞也罷，病也罷，死也罷，差不多莫不

12　關心！」

13　「哼，到處烏鴉一般黑，我們底××同志還不也是那樣！」

14　「說得好聽！階級友愛呀，甚麼呀──屁！好像連人對人的同情心都沒有！平常見

15　人裝得笑嘻嘻，其實是皮笑肉不笑，肉笑心不笑。稍不如意，就瞪起眼睛，搭出首長架

16　子來訓人。」

蓮步的升平氣象中，提到這樣的故事，似乎不太和諧，但當前的現實——請閉上眼睛想一想吧，每一分鐘，都有我們親愛的同志在血泊中倒下——似乎與這氣象也太不和諧！）

為了民族底利益，我們並不願再算階級仇恨的舊賬。我們是真正大公無私的。我們甚至盡一切力量拖曳着舊中國底代表者同我們一路走向光明。可是，在拖曳的過程中，舊中國底骯髒污穢也就沾染了我們自己，散佈細菌，傳染疾病。

我曾不止十次二十次地從李芬同志底影子汲取力量，生活的力量和戰鬥的力量。這次偶然想到她，使我決心寫一些雜文。野百合花就是它們的總標題。這有兩方面的含義：第一，這種花是延安山野間最美麗的野花，用以獻給那聖潔的影子；其次，據說這種花與一般百合花同樣有着鱗狀球莖，吃起來味雖略帶苦澀，不似一般百合花那樣香甜可口，但卻有更大的藥用價值——未知確否。

一九四二年二月廿六日

一、我們生活裏缺少什麼？

延安青年近來似乎生活有些不起勁，而且似乎肚子裏裝得有點不舒服。

為甚麼呢？我們生活裏缺少甚麼呢？有人會回答說：我們營養不良，我們缺少維他

野百合花

王實味

前記

在河邊獨步時，一位同志腳上的舊式棉鞋，使我又想起了曾穿過這種棉鞋的李芬同志——我所敬愛的生平第一個朋友。想起她，心臟照例震動一下。照例我覺到血液循環得更有力。

李芬同志是北大一九二六年級文預科學生，同年入黨，一九二八年犧牲于她底故鄉——湖南寶慶。她底死不是由於被捕，而是被她親舅父縛送給當地駐軍。這說明舊中國底代表者是如何殘忍。同時，在赴死之前，她曾把所有的三套襯衣褲都穿在身上，用針綫上下密密縫在一起；因爲，當時寶慶青年女共產黨員被捕槍決後，常由軍隊縱使流氓去奸屍！這又說明着中國是怎樣一個血腥、醜惡、骯髒、黑暗的社會！從聽到她底噩耗時起，我底血管裏便一直燃燒着最狂烈的熱愛與毒恨。每一想到她，我眼前便浮出那聖潔的女殉道者底影子，穿着三套密密縫在一起的襯衣褲，由自己的親舅父縛送去從容就義！每一想到她，我便心臟震動，血液循環的更有力！（在這歌囀玉堂春、舞廻金

菊花與金魚	秦牧	三八
「邯鄲學步」	秦牧	四三
河漢錯綜	秦牧	四六
毒物和藥	秦牧	五○
人和鬼	秦牧	五四
海瑞罵皇帝	吳晗	五八
說大話的故事	吳晗	六三
事事關心	鄧拓	六六
亂彈雜記	鄧拓	六九
爭鳴的風度	廖沫沙	八三
註 解	章白	九二

目錄

序	VII
緒論	XI
附錄	XIX
拼音對照表	XXXXIX
野百合花	王實味 一
三八節有感	丁玲 十一
了解作家，尊重作家	艾青 十七
蟬噪居漫筆	蕭軍 二一
從點戲說起	蕭軍 二四
論同志之「愛」與「耐」	夏衍 二九
白蟻宮的秘密	孟超 三二
張獻忠不殺人辨	孟超 三五

版權所有

中國現代文選

出版者　北歐亞洲問題研究所

編者　董培炎

承印者　香港新昌印刷有限公司

出版日期　一九七八年

董培炎編

中國現代文選

For Product Safety Concerns and Information please contact our EU representative GPSR@taylorandfrancis.com
Taylor & Francis Verlag GmbH, Kaufingerstraße 24, 80331 München, Germany

www.ingramcontent.com/pod-product-compliance
Lightning Source LLC
Chambersburg PA
CBHW070301010526
44108CB00039B/1438